C# 3.0 Design Patterns

Other Microsoft .NET resources from O'Reilly

C# 3.0 Design Patterns

Judith Bishop

O'REILLY®

Beijing · Cambridge · Farnham · Köln · Paris · Sebastopol · Taipei · Tokyo

C# 3.0 Design Patterns
by Judith Bishop

Published by O'Reilly Media, Inc., 1005 Gravenstein Highway North, Sebastopol, CA 95472.

O'Reilly books may be purchased for educational, business, or sales promotional use. Online editions are also available for most titles (*safari.oreilly.com*). For more information, contact our corporate/institutional sales department: (800) 998-9938 or *corporate@oreilly.com*.

Editor: John Osborn

Production Editor: Loranah Dimant

Copyeditor: Rachel Wheeler

Proofreader: Loranah Dimant

Indexer: John Bickelhaupt

Interior Designer: David Futato

Cover Illustrator: Karen Montgomery

Illustrator: Jessamyn Read

Printing History:

December 2007:   First Edition.

RepKover™
This book uses RepKover™, a durable and flexible lay-flat binding.

ISBN 13: 978-0-596-52773-0
[M]   [3/08]

In memory of my beloved father,
Tom Mullins (1920–2007).

Table of Contents

Foreword

When you're faced with a problem to solve (and frankly, who isn't these days?), the basic strategy usually taken by we computer people is called "divide and conquer." It goes like this:

- Conceptualize the specific problem as a set of smaller sub-problems.
- Solve each smaller problem.
- Combine the results into a solution of the specific problem.

Reducing complex problems down to the level of twiddling the states of a few billion bits is what we do all day. But "divide and conquer" is not the only possible strategy. We can also take a more generalist approach:

- Conceptualize the specific problem as a special case of a more general problem.
- Somehow solve the general problem.
- Adapt the solution of the general problem to the specific problem.

Design patterns are among the major tools in the toolboxes of those who espouse the generalist approach. If you look at samples from a broad spectrum of software solutions, you will find that though the specifics may vary widely, there is often an underlying structural similarity. (Searching a filesystem for a file with a particular attribute is in some sense structurally similar to searching an annotated parse tree for a symbol with a particular type.) *Design patterns codify general solutions to common problems.*

The ultimate example of the generalist approach is of course the design and implementation of programming languages themselves. As problem solving tools go, it is hard to get more general than a programming language like C#. When designing new programming languages (or new versions of old programming languages), we think about common problems that are faced every day by real developers and figure out how to create a language which solves them in a general, aesthetically pleasing, and powerful way that is broadly applicable.

We want to embed the most useful and powerful abstractions so deeply into the language infrastructure that you barely even consciously register them as being there anymore. Patterns like "local variable" or "procedure call" or "while loop" are so much a part of the air we all breathe that we don't even think of them as patterns anymore.

Furthermore, we want to make a language in which patterns which are useful but perhaps not quite so fundamental are nevertheless relatively straightforward to implement clearly and elegantly. A class in C# may be marked as "static," or "abstract," or "sealed," but not as "singleton." That was a deliberate choice of the language designers. However, implementing a singleton class in C# is still relatively easy.

The gray zone in between "clearly foundational" and "occasionally useful" is where the interesting design challenges lie. Our observations of design patterns used by real-world developers in C# (and other languages) strongly drive the design process for new versions.

Consider for example how you would implement an iterator pattern on a linked list in C# 1.0. You would end up defining an enumerator class to represent a position in the list containing a lot of boring boilerplate code (which impedes readability), and the solution would not be very reusable. The notion of "enumerate a set of things" is sufficiently applicable to a wide variety of problems that it met the bar for inclusion as a first class language concept. In C# 2.0 with its yield return statement the compiler can generate all the boring code for you, and the generic type system makes iterating over a set of things typesafe no matter what the "things" are.

All of this is a long way to say just why it is that I am so very excited about Language Integrated Query (LINQ) in C# 3.0. We believed that iterating over collections of things was a great start, but that we could do so much more. *Sorting, filtering, grouping, joining, projecting,* and *transforming* data are also fundamental operations that are useful in pretty much every domain. Whether you are writing a ray tracer, a compiler, an XML reader, or an online banking security system, odds are good that you are going to need to manipulate collections of *something* in a rich way.

By moving these concepts out of domain-specific object models and into a general-purpose programming language, we hopefully solve those more general problems. We additionally hope, though, that by adding C# 3.0's query expressions, lambda expressions, extension methods, initializer expressions, expression trees, and so on to the already rich set of C# 2.0 and 1.0 features, we make it easier to elegantly implement all sorts of other useful design patterns.

And that is also why I am excited about this book. *C# 3.0 Design Patterns* brings the frequently abstruse world of design patterns into sharp focus with pragmatic C# 3.0 implementations. I look forward to seeing where developers can go with these tools and this language, and what useful patterns we can build into the infrastructures of future languages.

—Eric Lippert
Senior Developer
C# Compiler Team
Seattle, Washington
November 30, 2007

Preface

Why I Wrote This Book

In 2002, Microsoft Research hosted an international meeting in Cambridge, U.K., to reveal its Rotor system, which would bring C# and .NET to non-Windows programmers. Once back home, writing software, papers, and a book on the topic, I came to realize that we had witnessed the beginning of a real revolution in programming. Since the advent of Java in 1996, programming had become *platform*-independent: with Java byte-code, programs could run anywhere. This independence, however, extended only to programs written in the Java language. .NET, on the other hand, was *language*-independent: it allowed programs in different languages to interact, but, up until that day, only on Windows.

In the ensuing five years, new platforms have come to support .NET (Mono, for example) and new hardware has come to support Intel chips (on which Windows runs). The result is that .NET now runs almost anywhere. Consequently, expertise in C# programming is a very transportable skill to acquire. But C# keeps improving as a language, and we are currently at the beginning of a new leap forward into C# 3.0, which offers enormous benefits in terms of productivity and ease of programming. Having already written an introductory C# text in 2003,* I realized that the benefits of the new features announced now in 2007, four years later, would be felt at a much more advanced level of software development. I wanted to write a second book that introduced C# 3.0 to developers who already knew the basic language—but what would be the formula that could introduce a language *and* address a reader's needs of precision, examples, and a heavy dose of reality?

Enter design patterns. Design patterns encapsulate common, accepted, and proven ways of using language features *together*. They form a level of discourse at a higher plane, and they exercise and promote good programming practices. However, there is an element of unreality surrounding design patterns, and one gets the impression

---

* Judith Bishop and Nigel Horspool, *C# Concisely* (Boston, MA: Addison-Wesley, 2003).

that they are more talked about than used. I wanted to change that and make design patterns really accessible to ordinary programmers, using the best language for them: C# 3.0. The result is this book.

Who This Book Is For

If you are a programmer who loves your code, for whom every line has a precise meaning and every feature has a correct place, this book is for you. It will help you with your primary job of making your code correct, elegant, extensible, and efficient. If you serve the business ends of your organization by focusing on the quality of your code, you need a book like *C# 3.0 Design Patterns*. Knowledge about design patterns is also a big step forward for those working up from low-level programmers to software engineers and architects.

Through reading this book, you will acquire skills in:

- Programming design patterns
- Basic UML modeling notation for representing patterns
- Selecting patterns appropriate for given scenarios and comparing alternative implementations
- Using advanced language features of C# 3.0 to realize patterns efficiently and elegantly

Although not written as a textbook, *C# 3.0 Design Patterns* could fit in very well for a mid-degree course on design patterns or advanced programming.

The diagrams and code for all the patterns and associated examples and case studies in this book can be found on the book's web site, *http://www.oreilly.com/catalog/9780596527730*.

What You Need to Know

This book is for programmers who know how to program in C# 1.0 or Java 1.4 and who would like to move on to the more modern features of the latest language. All the new features of C# 3.0, as well as many novel features from C# 2.0, are introduced by example and summarized in sidebars for easy reference. Thus, the book serves as a programmers' guide as well.

The book does not assume any acquaintance with design patterns. It covers the full set of 23 patterns that were originally proposed in Erich Gamma, Richard Helm, Ralph Johnson, and John Vlissides's *Design Patterns: Elements of Reusable Object-Oriented Software* in 1994 and now form a common introductory base to the patterns that are emerging in many other domains (such as security, concurrency, and architectural design). At the end of the book, the reader will have a thorough grounding in design patterns as they are commonly understood.

How This Book Is Organized

After the introduction in Chapter 1, the book takes a tour through the 23 core design patterns. Each chapter discusses two or three patterns, chosen because they have some common applicability and can be compared at the end of the chapter. The patterns are subdivided into three groups: *structural*, *creational*, and *behavioral*.

We begin with the structural patterns, studying the Decorator, Proxy, and Bridge patterns in Chapter 2; the Composite and Flyweight patterns in Chapter 3; and the Adapter and Façade patterns in Chapter 4. We then move on to the creational patterns, exploring the Prototype, Factory Method, and Singleton patterns in Chapter 5 and the Abstract Factory and Builder patterns in Chapter 6. The last four chapters deal with the largest category, the behavioral patterns: Chapter 7 focuses on the Strategy, State, and Template Method patterns; Chapter 8 on the Chain of Responsibility and Command patterns; Chapter 9 on the Iterator, Mediator, and Observer patterns; and Chapter 10 on the Visitor, Interpreter, and Memento patterns.

Our discussion of each pattern will consist of the following parts:

Role
> A short, high-level description of the pattern and what it is meant to achieve

Illustration
> An example of where the pattern might be used in programming a modern computer system, illustrating a real-world context with a photo or diagram to help you remember the pattern

Design
> An identification of the interconnected players in the pattern and their roles, explained in a UML diagram, with links back to the key players in the illustration

Implementation
> A stepwise refinement development of a short program that illustrates the pattern using the terms introduced in the "Design" section

Example
> A second program that gives an example of the pattern, usually in terms of the illustrative example, where the programming moves away from a strict adherence to the pattern terms

Use
> A discussion of real-world scenarios where the pattern might be used, ending with a table listing the conditions that would make its use applicable

Exercises
> A list of exercises of differing degrees of difficulty designed to enhance your understanding of the pattern under discussion

At the end of each chapter you will find a comparison of the patterns discussed therein and a discussion of how they fit in with those that have gone before.

The ordering of the patterns has been carefully chosen so as to represent a gradual progression in C# 3.0 maturity. Implementing the earlier patterns in each section requires very little that is not available in C# 1.0, while the later patterns are more sophisticated in their implementation and take advantage of more advanced features present in C# 3.0. This approach allows new features to be introduced inline, as they become relevant, rather than all at once at the start or end of the text.

This book is not intended to be a reference guide to the whole of C# or even C# 3.0, but rather to be a practical guide to using the most interesting features of the language. Although the emphasis is on developments in the most recent version, I also pick out some features of C# 1.0 and 2.0 that I think are really useful but that are not often employed in code. The list of C# features explicitly covered follows this Preface.

Special features of this book include:

- Pictorial illustrations of patterns, to help you focus on the meaning of what each pattern can accomplish in real life
- Quizzes that relate the illustrations to the UML diagrams
- Uncluttered "theory" code that can be adapted to many situations
- Tables that give guidance on when to choose a specific pattern
- Comparison tables for patterns that are similar, showing how they differ
- Lists of the advantages, disadvantages, and limitations of each pattern
- Challenges and exercises to help you take your knowledge further

What You Need to Use This Book

To run the programs in this book, you need:

- A computer that will run Windows XP or Vista. Compatible platforms are any PC or Intel-based Mac with a virtual machine.
- Microsoft's .NET Framework 3.5. As of October 2007, this version is still in Beta 2, but it is very stable now. It is available at *http://www.microsoft.com/downloads*.
- A program editor or programming environment. Visual Studio 2008 is an ideal companion to C# 3.0 programming, but it is not essential.
- The C# 3.0 reference documentation, available on the Microsoft web site (*http://msdn2.microsoft.com/vcsharp*, 529 pages).

All the programs in this book were prepared on an iMac Intel Core 2 Duo running Mac OS X 10.4 and 5 (Tiger and Leopard) and Windows XP on top of the Parallels virtual machine. The editor used was SciTE.

Finding What You Need

This book is intended to serve as a learning resource. In learning about C# 3.0 and design patterns, there will be times when you will need to find a particular feature or a related pattern. These tables are given in Chapter 11 for easy reference. The UML class diagram notation is covered in Chapter 1. You will also find that there are a few programs that, for space reasons, are not presented in full in the text. These are all included in the Appendix.

Conventions Used in This Book

The following typographical conventions are used in this book:

Italic
> Indicates new terms, URLs, and email addresses.

`Constant width`
> Indicates code examples and excerpts, commands, options, variables, attributes, functions, types, classes, namespaces, methods, properties, parameters, values, objects, events, and XML tags.

`Constant width bold`
> Used for emphasis or highlighting in code examples.

`Constant width italic`
> Shows text that should be replaced with user-supplied values.

 This icon signifies a tip, suggestion, or general note.

 This icon indicates a warning or caution.

Using Code Examples

This book is here to help you get your job done. In general, you may use the code in this book in your programs and documentation. You do not need to contact us for permission unless you're reproducing a significant portion of the code. For example, writing a program that uses several chunks of code from this book does not require permission. Selling or distributing a CD-ROM of examples from O'Reilly books *does* require permission. Answering a question by citing this book and quoting example code does not require permission. Incorporating a significant amount of example code from this book into your product's documentation *does* require permission.

We appreciate, but do not require, attribution. An attribution usually includes the title, author, publisher, and ISBN. For example: "*C# 3.0 Design Patterns*, by Judith Bishop. Copyright 2008 Judith Bishop, 978-0-596-52773-0."

If you think your use of code examples falls outside fair use or the permission given above, feel free to contact us at *permissions@oreilly.com*.

Comments and Questions

The author would be delighted to hear what you think of the book and whether you have any good ideas to extend the presentation of C# design patterns. Please address comments and questions concerning this book to the publisher:

O'Reilly Media, Inc.
1005 Gravenstein Highway North
Sebastopol, CA 95472
800-998-9938 (in the United States or Canada)
707-829-0515 (international or local)
707-829-0104 (fax)

We have a web page for this book, where we list errata, examples, and any additional information. You can access this page at:

http://www.oreilly.com/catalog/9780596527730

To comment or ask technical questions about this book, send email to:

bookquestions@oreilly.com

For more information about our books, conferences, Resource Centers, and the O'Reilly Network, see our web site at:

http://www.oreilly.com

The author also has a site for the book at:

http://patterns.cs.up.ac.za

Safari® Books Online

When you see a Safari® Books Online icon on the cover of your favorite technology book, that means the book is available online through the O'Reilly Network Safari Bookshelf.

Safari offers a solution that's better than e-books. It's a virtual library that lets you easily search thousands of top tech books, cut and paste code samples, download chapters, and find quick answers when you need the most accurate, current information. Try it for free at *http://safari.oreilly.com*.

Acknowledgments

My first thanks are to John Osborn, my editor at O'Reilly, for keeping the faith and getting this book out on time. His care and expertise are much appreciated. To Jeff Pepper, who signed up the book quite a while ago, thanks as well. I'm sorry we could not see the project through together. Thanks also to the reviewers, Eric Lippert, Jim Whitehead, Stefan Gruner, and Pierre-Henri Kuaté, whose insightful comments—no holds barred—led to many revisions but an ultimately much better book. My department at the University of Pretoria provided me with the latest equipment, and my colleagues gave me the time to really concentrate when I needed to. In particular I thank Jan Eloff for his support and friendship. To Carlo Ghezzi of the Politecnico di Milano, who graciously hosted me for the summer of 2007, when much of the first draft was written, *grazie mille*. My former students Hans Lombard and D-J Miller helped at very short notice with some of the examples, and I really appreciated their fresh minds and dedication to the task.

Writing this book would have been a much less enjoyable experience without the constant support and interest of my talented friends Nigel Horspool, Rob Koenig, and Rudolph Vosser. They never knew quite when the book would really be finished, but now it is. And finally, to my mother, my sons, and my family, whose love and *joie de vivre* kept me going on this (yet another) book—thank you.

—Judith Bishop
Pretoria, South Africa
October 2007

CHAPTER 1

C# Meets Design Patterns

What makes a successful and happy programmer? What contributes to that wonderful "gotcha!" feeling you get when your program finally compiles and runs correctly, and you know that it is as elegant as it can be? How did you manage to make it elegant while at the same time satisfying all the normal "-ilities" (flexibility, maintainability, reliability, and reusability, to name a few)? And why are some programmers able to attain this level of elegance so much quicker than others?

It would be easy to say that some are born to program and some are not. Yet even the best programmers will sit for hours or even days poring over a single screen of code, knowing it is not quite right and struggling to make it better. The answer is that a successful programmer has two primary tools: a good programming language and design patterns. This book is devoted to showing how this winning combination works together to launch ordinary programmers into the realm of experts.

Those who have long-term programming experience will appreciate that time brings improvements to a language. Simple things that we take for granted today—like type checking of variables—were nonexistent or optional in the languages of the 1970s. Object orientation, which is the basis for programming these days, only came into vogue in the 1990s, and generics—on which our modern collection classes for stacks, maps, and lists are based—were just a research project five years ago.

Successful programmers keep abreast of improvements in languages, but often it is not obvious even to a seasoned professional how a particular new feature will be useful. Some features, such as automatic properties (Chapter 3) and collection initializers (Chapter 3), are likely to immediately find a home in your toolbox; others, such as extension methods (Chapter 2), are somewhat more abstract.

Examples are needed to illustrate the utility of many emerging language features—but while examples illustrate, they can also obscure because they are directed toward solving particular problems. Given an example of how iterators work with a family tree manager (Chapter 9), would you be able to reuse them for a chat room program? The connection is not at all obvious and could easily be missed. Enter *design patterns*, the ultimate in mind connectors for successful programmers.

Design patterns encapsulate common ways of solving problems using language features together.

Design patterns provide a high-level language of discourse for programmers to describe their systems and to discuss solutions to common problems. This language comprises the names of recognizable patterns and their elements. The proper and intelligent use of patterns will guide a developer into designing a system that conforms to well-established prior practices, without stifling innovation. In the marketplace, design patterns greatly enhance practitioners' mobility and the value of their knowledge, as they provide a common, recognizable basis for tackling problems.

The patterns have illustrative *names* and are described with *diagrams* illustrating their *role players*. There are only 23 classic patterns (fewer than the letters of the English alphabet), and a good programmer can learn the names and uses of all of them with some practice. When faced with design choices, such programmers are no longer left to select language features, such as inheritance, interfaces, or delegates. They can instead hone in on the bigger picture: a blog would match an Observer pattern (Chapter 9), a community network system would need a Proxy (Chapter 2), and so on. The element of decision making is not removed, but it is raised to a higher level.

So, who decides how a design pattern is implemented in a given language? Books such as this one and writings on web sites present the implementations of the patterns, together with guidance on how to choose a pattern and even how to select among alternative implementations (if there are any). However, the pull of custom is very strong, and often patterns are presented using only the language features of the 1980s. Not so in this book. *C# 3.0 Design Patterns* aims to present the 23 classic patterns in the best possible C# 3.0 style, ensuring that what you learn here will be of real value to you for many years to come.

About Patterns

Design patterns were introduced in Erich Gamma, Richard Helm, Ralph Johnson, and John Vlissides's seminal work *Design Patterns: Elements of Reusable Object-Oriented Software* (Addison-Wesley). The book specifies and describes 23 patterns that form the foundation of any study of the subject, which are still regarded as the essential core patterns today.

These core patterns address issues in mainline object-oriented programming (OOP), and the original implementations were presented in C++ and Smalltalk (the primary OOP languages at the time they were developed). Since then, other books have implemented the patterns in Java, Visual Basic, and C#. As the value of the pattern concept has become accepted, new patterns have been proposed to add to the original list. In addition, there are now patterns that are applicable to specific areas, such as software architecture, user interfaces, concurrency, and security. Although these patterns are extremely important in their areas, their adherents are fragmented, and the core set of universally accepted patterns has not been expanded.

As outlined in the Preface, the discussion of each pattern in this book consists of a brief description of its role, an illustration, a look at its design and implementation, and an example, followed by a discussion of its uses and some exercises. New features of the C# language are introduced where patterns draw upon them; thus, you will learn more about the language as you learn about the patterns.

The 23 patterns are divided into three groups: *creational*, *structural*, and *behavioral*. Within a group, though, there is no inherent ordering, and alphabetical ordering has traditionally been the default. In this book, we take an innovative approach by relating the patterns to the language features they require and introducing them in order of increasing language complexity. Several of the patterns in each group need only inheritance or interfaces, and it makes sense to deal with these first so that the focus can be on the patterns themselves and not on the language. The patterns that make use of more advanced language features (generics, indexers, and delegates) are then presented later. Novel features of C# can thus be introduced as we go along, rather than in a standalone introduction or appendix. A comprehensive index complements this approach.

A key feature of any pattern handbook is the insight that it gives as to the use of patterns in real systems. Knowing that the Façade pattern is frequently used in compiler construction, or that adapters are prevalent in well-known graphical frameworks, reinforces their importance and helps to direct their use. However, in large systems patterns are seldom found in isolation, and often they work together. The Singleton pattern, for example, is often used in conjunction with other patterns when it is necessary to create only one version of a component. Thus, considerable attention is given at the end of each chapter to the comparative merits of the patterns explored.

About UML

An important part of each pattern's description is a Unified Modeling Language* (UML) class diagram. UML is a universally accepted way of describing software in diagrammatic form. The diagrams in the book make use of the UML features itemized in Table 1-1.

---

* Defined by the Object Management Group (see *http://www.uml.org*).

Table 1-1. UML class diagram notation

Program element	Diagram element	Meaning
Class	**Class** −attribute +operation( )	Types and parameters specified when important; access indicated by + (public), (private), and # (protected).
Interface	<<interface>> **IClass** +operation( )	Name starts with I. Also used for abstract classes.
Note	descriptive text	Any descriptive text.
Package	Package	Grouping of classes and interfaces.
Inheritance	A △ ↑ B	B inherits from A.
Realization	A △ ┆ B	B implements A.
Association	A ——— B	A and B call and access each other's elements.
Association (one way)	A ——→ B	A can call and access B's elements, but not vice versa.
Aggregation	A ◇— B	A has a B, and B can outlive A.

Table 1-1. UML class diagram notation (continued)

Program element	Diagram element	Meaning
Composition	A ◆——— B	A has a B, and B depends on A.

There are three kinds of blocks, for classes, interfaces/abstract classes, and packages. The class is the most common diagram element and contains details of some of its corresponding C# class's more important *attributes* (or fields) and *operations* (or methods). A UML diagram is not meant to be an exact copy of a program, and thus only the elements that are important to the pattern under consideration are shown. The accessibility of all attributes and operations (private, public, or protected) is indicated. The default for attributes is private and for operations is public. Deviations from the defaults will be highlighted as they occur.

The types associated with attributes and operations are not usually given. However, when these are important, they can be inserted after the identifier, separated by a colon. The same relaxed approach applies to parameters of methods, which are not usually shown in a diagram.

Notes are very useful for explaining relationships, such as when a method in one class calls a particular method in another, when this information is directly relevant to the pattern. In most cases, though, six types of lines give enough information. The Decorator pattern, which we will consider first, has a reasonably rich diagram, and it will be used to explain the lines in more detail.

About C# 3.0

An objective of this book is to present C# in its very best style. The version we are using is C# 3.0 on the .NET 3.5 Beta 2 Framework (August 2007).

C# 1.0 came out in December 2002, embodying much of the research in OOP that had taken place since Java was launched seven years previously. C# 2.0 was released in final form in September 2005, and the ECMA standard was made available in June 2006. C# 2.0 added five significant features to C# 1.0, most of which are used in the patterns in this book:

- Generics that allow classes, structs, interfaces, delegates, and methods to be parameterized by the types of data they store and manipulate

- Anonymous methods that allow code blocks to be written "inline" where delegate values are expected

- Iterators, which are methods to incrementally compute and yield sequences of values

- Partial types that allow classes, structs, and interfaces to be broken into multiple pieces stored in different source files for easier development and maintenance
- Nullable types that represent values that possibly are unknown; they support all possible values of an underlying type plus an additional null state

Within Microsoft, work continued on the language, with a particular emphasis on the integration of SQL database interfacing and the associated dynamic typing required. The report on Version 3.0 of the language, finalized in May 2006, includes substantial advances in integrating the functional and database programming paradigms into mainline object-orientation:

- Implicit typing of local variables, which permits the types of local variables to be inferred from the expressions used to initialize them
- Extension methods, which make it possible to extend existing types and constructed types with additional methods, outside their definitions
- Lambda expressions, an evolution of anonymous methods that provide improved type inference and conversions to both delegate types and expression trees
- Object initializers, which ease construction and initialization of objects
- Anonymous types, which are tuple types automatically inferred and created from object initializers
- Implicit typing of arrays, which is a form of array creation and initialization together where the element type of the array is inferred from the initializer
- Query expressions, which provide a language-integrated syntax for queries that is similar to relational and hierarchical query languages, such as SQL and XQuery

All these new features are used in a natural way in this book. For full details on the entire C# 3.0 language, see the reference documentation available at *http://msdn2. microsoft.com/vcsharp*.

About the Examples

The nearly 40 full example programs in this book have been carefully crafted to satisfy the following criteria:

- They are programmable in no more than 180 lines, and usually 100.
- They are related to real computer systems.
- They are extensible with more functionality.

You'll find programs related to real-world systems, such as Flickr and Facebook, as well as chat rooms, games, and blogs. We'll also tackle topics such as embedded systems and manufacturing. Some traditional examples (to do with banking and student marks, for instance) are included as well, but for the most part, the examples are new and have not been seen before in books of this nature. A key factor is that, thanks to the incorporation of design patterns and the deft use of C# 3.0, the programs are remarkably short. Examples that would not have been feasible to show in full in a book before are now perfectly reasonable.

CHAPTER 2

Structural Patterns: Decorator, Proxy, and Bridge

We start our tour of design patterns with the group known as the structural patterns. There are seven patterns that make up the structural group, each with the role of building flexibility, longevity, and security into computer software. The names of the patterns are important, so I'll introduce them immediately. They are:

- Decorator
- Proxy
- Bridge
- Composite
- Flyweight
- Adapter
- Façade

Structural patterns are concerned with how classes and objects are composed to form larger structures. Of the many purposes of the seven structural patterns, here are 10:

- Add new functionality dynamically to existing objects, or remove it (Decorator).
- Control access to an object (Proxy).
- Create expensive objects on demand (Proxy).
- Enable development of the interface and implementation of a component to proceed independently (Bridge).
- Match otherwise incompatible interfaces (Adapter).
- Reduce the cost of working with large numbers of very small objects (Flyweight).
- Reorganize a system with many subsystems into identifiable layers with single entry points (Façade).
- Select or switch implementations at runtime (Bridge).
- Simplify the interface to a complex subsystem (Façade).
- Treat single objects and composite objects in the same way (Composite).

Structural patterns can be employed while a system is being designed, or later on during maintenance and extension. In fact, some of them are specifically useful in the post-production stages of the lifecycle of a software system, when changes are introduced that were not foreseen and when even the interfaces between components need updating. Thus, sometimes when you want to add functionality, you will be working with existing classes that cannot be changed. The Decorator pattern is useful here. Alternatively, you might be able to design a whole system from scratch so that it works in a particularly usable way, with the Composite pattern.

Our exploration of the structural design patterns will span three chapters. In this chapter, we'll look at the Decorator, Proxy, and Bridge patterns. In Chapter 3, we'll tackle the Composite and Flyweight patterns, and in Chapter 4, we'll examine the Adapter and Façade patterns.

Our first three patterns provide ways of adding state and behavior dynamically, controlling the creation and access of objects, and keeping specifications and implementations separate. They do not draw upon any advanced features of C#, relying only on interfaces for structuring; however, at the end of this chapter, I introduce *extension methods* as an interesting way to implement the Bridge pattern.

For each pattern, we will examine its role, an illustration of where it might be used in programming, and its design (what the major players are and what roles they play in the pattern). We will then look at some simple code illustrating the implementation of the pattern and at a more concrete example. Finally, we will consider some additional real-world uses for the pattern and some exercises that you can work through to enhance your understanding of it. Also, at the end of this and every chapter, you will find a more detailed discussion of when the individual patterns might be used and a comparison of their intent and applicability.

Decorator Pattern

Role

The role of the Decorator pattern is to provide a way of attaching new state and behavior to an object dynamically. The object does not know it is being "decorated," which makes this a useful pattern for evolving systems. A key implementation point in the Decorator pattern is that decorators both inherit the original class and contain an instantiation of it.

Illustration

As its name suggests, the Decorator pattern takes an existing object and adds to it. As an example, consider a photo that is displayed on a screen. There are many ways to add to the photo, such as putting a border around it or specifying tags related to the content. Such additions can be displayed on top of the photo, as shown in Figure 2-1.

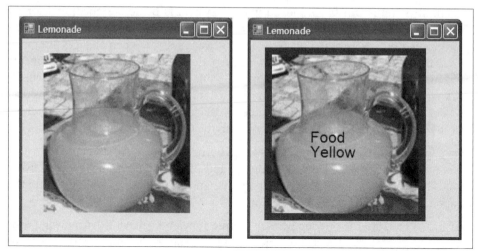

Figure 2-1. Decorator pattern illustration—(a) plain photograph and (b) photograph with tags

The combination of the original photo and some new content forms a new object. In the second image shown in Figure 2-1, there are four objects: the original photo as shown to the left, the object that provides a border, and two tag objects with different data associated with them. Each of them is a `Decorator` object. Given that the number of ways of decorating photos is endless, we can have many such new objects. The beauty of this pattern is that:

- The original object is unaware of any decorations.
- There is no one big feature-laden class with all the options in it.
- The decorations are independent of each other.
- The decorations can be composed together in a mix-and-match fashion.

Design

Now, we can specify the players in the Decorator pattern in a UML diagram, shown in Figure 2-2. Because this is the first pattern we are describing in UML, we'll take it slowly. (The UML that we need for patterns in this book is covered in Chapter 1 and summarized in Table 1-1.) The essential players in this UML diagram are:

Component
    An original class of objects that can have operations added or modified (there may be more than one such class)

Operation
    An operation in `IComponent` objects that can be replaced (there may be several operations)

IComponent

The interface that identifies the classes of objects that can be decorated (Component is one of these)

Decorator

A class that conforms to the IComponent interface and adds state and/or behavior (there may be more than one such class)

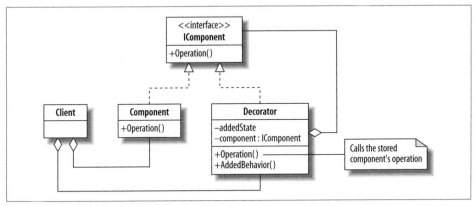

Figure 2-2. Decorator pattern UML diagram

The center of the UML diagram is the Decorator class. It includes two types of relationships with the IComponent interface:

Is-a

The is-a relationship is shown by a dotted arrow from the Decorator to IComponent, indicating that Decorator realizes the IComponent interface. The fact that Decorator implements IComponent means that Decorator objects can be used wherever IComponent objects are expected. The Component class is also in an is-a relationship with IComponent, and therefore the client can use Component and Decorator objects interchangeably—the heart of the Decorator pattern.

Has-a

The has-a relationship is shown by an open diamond on the Decorator, linked to IComponent. This indicates that the Decorator instantiates one or more IComponent objects and that decorated objects can outlive the originals. The Decorator uses the component attribute (of type IComponent) to invoke any replacement Operation it might wish to override. This is the way the Decorator pattern achieves its objective.

The addedBehavior operation and the addedState attribute in the Decorator class are other optional ways of extending what is in the original Component objects. We'll look at some examples momentarily.

Match the Decorator Pattern Players with the Photo Decorator Illustration

To test whether you understand the Decorator pattern, cover the lefthand column of the table below and see if you can identify the players among the items from the illustrative example (Figure 2-1), as shown in the righthand column. Then check your answers against the lefthand column.

IComponent	Any photo
Component	A plain photo
Operation	To display a photo
Decorator	A tagged photo
Client	Creator of photos and tagged photos
IComponent	Any photo

From this list, we can see that the following would be valid statements in a Client wanting to put two tags on a photo:

```
Photo photo = new Photo( );
Tag foodTag = new Tag (photo, "Food",1);
Tag colorTag = new Tag (foodTag, "Yellow",2);
```

By the is-a relationship, photo, foodTag, and colorTag are all IComponent objects. Each of the tags (the decorators) is created with a Component, which might be a photo or an already tagged photo. The resulting object diagram is shown in Figure 2-3. As you can see, there are actually three separate photo objects in the system. How they interact is discussed in the upcoming "Implementation" section.

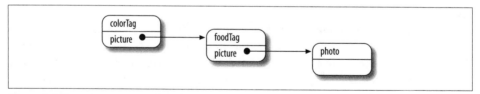

Figure 2-3. Decorator pattern objects

In most of the patterns we will encounter, the players can appear in multiple guises. To keep the UML diagrams clear and simple, not all of the options will be shown. However, we should consider the implications of these multiple players on the design of the pattern:

Multiple components

> Different components that conform to the interface can also be decorated. For example, we could have a class that draws people, houses, ships, and so on from simple shapes and lines. They too could be tagged. It is for this reason that the IComponent interface is important, even if it does not contain any operations. In the case where we are sure there will only ever be one class of components, we can dispense with the IComponent interface and have the decorators directly inherit from Component.

Multiple decorators

> We have seen that we can create different instances of a Tag decorator. We can also consider having other types of decorators, such as Border decorators or even decorators that make the photo invisible. No matter what the decorators are, each contains a component object, which might itself be a decorator, setting off a chain of changes (as suggested in Figure 2-3). Some Decorator pattern designs include an IDecorator interface, but it generally serves no purpose in C# implementations.

Multiple operations

> Our illustration focuses on drawing as the chief operation for photos and decorations. Other examples will lend themselves to many more optional operations. Some of these will be part of the original component and its interface, whereas some will be added behaviors in certain decorators only. The client can call any of the operations individually on any of the components (decorated or otherwise) to which it has access.

Implementation

The Decorator pattern's key feature is that it does not rely on inheritance for extending behavior. If the Tag class had to inherit from the Photo class to add one or two methods, Tags would carry everything concerned with Photos around with them, making them very heavyweight objects. Instead, having the Tag class implement a Photo interface and then add behavior keeps the Tag objects lean. They can:

- Implement any methods in the interface, changing the initial behavior of the component
- Add any new state and behavior
- Access any public members via the object passed at construction

Before we carry on with the photo example, consider the theoretical version of the Decorator pattern in Example 2-1. Short examples such as this one are useful for showing the interaction between classes and objects of a pattern in a direct mapping to the UML. Once we move on to a real-world example, optimizations and extensions might be employed that make it more difficult to detect and visualize the pattern. Moreover, in a real-world example, the names of the players can be completely different than those in the pattern description.

Example 2-1. Decorator pattern theory code

```csharp
1    using System;
2
3    class DecoratorPattern {
4
5      // Decorator Pattern              Judith Bishop  Dec 2006
6      // Shows two decorators and the output of various
7      // combinations of the decorators on the basic component
8
9      interface IComponent {
10       string Operation();
11     }
12
13     class Component : IComponent {
14       public string Operation () {
15         return "I am walking ";
16       }
17     }
18
19     class DecoratorA : IComponent {
20       IComponent component;
21
22       public DecoratorA (IComponent c) {
23         component = c;
24       }
25
26       public string Operation() {
27         string s = component.Operation();
28         s += "and listening to Classic FM ";
29         return s;
30       }
31     }
32
33     class DecoratorB : IComponent {
34       IComponent component;
35       public string addedState = "past the Coffee Shop ";
36
37       public DecoratorB (IComponent c) {
38         component = c;
39       }
40
41       public string Operation () {
42         string s = component.Operation ();
43         s += "to school ";
44         return s;
45       }
46
47       public string AddedBehavior() {
48         return "and I bought a cappuccino ";
49       }
50     }
51
52     class Client {
53
54       static void Display(string s, IComponent c) {
```

Example 2-1. Decorator pattern theory code (continued)

```
55            Console.WriteLine(s+ c.Operation( ));
56        }
57
58    static void Main( ) {
59        Console.WriteLine("Decorator Pattern\n");
60
61        IComponent component = new Component( );
62        Display("1. Basic component: ", component);
63        Display("2. A-decorated : ", new DecoratorA(component));
64        Display("3. B-decorated : ", new DecoratorB(component));
65        Display("4. B-A-decorated : ", new DecoratorB(
66                new DecoratorA(component)));
67        // Explicit DecoratorB
68        DecoratorB b = new DecoratorB(new Component( ));
69        Display("5. A-B-decorated : ", new DecoratorA(b));
70        // Invoking its added state and added behavior
71        Console.WriteLine("\t\t\t"+b.addedState + b.AddedBehavior( ));
72    }
73  }
74 }
75 /* Output
76 Decorator Pattern
77
78 1. Basic component: I am walking
79 2. A-decorated : I am walking and listening to Classic FM
80 3. B-decorated : I am walking to school
81 4. B-A-decorated : I am walking and listening to Classic FM to school
82 5. A-B-decorated : I am walking to school and listening to Classic FM
83            past the Coffee Shop and I bought a cappuccino
84 */
```

The example starts off with the IComponent interface and a simple Component class that implements it (lines 9–17). There are two decorators that also implement the interface; each of them includes a declaration of an IComponent, which is the object it will decorate. DecoratorA (lines 19–31) is fairly plain and simply implements the Operation by calling it on the component it has stored, then adding something to the string it returns (line 28). DecoratorB (lines 33–50) is more elaborate. It also implements the Operation in its own way, but it offers some public addedState (line 35) and addedBehavior (lines 47–49) as well. In both implemented operations, the component's Operation method is called first, but this is not a requirement of the pattern; it merely makes for more readable output in this example.

The Client class is responsible for creating components and decorators in various configurations and displaying the result of calling the Operation in each case. Cases 2 and 3 (lines 63–64) decorate the basic component in different ways, as shown in the output on lines 79–80. Cases 4 and 5 apply two decorators, a B and an A, in different orders. In cases 2–4, the decorator objects are instantiated and used immediately, then discarded. In case 5, we create a DecoratorB object and keep this instance in a variable of the same type (instead of IComponent), so we can invoke the new behavior:

```
DecoratorB b = new DecoratorB(new Component( ));
Display("5. A-B-decorated : ", new DecoratorA(b));
// Invoking its added state and added behavior
Console.WriteLine("\t\t\t"+b.addedState + b.AddedBehavior( ));
```

**5. A-B-decorated : I am walking to school and listening to Classic FM
         past the Coffee Shop and I bought a cappuccino**

There are three objects here: the explicitly declared b and the implicitly declared
DecoratorA and Component objects. The Display method receives the DecoratorA
object and invokes its Operation method (line 55). This takes it to the DecoratorB
object. On line 42, the object that DecoratorB was composed with has its Operation
invoked, and the basic string "I am walking" was returned (line 15). Continuing on,
DecoratorB adds the bit about walking to school (line 43), and then DecoratorA adds
"listening to Classic FM" (line 28). This completes the call to Display. As can be seen
on line 82, the result is the opposite of line 81 because the decorators were composed in a different order.

However, that is not all. Decorators can define new behavior, which can be invoked
explicitly. We do this on line 71, which results in the second line of output (line 83)
about buying a cappuccino.

That, in a nutshell, is how decorators work. Decorators do not need any advanced
language features; they rely on object aggregation and interface implementation.
Now, let's consider a real-world example.

Example: Photo Decorator

In this section, we'll consider how to implement a photo decorator system, as
described in the "Illustration" section, earlier. To emphasize that the original component was written previously and is not available for altering, we'll place it in a separate namespace called Given:

```
using System.Windows.Forms;

namespace Given {
  // The original Photo class
  public class Photo : Form {
    Image image;

    public Photo () {
      image = new Bitmap("jug.jpg");
      this.Text = "Lemonade";
      this.Paint += new PaintEventHandler(Drawer);
    }

    public virtual void Drawer(Object source, PaintEventArgs e) {
      e.Graphics.DrawImage(image,30,20);
    }
  }
}
```

Photo inherits from System.Windows.Forms so that it can be displayed. The constructor sets up the Drawer method as the target of the PaintEventHandler that will be called when the Form is activated by a Main method. In C#, a call to Application.Run will start up a window in this way, so a basic client can look like this:

```
static void  Main () {
  // Application.Run acts as a simple client
  Application.Run(new Photo( ));
}
```

Now, without altering anything in the Photo class, we can start adding decorators. The first draws a blue border around the photo (we'll assume the size is known to keep things simple):

```
// This simple border decorator adds a colored border of fixed size
class BorderedPhoto : Photo {
  Photo photo;
  Color color;
  public BorderedPhoto (Photo p, Color c) {
    photo = p;
    color=c;
  }

  public override void Drawer(Object source, PaintEventArgs e) {
    photo.Drawer(source, e);
    e.Graphics.DrawRectangle(new Pen(color, 10),25,15,215,225);
  }
}
```

Notice that this code deviates from the pattern laid out in Figure 2-2, in that there is no IComponent interface. This is perfectly acceptable; the decorators can inherit directly from the component and maintain an object of that class as well. We see now that Drawer is the operation that is to be called from one decorator to the next. However, this code does rely on the original Component declaring Drawer as virtual. If this is not the case, and we cannot go in and change the Component class, an interface is necessary. This arrangement is shown in Example 2-1.

The Tag decorator follows a similar form, so we can put together the following composition:

```
// Compose a photo with two tags and a blue border
foodTag = new Tag (photo, "Food", 1);
colorTag = new Tag (foodTag, "Yellow", 2);
composition = new BorderedPhoto(colorTag, Color.Blue);
Application.Run(composition);
```

The result of this sequence of decorations is shown in Figure 2-1(b). Notice that Decorators can be instantiated with different parameters to give different effects: the foodTag object has a second parameter of "Food", and the colorTag's second parameter is "Yellow".

Finally, let's examine the added state and behavior that is in the Tags. A Tag class declares a static array and counter that stores the tag names as they come in. Any tag decorator object can then call the ListTags method to show all the tags currently in play. The full program is given in Example 2-2.

Example 2-2. Decorator pattern example code—Photo Decorator

```
using System;
  using System.Drawing;
  using System.Drawing.Drawing2D;
  using System.Windows.Forms;
  using System.Collections.Generic;
  using Given;

  // Decorator Pattern Example        Judith Bishop  Aug 2007
  // Draws a single photograph in a window of fixed size
  // Has decorators that are BorderedPhotos and TaggedPhotos
  // that can be composed and added in different combinations

  namespace Given {

    // The original Photo class
    public class Photo : Form {
      Image image;
      public Photo () {
        image = new Bitmap("jug.jpg");
        this.Text = "Lemonade";
        this.Paint += new PaintEventHandler(Drawer);
      }

      public virtual void Drawer(Object source, PaintEventArgs e) {
        e.Graphics.DrawImage(image,30,20);
      }
    }
  }

  class DecoratorPatternExample {

    // This simple BorderedPhoto decorator adds a colored border of fixed size
    class BorderedPhoto : Photo {
      Photo photo;
      Color color;

      public BorderedPhoto (Photo p, Color c) {
        photo = p;
        color=c;
      }

      public override void Drawer(Object source, PaintEventArgs e) {
        photo.Drawer(source, e);
        e.Graphics.DrawRectangle(new Pen(color, 10),25,15,215,225);
      }
    }
```

Example 2-2. Decorator pattern example code—Photo Decorator (continued)

```
// The TaggedPhoto decorator keeps track of the tag number which gives it
// a specific place to be written

class TaggedPhoto : Photo {
 Photo photo;
  string tag;
  int number;
  static int count;
  List <string> tags = new List <string> ();

  public TaggedPhoto(Photo p, string t) {
    photo = p;
    tag = t;
    tags.Add(t);
    number = ++count;
  }

  public override void Drawer(Object source, PaintEventArgs e) {
    photo.Drawer(source,e);
    e.Graphics.DrawString(tag,
        new Font("Arial", 16),
        new SolidBrush(Color.Black),
        new PointF(80,100+number*20));
  }

  public string ListTaggedPhotos( ) {
    string s = "Tags are: ";
    foreach (string t in tags) s +=t+" ";
    return s;
  }
}

static void Main () {
  // Application.Run acts as a simple client
  Photo photo;
  TaggedPhoto foodTaggedPhoto, colorTaggedPhoto, tag;
  BorderedPhoto composition;

  // Compose a photo with two TaggedPhotos and a blue BorderedPhoto
  photo = new Photo();
  Application.Run(photo);
  foodTaggedPhoto = new TaggedPhoto (photo,"Food");
  colorTaggedPhoto = new TaggedPhoto (foodTaggedPhoto,"Yellow");
  composition = new BorderedPhoto(colorTaggedPhoto, Color.Blue);
  Application.Run(composition);
  Console.WriteLine(colorTaggedPhoto.ListTaggedPhotos());

  // Compose a photo with one TaggedPhoto and a yellow BorderedPhoto
  photo = new Photo();
  tag = new TaggedPhoto (photo,"Jug");
  composition = new BorderedPhoto(tag, Color.Yellow);
  Application.Run(composition);
```

Example 2-2. Decorator pattern example code—Photo Decorator (continued)

```
    Console.WriteLine(tag.ListTaggedPhotos());
  }
 }
/* Output
TaggedPhotos are: Food Yellow
TaggedPhotos are: Food Yellow Jug
*/
```

An important point about the Decorator pattern is that it is based around new *objects* being created with their own sets of operations. Some of these might be inherited, but only down one level. For example, when implementing the Photo Decorator program, we could try to alter properties of the Windows Form class, such as Height and Width, from within a decorator object. For the component itself and for a first-level decorator, this would work. But as soon as there was a second level of decorators, the changes would not get through. The reason is evident from the object diagram in Figure 2-3: the first decorator holds a reference to the actual Windows Form object, but the second-level decorator does not. For this kind of manipulation a different pattern, such as Strategy (discussed in Chapter 7), would be more fitting.

In the example of the Photo Decorator program, we did not actually add any behavior; we only overrode it. A Client implemented as the Application.Run harness uses the event model to invoke the PaintEventHandler implicitly. It does not give an opportunity for calling other methods explicitly. Of course, other events (such as MouseMove and OnClick) can be programmed, and then the other behaviors in the decorators will make sense (see the "Exercises" section later).

Use

Here are four ways the Decorator pattern is used in the real world:

- As our small example illustrated, the Decorator pattern fits well in the graphics world. It is equally at home with video and sound; for instance, video streaming can be compressed at different rates, and sound can be input to a simultaneous translation service.

- At a more mundane level, decorators abound in the I/O APIs of C#. Consider the following hierarchy:

```
System.IO.Stream
  System.IO.BufferedStream
  System.IO.FileStream
  System.IO.MemoryStream
  System.Net.Sockets.NetworkStream
  System.Security.Cryptography.CryptoStream
```

  The subclasses decorate Stream because they inherit from it, and they also contain an instance of a Stream that is set up when an object is constructed. Many of their properties and methods relate to this instance.

- In today's world of mobile devices, web browsers and other mobile applications thrive on the Decorator pattern. They can create display objects suitable for smaller screens that include scroll bars and exclude banners that would be standard on desktop display browsers, for example.

- The Decorator pattern is so useful that there are now actual Decorator classes in .NET 3.0. The one in System.Windows.Controls "provides a base class for elements that apply effects onto or around a single child element, such as Border or Viewbox."

The following table summarizes when, in general, to use the Decorator pattern.

Use the Decorator pattern when…
You have:
• An existing component class that may be unavailable for subclassing.
You want to:
• Attach additional state or behavior to an object dynamically.
• Make changes to some objects in a class without affecting others.
• Avoid subclassing because too many classes could result.
But consider using instead:
• The Adapter pattern, which sets up an interface between different classes.
• The Composite pattern, which aggregates an object without also inheriting its interface.
• The Proxy pattern, which specifically controls access to objects.
• The Strategy pattern, which changes the original object rather than wrapping it.

Exercises

1. Assume that the Photo class was written with Drawer as a plain (not virtual) method and it cannot be altered. Reconstruct Example 2-2 so that it works under this constraint. (Hint: use an interface as in the theory example.)

2. Add to the Photo Decorator system a second type of component called Hominid. Use the drawing methods for ovals and lines to draw an approximation of a person. Then, use the same two decorators—Tag and Border—to decorate Hominid objects.

3. Add other event handlers to the constructors of the decorators, together with additional behavior. For example, an OnClick event could cause a tag to appear, rather than having it appear automatically.

4. Decorate the Console class so that Write and WriteLine methods are trapped and the output is reformatted for lines of a given size, avoiding unsightly wraparounds. Test your decorator with the program in Example 2-1.

5. Write a program that decorates the Stream class and shows how much of a file has been read in, using a trackbar.

6. Write a program that decorates the Stream class and asks for a password before allowing reading to continue.

7. Write a program that decorates a text message with a simple cipher. Include a second decorator that transforms the encrypted message back to plain text.

Proxy Pattern

Role

The Proxy pattern supports objects that control the creation of and access to other objects. The proxy is often a small (public) object that stands in for a more complex (private) object that is activated once certain circumstances are clear.

Illustration

A major phenomenon in the world today is the rise in popularity of community networking systems, the most prominent of which is Facebook. A session from Facebook is shown in Figure 2-4.

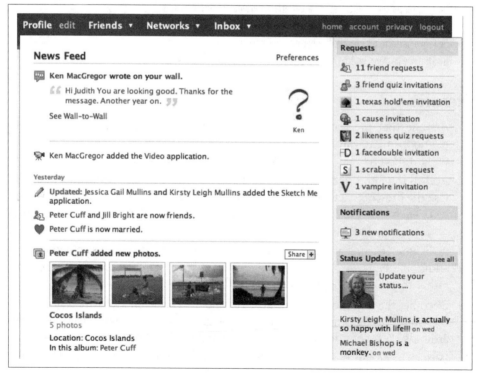

Figure 2-4. Proxy pattern illustration—a page in a social networking system

A feature of such systems is that many people who sign up do so only to view what others are up to and do not actively participate or add content. It might therefore be a good policy to start every newcomer with a plain page and not grant users any actual storage space or access to any facilities until they start adding friends and messages.

Another feature of these systems is that you have to first register with the system and then log on at each session. Once logged on, you have access to your friends' pages. All the actions you can perform (poke, write on walls, send gifts, etc.) originate at your browser and are sent across the network to the nearest Facebook server. The objects are the Facebook pages; the proxies are the mechanisms that allow registration and login.

Design

The design of a proxy and its players is shown in the UML diagram in Figure 2-5.

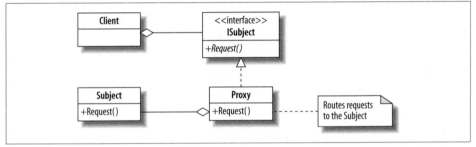

Figure 2-5. Proxy pattern UML diagram

The players in the pattern are:

ISubject
    A common interface for subjects and proxies that enables them to be used interchangeably

Subject
    The class that a proxy represents

Proxy
    A class that creates, controls, enhances, and authenticates access to a Subject

Request
    An operation on the Subject that is routed via a proxy

The central class, Proxy, implements the ISubject interface. The Client can use ISubject to abstract away from proxies. However, as we shall see in the upcoming SpaceBook example, sometimes we can dispense with this interface. Each Proxy object maintains a reference to a Subject, which is where the action really takes place. The Proxy performs frontend work. Its value can be enhanced by making the Subject a private class so that the Client cannot get to the Subject except via the Proxy.

There are several kinds of proxies, the most common of which are:

Virtual proxies
> Hands the creation of an object over to another object (useful if the creation process might be slow or might prove unnecessary)

Authentication proxies
> Checks that the access permissions for a request are correct

Remote proxies
> Encodes requests and send them across a network

Smart proxies
> Adds to or change requests before sending them on

Within the scope of the social networking system mentioned earlier, these map as follows:

- Delaying the creation of a rich environment (virtual proxy)
- Logging in users (authentication proxy)
- Sending requests across the network (remote proxy)
- Performing actions on friends' books (smart proxy

Implementation

A major aim of this book is to introduce interesting features of C# and show how they can make writing patterns easier, clearer, and more secure. As each new feature finds a place in a pattern, I will introduce it via a sidebar. This example illustrates the use of some of C#'s *access modifiers*—the focus of our first sidebar.

Table 2-1. Access modifiers

Modifier	Effect	Default for
private	Accessible within the method or type in which it is declared	Members of classes and structs; nested types
internal	Accessible within the assembly	Non-nested types
protected	Accessible within a class and its derived classes	–
protected internal	Accessible within a class, its derived classes, or an assembly	–
public	Accessible everywhere	Members of enums and interfaces

Now, let's look at a small theoretical example of the pattern that aims to show:

- How the division between the Client on the one hand and the proxies and the Subject on the other can be implemented with the strictest access modifiers possible
- How virtual and protection proxies perform their work and route requests onward

The nub of the virtual proxy code is this:

```
public class Proxy : ISubject {
  Subject subject;

  public string Request() {
    // A virtual proxy creates the object only on its first method call
    if (subject == null)
      subject = new Subject();
    return subject.Request();
  }
}
```

The Client can create the Proxy at any time using a normal instantiation. Because a default constructor is used, the reference to a Subject is not made at this time. It is only when the Request method is called that the Subject reference is checked and, if null, assigned to an instantiated object.

The full code for the theory example is shown in Example 2-3. The example emphasizes that all instances in the client are declared of the interface type, ISubject. This means that access to additional operations in proxies, such as Authenticate, will require the ISubject object to be suitably type-cast, as happens on lines 63 and 64. The example includes the second proxy in the ProtectionProxy class (lines 31–50). This proxy is independent of the other one. If a ProtectionProxy object is declared, as on line 61, all first requests will be met by an instruction to authenticate. In this example, Authenticate is a separate method that must be called, as in lines 63 and 64. In the next example, registrations and authentication will start up automatically when Request is called.

C# Feature—Access Modifiers

At the physical level, a C# program consists of one or more compilation units, each contained in a separate source file. When a C# program is compiled, all of the compilation units are processed together. Thus, compilation units can depend on each other, possibly in a circular fashion. An *assembly* is a physical container for types and the resources associated with them.

At the logical level, C# programs are organized using *namespaces*. Namespaces are used as a way of presenting program elements that are exposed to other programs in the same or different assemblies. Access modifiers are a way of specifying which members of a namespace will be exposed and to what degree.

In C#, an access modifier alters the default accessibility of a type or its members. The available modifiers and the defaults that are applied are shown in Table 2-1. In this table, *types* include classes, structs, interfaces, enums, and delegates. The interpretation of this table for classes is as follows:

- A *non-nested class* is by default visible to other classes in the same assembly.
- A *nested class* is by default private and can have no more accessibility than its enclosing class.
- A *member* of a class (e.g., field, method, property) is by default private.
- An *inherited class* can have special access to a member in its superclass that has been tagged with the protected modifier.

Unless you are going to do cross-assembly development, the public modifier is not strictly necessary; however, it has a currency in programming that the internal modifier does not. It is therefore acceptable to use public when tagging members for access outside of classes. The real need for the more restrictive internal modifier is illustrated in the "Example" section.

There are some restrictions as to where and how access modifiers can be placed. Interface members are always public, and no modifiers are allowed. Namespaces cannot have private or protected members. Modifiers can only be added to types and members to make them as accessible as their enclosing methods or classes.

cf. C# Language Specification Version 3.0, September 2007, Section 10.3.5

Example 2-3. Proxy pattern theory code

```
1    using System;
2
3       // Proxy Pattern                    Judith Bishop  Dec 2006
4       // Shows virtual and protection proxies
5
6       class SubjectAccessor {
7         public interface ISubject {
8           string Request ();
9         }
10
```

Example 2-3. Proxy pattern theory code (continued)

```
11      private class Subject {
12          public string Request( ) {
13            return "Subject Request " + "Choose left door\n";
14          }
15      }
16
17      public class Proxy : ISubject {
18          Subject subject;
19
20          public string Request( ) {
21            // A virtual proxy creates the object only on its first method call
22            if (subject == null) {
23              Console.WriteLine("Subject inactive");
24              subject = new Subject( );
25            }
26            Console.WriteLine("Subject active");
27            return "Proxy: Call to " + subject.Request( );
28          }
29      }
30
31      public class ProtectionProxy : ISubject {
32          // An authentication proxy first asks for a password
33          Subject subject;
34          string password = "Abracadabra";
35
36          public string Authenticate (string supplied) {
37            if (supplied!=password)
38              return "Protection Proxy: No access";
39            else
40              subject = new Subject( );
41              return "Protection Proxy: Authenticated";
42          }
43
44          public string Request( ) {
45            if (subject==null)
46              return "Protection Proxy: Authenticate first";
47            else return "Protection Proxy: Call to "+
48              subject.Request( );
49          }
50      }
51    }
52
53    class Client : SubjectAccessor {
54      static void Main( ) {
55        Console.WriteLine("Proxy Pattern\n");
56
57        ISubject subject = new Proxy( );
58        Console.WriteLine(subject.Request( ));
59        Console.WriteLine(subject.Request( ));
60
61        subject = new ProtectionProxy( );
62        Console.WriteLine(subject.Request( ));
```

Example 2-3. Proxy pattern theory code (continued)

```
63          Console.WriteLine((subject as ProtectionProxy).Authenticate("Secret"));
64          Console.WriteLine((subject as ProtectionProxy).Authenticate("Abracadabra"));
65          Console.WriteLine(subject.Request());
66       }
67    }
68
69    /* Output
70
71    Proxy Pattern
72
73    Subject inactive
74    Subject active
75    Proxy: Call to Subject Request Choose left door
76
77    Subject active
78    Proxy: Call to Subject Request Choose left door
79
80    Protection Proxy: Authenticate first
81    Protection Proxy: No access
82    Protection Proxy: Authenticated
83    Protection Proxy: Call to Subject Request Choose left door
84    */
```

The program is structured with an enclosing class called SubjectAccessor that is there to group the types of the proxies and subjects. The interface and the proxies are all declared as public (lines 7, 17, and 31), so that they and their publicly modified members are fully accessible to clients. The intention of both the virtual and protection proxies is to provide a frontend to the Subject. For this reason, the Subject is declared as private (line 11). Its Request method is public, but it is only visible to classes that can see the class—i.e., those within SubjectAccessor.

We can perform two tests to check that the accessibility is set up just right:

- A more natural grouping for proxies and subjects would have been a namespace, but classes within namespaces are not permitted to be private. See what happens when you change line 6 to namespace SubjectAccessor and add a using SubjectAccessor statement after line 1. The same applies if you remove the SubjectAccessor class altogether, as then the types all belong to the default namespace.

- Add the following statement in the Main method (at line 56):

  ```
  ISubject test = new Subject();
  ```

  The code for a client to declare a real subject will not compile because the program is organized so that it can only declare proxies. However, if you remove the private modifier from Subject (line 11), the instantiation will be accepted. The reason for this is that in order to gain access to the classes in SubjectAccessor, the client inherits from it, thus giving it access to internal members. An alternative way of composing the program is discussed in the exercises.

As this discussion has illustrated, you can make the proxies and the Subject available for use in just the ways you need. They are not intended to be independent of each other—hence their grouping in a class. The proxies are free to aggregate objects of the Subject. They keep them in line with each other and with what they offer to the Client.

Example: SpaceBook

To further investigate proxies, we'll postulate a rudimentary social networking system called *SpaceBook*. SpaceBook keeps pages of text that people enter under their login names, so both authentication and lazy creation of pages are required. As suggested in the earlier "Illustration" section, simply registering for SpaceBook will not give users any space on the system; to gain space, they must first add some content. Therefore, the system should, from the start, enable people to write on others' pages. The SpaceBook class looks like this:

```
// The Subject
private class SpaceBook {
    static SortedList <string,SpaceBook> community =
        new SortedList <string,SpaceBook> (100);
    string pages;
    string name;
    string gap = "\n\t\t\t\t";

    static public bool IsUnique (string name) {
        return community.ContainsKey(name);
    }

    internal SpaceBook (string n) {
        name = n;
        community [n] = this;
    }

    internal void Add(string s) {
        pages += gap+s;
        Console.WriteLine(gap+"======== "+name+"'s SpaceBook =========");
        Console.WriteLine(pages);
        Console.WriteLine(gap+"=========================");
    }

    internal void Add(string friend, string message) {
        community[friend].Add(message);
    }

    internal void Poke (string who, string friend) {
        community[who].pages += gap + friend + " poked you";
    }
}
```

The class maintains a static list of all current users. We use the built-in SortedList class here from System.Collections.Generic and index it with a string, which is the user's name. The constructor enters this SpaceBook object into the collection under the given name. There are two Add methods: one for the user and one to add to another user's pages. Then there is the popular Poke method, which enters a fixed message on another page.

SpaceBook has one public method, which might be unexpected: the static Unique method, which checks whether a name has been used before. It enables us to keep the community list completely private (which it is by default inside the class).

Now, we turn to the client. It shows a few tests of activity on Spacebook by Judith and Tom:

```
// The Client
class ProxyPattern : SpaceBookSystem {
  static void Main () {
    MySpaceBook me = new MySpaceBook();
    me.Add("Hello world");
    me.Add("Today I worked 18 hours");

    MySpaceBook tom = new MySpaceBook();
    tom.Poke("Judith");
    tom.Add("Judith","Poor you");
    tom.Add("Off to see the Lion King tonight");
  }
}
```

The first user, whom we deduce is Judith, creates a MySpaceBook (not a SpaceBook) and adds two messages to it. Then, Tom also creates a MySpaceBook, pokes Judith, and adds a message to her page and to his page.

Note that neither the client nor the actual SpaceBook system has any authentication code. This will all be handled in the proxy, whose name is now obvious—MySpaceBook. The output for the preceding client code is:

```
Let's register you for SpaceBook
All SpaceBook names must be unique
Type in a user name: Judith
Type in a password: haha
Thanks for registering with SpaceBook
Welcome Judith. Please type in your password: haha
Logged into SpaceBook

        ======== Judith's SpaceBook =========
        Hello world
        ==================================

        ======== Judith's SpaceBook =========
        Hello world
            Today I worked 18 hours
        ==================================
```

```
Let's register you for SpaceBook
All SpaceBook names must be unique
Type in a user name: Tom
Type in a password: yey
Thanks for registering with SpaceBook
Welcome Tom. Please type in your password: yey
Logged into SpaceBook

          ======== Judith's SpaceBook =========
          Hello world
          Today I worked 18 hours
          Tom poked you
          eTom said: Poor you
          ===================================

          ======== Tom's SpaceBook =========
          Off to see the Lion King tonight
          ===================================
```

We can distinguish between the output from SpaceBook itself, which is centered within lines, and the interaction initiated by the proxies.

SpaceBook does not have a constructor, so apart from obtaining a reference, nothing happens when the client instantiates a SpaceBook. The heart of the proxy is here:

```
public void Add(string message) {
  Check();
  if (loggedIn) mySpaceBook.Add(message);
}


void Check() {
  if (!loggedIn) {
    if (password==null)
    Register();
    if (mySpaceBook == null)
    Authenticate();
  }
}
```

The first point of contact by the client is a call on Add. Add immediately checks the status of the user and takes him through the steps of registering and supplying a password, and then authenticating against this password. Check is also called from the other Add methods and the Poke method. We can now consider the full program, shown in Example 2-4.

Example 2-4. Proxy pattern example code—SpaceBook

```
using System;
using System.Collections.Generic;

  // Proxy Pattern Example          Judith Bishop  Aug 2007
 // Sets up a SpaceBook page with registration and authentication
```

Example 2-4. Proxy pattern example code—SpaceBook (continued)

```
class SpaceBookSystem {

  // The Subject
  private class SpaceBook {
    static SortedList <string,SpaceBook> community =
        new SortedList <string,SpaceBook> (100);
    string pages;
    string name;
    string gap = "\n\t\t\t\t";

    static public bool IsUnique (string name) {
      return community.ContainsKey(name);
    }

    internal SpaceBook (string n) {
      name = n;
      community [n] = this;
    }

    internal void Add(string s) {
      pages += gap+s;
      Console.Write(gap+"======== "+name+"'s SpaceBook =========");
      Console.Write(pages);
      Console.WriteLine(gap+"===================================");

    }

    internal void Add(string friend, string message) {
      community[friend].Add(message);
    }

    internal void Poke (string who, string friend) {
      community[who].pages += gap + friend + " poked you";
    }
  }

    // The Proxy
    public class MySpaceBook {
      // Combination of a virtual and authentication proxy
      SpaceBook mySpaceBook;
      string password;
      string name;
      bool loggedIn = false;

      void Register () {
        Console.WriteLine("Let's register you for SpaceBook");
        do {
          Console.WriteLine("All SpaceBook names must be unique");
          Console.Write("Type in a user name: ");
          name = Console.ReadLine();
        } while (SpaceBook.Unique(name));
        Console.Write("Type in a password: ");
```

Example 2-4. Proxy pattern example code—SpaceBook (continued)

```
      password = Console.ReadLine( );
      Console.WriteLine("Thanks for registering with SpaceBook");
    }

  bool Authenticate ( ) {
    Console.Write("Welcome "+name+". Please type in your password: ");
    string supplied = Console.ReadLine( );
    if (supplied==password) {
      loggedIn = true;
      Console.WriteLine("Logged into SpaceBook");
      if (mySpaceBook == null)
        mySpaceBook = new SpaceBook(name);
      return true;
    }
    Console.WriteLine("Incorrect password");
    return false;
  }

  public void Add(string message) {
    Check( );
    if (loggedIn) mySpaceBook.Add(message);
  }

  public void Add(string friend, string message) {
    Check( );
    if (loggedIn)
      mySpaceBook.Add(friend, name + " said: "+message);
  }

  public void Poke(string who) {
    Check( );
    if (loggedIn)
      mySpaceBook.Poke(who,name);
  }

  void Check( ) {
    if (!loggedIn) {
      if (password==null)
        Register( );
      if (mySpaceBook == null)
        Authenticate( );
    }
  }
}

// The Client
class ProxyPattern : SpaceBookSystem {
  static void Main ( ) {
    MySpaceBook me = new MySpaceBook( );
    me.Add("Hello world");
    me.Add("Today I worked 18 hours");
```

Example 2-4. Proxy pattern example code—SpaceBook (continued)

```
        MySpaceBook tom = new MySpaceBook( );
        tom.Poke("Judith");
        tom.Add("Judith","Poor you");
        tom.Add("Off to see the Lion King tonight");
    }
  }
/* Output
Let's register you for SpaceBook
All SpaceBook names must be unique
Type in a user name: Judith
Type in a password: haha
Thanks for registering with SpaceBook
Welcome Judith. Please type in your password: haha
Logged into SpaceBook


            ======== Judith's SpaceBook =========
            Hello world
            =================================


            ======== Judith's SpaceBook =========
            Hello world
                  Today I worked 18 hours
            =================================
Let's register you for SpaceBook
All SpaceBook names must be unique
Type in a user name: Tom
Type in a password: yey
Thanks for registering with SpaceBook
Welcome Tom. Please type in your password: yey
Logged into SpaceBook


            ======== Judith's SpaceBook =========
            Hello world
            Today I worked 18 hours
            Tom poked you
            eTom said: Poor you
            =================================


            ======== Tom's SpaceBook =========
            Off to see the Lion King tonight
            =================================


*/
```

Notice that in this program there is no need for the ISubject interface. SpaceBook and
MySpaceBook reside within the SpaceBookSystem and handle interaction through aggregation (MySpaceBook has a reference to a SpaceBook object) and accessibility modifiers, as discussed earlier.

Use

Proxies are frontends to classes that have sensitive data or slow operations. They are often found in image-drawing systems, where the proxy places a placeholder on the screen and then activates a real drawer to fetch and render the image. In the same way, they can be involved in initiating the buffering associated with video streaming.

Proxies, like decorators, forward requests on to another object. The difference is that the proxy relationship is set up at design time and is well-known in advance, even though the Subject is not an active participator in the relationship. Decorators, on the other hand, can be added dynamically.

We have not examined remote proxies in detail in this section, but they can be found in any client/server system running on the .NET Framework (see "Exercises," later).

Use the Proxy pattern when...

You have objects that:
- Are expensive to create.
- Need access control.
- Access remote sites.
- Need to perform some action whenever they are accessed.

You want to:
- Create objects only when their operations are requested.
- Perform checks or housekeeping on objects whenever accessed.
- Have a local object that will refer to a remote object.
- Implement access rights on objects as their operations are requested.

Exercises

1. Change Example 2-3 so that the Client does not inherit from the Program, but rather creates an instance of it.

2. If you are a GUI programmer, turn the SpaceBook system into something more visually appealing. You can either replace the methods in SpaceBook (the subject) to draw frames in windows and so on, or add decorators, leaving the existing component as it is.

3. The SpaceBook system as it stands lacks a real "friends" facility; at the moment, a user has access to all the other books on the system. Improve SpaceBook so that friends can be added and then operations such as Poke can be done only on users who have been declared (and accepted as) your friends. Carefully design your improvements so that code goes in the right place—SpaceBook (the subject) or MySpaceBook (the proxy).

4. Another type of online community network holds photos (an example is Flickr). Users upload photos, which all others can view but only friends can download or comment on. Sketch out the use of the Proxy pattern for such a system.

5. Consider how to monitor an activity on a library. For example, supposing a third-party library expects a `Stream` class, you could implement your own `MyStream` class that intercepts, monitors, and logs every call to Stream methods. Write a short test program that uses the Proxy pattern to illustrate this idea.

Bridge Pattern

Role

The Bridge pattern decouples an abstraction from its implementation, enabling them to vary independently. The Bridge pattern is useful when a new version of software is brought out that will replace an existing version, but the older version must still run for its existing client base. The client code will not have to change, as it is conforming to a given abstraction, but the client will need to indicate which version it wants to use.

Illustration

Consider the rolling out of a new version of the .NET Framework used to compile and run C# 3.0. You can have several versions of the Framework loaded on your computer at any time and can select which one to use by externally setting a path to it in the Windows operating system. Setting the path is the *bridge* between what applications want from the Framework and the actual version they will get. Figure 2-6 shows that the one the system is being directed to is Version 3.5, which includes the C# 3.0 compiler. In Figure 2-7, you can see that there are five versions of the Framework loaded on my computer.

Design

Inheritance is a common way to specify different implementations of an abstraction. However, the implementations are then bound tightly to the abstraction, and it is difficult to modify them independently. The Bridge pattern provides an alternative to inheritance when there is more than one version of an abstraction. Consider the UML diagram in Figure 2-8. The two implementations, A and B, implement an interface called the `Bridge`. The `Abstraction` includes an attribute of type `Bridge` but is not otherwise in a relationship with the implementations.

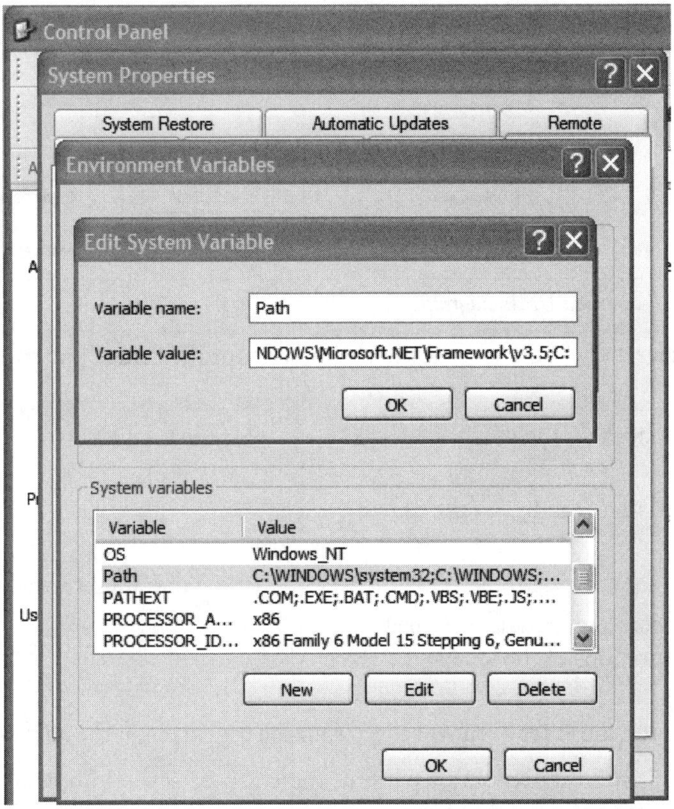

Figure 2-6. Bridge pattern illustration (a)—environment Path variable set to Version 3.5

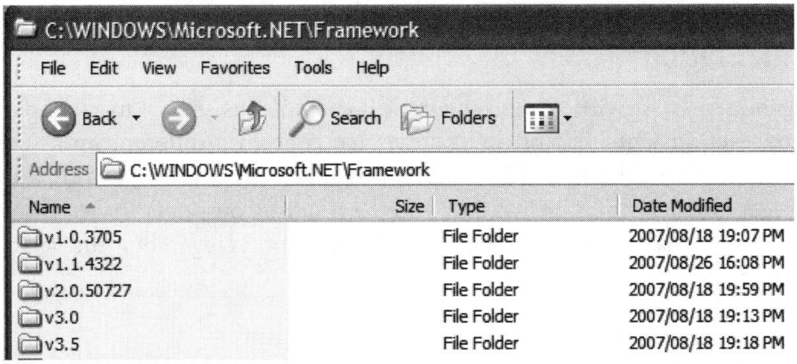

Figure 2-7. Bridge pattern illustration (b)—five versions of the .NET Framework loaded

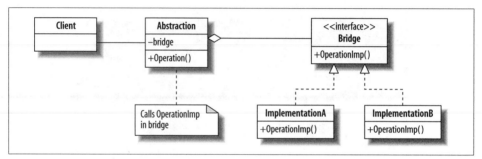

Figure 2-8. Bridge pattern UML diagram

From this diagram, we can see that the role players for the Bridge pattern are:

Abstraction
> The interface that the client sees

Operation
> A method that is called by the client

Bridge
> An interface defining those parts of the Abstraction that might vary

ImplementationA *and* ImplementationB
> Implementations of the Bridge interface

OperationImp
> A method in the Bridge that is called from the Operation in the Abstraction

As we noticed with the Decorator pattern, there can be several implementations for the one abstraction. Legacy implementations do not have to implement the Bridge if they are still going to be instantiated in the old way; they need to do so only if they must be used interchangeably with the new implementations.

Implementation

Once again, let's start with a small theoretical example, as shown in Example 2-5. In the client, each instantiation of the Abstraction is given a different implementation (lines 36–37). Then, the Operations are called. Each invocation goes to a different OperationImp method (lines 23 and 29), and the resulting output is shown below (lines 43–44). Notice that the implementations implement Bridge, but the Abstraction aggregates it.

Example 2-5. Bridge pattern theory code

```
1    using System;
2
3    class BridgePattern {
4
5    // Bridge Pattern          Judith Bishop  Dec 2006, Aug 2007
6    // Shows an abstraction and two implementations proceeding independently
7
```

Example 2-5. Bridge pattern theory code (continued)

```
8      class Abstraction {
9        Bridge bridge;
10       public Abstraction (Bridge implementation) {
11         bridge = implementation;
12       }
13       public string Operation () {
14         return "Abstraction" +" <<< BRIDGE >>>> "+bridge.OperationImp();
15       }
16     }
17
18     interface Bridge {
19       string OperationImp();
20     }
21
22     class ImplementationA : Bridge {
23       public string  OperationImp () {
24         return "ImplementationA";
25       }
26     }
27
28     class ImplementationB : Bridge {
29       public string OperationImp () {
30         return "ImplementationB";
31       }
32     }
33
34     static void Main () {
35       Console.WriteLine("Bridge Pattern\n");
36       Console.WriteLine(new Abstraction (new ImplementationA()).Operation());
37       Console.WriteLine(new Abstraction (new ImplementationB()).Operation());
38     }
39   }
40   /* Output
41   Bridge Pattern
42
43   Abstraction <<< BRIDGE >>>> ImplementationA
44   Abstraction <<< BRIDGE >>>> ImplementationB
45   */
```

Example: OpenBook

The Bridge pattern gives us a nice opportunity to extend a previous example and to show different patterns interacting. Let's consider the SpaceBook system again. Suppose a developer is working on a new version of SpaceBook called OpenBook. The main feature of OpenBook is that it does not require password authentication. It also does not bother with lazy instantiation, as it is assumed that all OpenBook users will get onto the system straightaway. OpenBook is thus replacing the proxy level of SpaceBook but not the guts of it, and it is certainly the intention that users of both systems should be able to see each other's pages.

Therefore, we have a design where MyOpenBook and MySpaceBook need to implement a common interface. We shall call this the Bridge interface. The Abstraction is what is commonly called a Portal. It keeps a copy of the appropriate type of book object and routes each of the methods in the interface to the versions in that book object. The main program then reflects these changes:

```
class BridgePattern : SpaceBookSystem {
  static void Main () {
    MySpaceBook me = new MySpaceBook();
    me.Add("Hello world");
    me.Add("Today I worked 18 hours");

    Portal tom = new Portal(new MyOpenBook("Tom"));
    tom.Poke("Judith");
    tom.Add("Judith","Poor you");
    tom.Add("Hey, I'm also on OpenBook - it was so easy!");
  }
}
```

Users like Judith can continue to use the old SpaceBook, as nothing has changed, but Tom can now go in through the Portal (the Abstraction) and link up via the Bridge to the new OpenBook access to SpaceBook. The resulting output starts off as before, but then we see that Tom did not have to register or authenticate:

```
Let's register you for SpaceBook
All SpaceBook names must be unique
Type in a user name: Judith
Type in a password: yey
Thanks for registering with SpaceBook
```

```
Welcome Judith. Please type in your password: yey
Logged into SpaceBook


                ======== Judith's SpaceBook =========
Hello world
                   Today I worked 18 hours
                   Tom poked you
                   Tom : hugged you


                =================================

                ======== Judith's SpaceBook =========
Hello world
                   Today I worked 18 hours
                   Tom poked you
                   Tom : hugged you
                   Tom : Poor you


                =================================

                ======== Tom-1's SpaceBook =========
Hey, I'm on OpenBook - it was so easy!


                =================================
```

Here, we'll assume that the developer decided to avoid conflicting names by adding a serial number to each user's ID—if the next user is Pat, her name will be Pat-2. At the moment, Tom's output still refers to SpaceBook because the new system is still using all of SpaceBook's facilities. Once OpenBook has been customized further, this will change. The frontend is encapsulated in the Bridge interface:

```
interface Bridge {
  void Add(string message);
  void Add(string friend, string message);
  void Poke(string who);
}
```

The Portal is very simple and performs the duties of the abstraction exactly as they were laid out in Example 2-5. However, it has three operations to route instead of one:

```
class Portal {
  Bridge bridge;
  public Portal (Bridge aSpaceBook) {
    bridge = aSpaceBook;
  }
  public void Add(string message)
    {bridge.Add(message);}
  public void Add(string friend, string message)
    {bridge.Add(friend,message);}
  public void Poke(string who)
    {bridge.Poke(who);}
}
```

The second implementation of the `Bridge` interface in this example also happens to be a Proxy to SpaceBook. Most of the Proxy mechanisms have been stripped out, and all that remains is the smart proxy operation of keeping a serial count of users. Here is OpenBook in its most rudimentary form:

```
public class MyOpenBook : Bridge {
  // Combination of a virtual and authentication proxy
  SpaceBook mySpaceBook;
  string name;
  static int users;

  public MyOpenBook (string n) {
    name = n;
    users++;
    mySpaceBook = new SpaceBook(name+"-"+users);
  }

  public void Add(string message) {
    mySpaceBook.Add(message);
  }

  public void Add(string friend, string message) {
    mySpaceBook.Add(friend, name + " said: "+message);
  }

  public void Poke(string who) {
    mySpaceBook.Poke(who,name);
  }
}
```

Note that the `Bridge` defines the operations that will be supported by all `Portal` members. Now, suppose OpenBook wanted to add some cool operations, like `SuperPoke`:

```
public void SuperPoke (string who, string what) {
  myOpenBook.Add(who, what+" you");
}
```

`SuperPoke` is implemented rather crudely on top of `Add`, as this is a SpaceBook-supported feature. If we put `SuperPoke` in OpenBook, the compiler will accept it, but we won't be able to call it because in the main program tom is a reference to a `Portal` object and `SuperPoke` is not in the `Portal`. We can solve this problem in two ways:

- Add the new operation to the `Portal` (Abstraction), but not to the `Bridge`, so it does not affect other implementations.

- If we cannot alter the `Portal`, we can create an extension method to extend it as follows:

```
static class OpenBookExtensions {
  public static void SuperPoke (this Portal me, string who, string what) {
    me.Add(who, what+" you");
  }
}
```

and call it the same way we call the other methods:

```
tom.SuperPoke("Judith-1","hugged");
```

Extension methods are one of the new features in C# 3.0.

C# 3.0 Feature—Extension Methods

Extension methods allow developers to add new methods to an existing type without having to create an inherited class or to recompile the original. Thus, you can add methods to classes for which you might not even have the sources (e.g., System. String). An extension method is defined the same way as any other, with two stipulations:

- It is declared as static in an outer-level static, nongeneric class.
- The type it is extending is declared as the first parameter, preceded by this.

The method can then be called as an instance method on an object of the type that has been extended.

cf. C# Language Specification Version 3.0, September 2007, Section 10.6.9

The full program for the OpenBook extension is given in Example 2-6. The SpaceBook and MySpaceBook classes from Example 2-4 were not altered in any way and are given as headers only to save space. In this output, Judith has switched to Open-Book and therefore has the name Judith-1. Tom, as the second OpenBook user, is given the name Tom-2.

Example 2-6. Bridge pattern example code—OpenBook

```
using System;
  using System.Collections.Generic;

  // Bridge Pattern Example      Judith Bishop  Dec 2006, Aug 2007
  // Extending SpaceBook with a second implementation via a Portal

  // Abstraction
  class Portal {
    Bridge bridge;
    public Portal (Bridge aSpaceBook) {
      bridge = aSpaceBook;
    }
    public void Add(string message)
      {bridge.Add(message);}
    public void Add(string friend, string message)
      {bridge.Add(friend,message);}
    public void Poke(string who)
      {bridge.Poke(who);}
    }
```

Example 2-6. Bridge pattern example code—OpenBook (continued)

```
  // Bridge
  interface Bridge {
    void Add(string message);
    void Add(string friend, string message);
    void Poke(string who);
  }

  class SpaceBookSystem {

  // The Subject
  private class SpaceBook { ... }

  // The Proxy
  public class MySpaceBook { ... }

  // A Proxy with little to do
  // Illustrates an alternative implementation of the Bridge pattern

  public class MyOpenBook : Bridge {
    // Combination of a virtual and authentication proxy
    SpaceBook myOpenBook;
    string name;
    static int users;

    public MyOpenBook (string n) {
      name = n;
      users++;
      myOpenBook = new SpaceBook(name+"-"+users);
    }

    public void Add(string message) {
      myOpenBook.Add(message);
    }

    public void Add(string friend, string message) {
      myOpenBook.Add(friend, name + " : "+message);
    }

    public void Poke(string who) {
      myOpenBook.Poke(who,name);
    }
  }
}

static class OpenBookExtensions {
  public static void SuperPoke (this Portal me, string who, string what) {
    me.Add(who, what+" you");
  }
}

// The Client
class BridgePattern : SpaceBookSystem {
  static void Main () {
```

Example 2-6. Bridge pattern example code—OpenBook (continued)

```
        Portal me = new Portal(new MyOpenBook("Judith"));
        me.Add("Hello world");
        me.Add("Today I worked 18 hours");

        Portal tom = new Portal(new MyOpenBook("Tom"));
        tom.Poke("Judith-1");
        tom.SuperPoke("Judith-1","hugged");
        tom.Add("Judith-1","Poor you");
        tom.Add("Hey, I'm on OpenBook - it's cool!");
    }
  }
/* Output
        ======== Judith-1's SpaceBook =========
        Hello world


        ===================================

        ======== Judith-1's SpaceBook =========
        Hello world
        Today I worked 18 hours


        ===================================

        ======== Judith-1's SpaceBook =========
        Hello world
        Today I worked 18 hours
        Tom poked you
        Tom : hugged you


        ===================================

        ======== Judith-1's SpaceBook =========
        Hello world
        Today I worked 18 hours
        Tom poked you
        Tom : hugged you
        Tom : Poor you


        ===================================

        ======== Tom-2's SpaceBook =========
        Hey, I'm on OpenBook - it's cool!


        ===================================

*/
```

Use

Bridge is a very simple, but very powerful pattern. Given a single implementation, we can add a second one together with a `Bridge` and an `Abstraction` and achieve considerable generality over the original design.

A well-quoted use of the Bridge pattern is in graphics, where different displays have different capabilities and drivers. These would be the implementations of the Bridge pattern, and the `Bridge` would be an interface of their essential capabilities. The `Client` calls the `Abstraction` to display something, and the `Abstraction` can examine the properties of the one or more `Bridge` instances (drivers) it is holding and select the most appropriate one for the task.

Use the Bridge pattern when...

You can:
- Identify that there are operations that do not always need to be implemented in the same way.

You want to:
- Completely hide implementations from clients.
- Avoid binding an implementation to an abstraction directly.
- Change an implementation without even recompiling an abstraction.
- Combine different parts of a system at runtime.

Exercise

1. Although some limited operations can be added to OpenBook, the fact that some fundamental ones, such as the page header, are embedded in the private SpaceBook class makes real change difficult. Assuming that you can negotiate an upgrade with the developers of SpaceBook, make a proposal, including a UML diagram, for the long-term design of an extensible system. Implement it.

Pattern Comparison

The careful reader might have noticed that the three patterns described in this chapter seem to offer much the same service. At a high level, they are all helping to extend classes in novel ways, and they all provide alternatives to inheritance. A summary of when each pattern might be used was provided at the end of each section. Because this is also a programming book, we'll now summarize the object mechanisms the patterns use (see Table 2-2) and draw conclusions about their comparative operation. This summary is based on the UML diagrams and theory code for each of the patterns.

In each pattern, we can identify four roles, which can fall under the headings *original*, *new*, *interface*, and *client*. The actual names given to these meta-roles are shown in the first three rows of the table. Note that the Bridge pattern can work in two ways. In our examples, we used the "Bridge-up" option. We assumed that we had

---

one implementation already and wanted to share its interface with other implementations yet to be built. To do so, we needed to create an `Abstraction` that was closely connected to the `Bridge` interface. An equally valid application for the Bridge pattern would be to have an original abstraction in mind and to build it hand-in-hand with the implementations (the "Bridge-down" approach).

Table 2-2. Comparison of Decorator, Proxy, and Bridge patterns

	Decorator	**Proxy**	**Bridge-down**	**Bridge-up**
Original	Component	Subject	Abstraction	Implementation
Interface	IComponent	ISubject	Bridge	Bridge
New	Decorator	Proxy	Implementation	Abstraction
Client aggregates	New with interface	New	Original with new	New with original
Client activates	Original and new	New	Original	New
Original changed by	Implementing the interface	No change	Aggregating the interface	Implementing the interface
New classes	Aggregate the interface	Aggregate the original	Implement the interface	Aggregate the interface
	Implement the interface	Implement the interface		
Operation routed	From new to original	From new to original	From original to new	From new to original

As you can see in the fourth row of the table, variations are found in the clients. For example, the Decorator pattern aggregates the interface so that it can share decorations; it provides the original as a construction parameter. The Bridge-up pattern does the same. To make this more concrete, here are the two statements from the clients:

```
// Decorator
Display(new DecoratorA(new IComponent()));

// Bridge-up
Console.WriteLine(new Abstraction(new ImplementationA()).Operation());
```

The fifth row shows what objects are invoked in the pattern. The Decorator pattern can call the original components or the decorators, but the Bridge pattern variations only call one or the other. The Proxy pattern both aggregates and invokes only the new classes.

The next row itemizes how the original changes as a result of the pattern. Only the Proxy pattern enables the original to remain completely unchanged. The Decorator pattern relies on there being an interface that everyone implements, which might have to be added after the original classes are developed. The Bridge pattern is more closely coupled, and there is an understanding that the original must incorporate considerable references to the rest of the system.

All the patterns rely on rerouting operations. The last row in the table shows that the rerouting is always done from the new code back to the original; in the case of the Bridge pattern, it just depends on which class is called new and which class is called the original. It is worth noting that in real-time applications, where reaction time is important, the overhead of the time for rerouting the operations might not be acceptable.

CHAPTER 3

Structural Patterns: Composite and Flyweight

The Composite and Flyweight structural patterns apply to systems that have many data objects. The Composite pattern has wide applicability, and its composite lists can also make use of the Flyweight pattern. The Flyweight pattern shares identical objects behind the scenes to save space. In their implementations, these patterns make use of the following novel C# features:

- Generics
- Properties
- Structs
- Indexers
- Implicit typing
- Initializers
- Anonymous types

Composite Pattern

Role

The Composite pattern arranges structured hierarchies so that single components and groups of components can be treated in the same way. Typical operations on the components include add, remove, display, find, and group.

Illustration

Computer applications that specialize in grouping data abound these days. Consider a music playlist in iTunes or a digital photo album in Flickr or iPhoto (Figure 3-1). Items are put in a large list, which is then given structure separately.

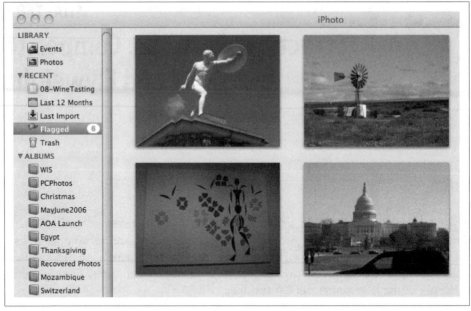

Figure 3-1. Composite pattern illustration—iPhoto

Looking at the screenshot from iPhoto, we can see that there are different ways of viewing the photos that have been imported: chronologically or by named event. A single photo can appear in many albums ("Last Roll," "2007," and "Switzerland," for example). Creating an album forms a composite object but does not entail actually copying the photos. In this context, the important point about the Composite pattern is that the operations carried out on photos and albums of photos should have the same names and effects, even though the implementations are different. For example, the user should be able to display a photo or an album (that contains photos). Similarly, deletions of a single photo or an album should behave in the same way.

Design

The Composite pattern is one of the simplest there is, on the face of it. It has to deal with two types: Components and Composites of those components. Both types agree to conform to an interface of common operations. Composite objects consist of Components, and in most cases, operations on a Composite are implemented by calling the equivalent operations for its Component objects. See Figure 3-2 for the UML diagram for this pattern.

The essential players in the Composite pattern UML diagram are:

IComponent

> Defines the operations for objects in the composition, and any default behavior that will be applicable across objects of both types

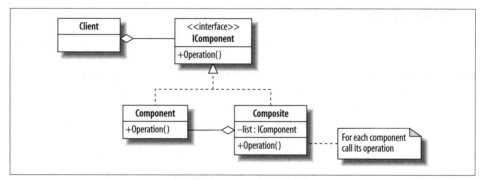

Figure 3-2. Composite pattern UML diagram

Operation
> Performs an operation on IComponent-conforming objects

Component
> Implements the operations as applicable to single objects that cannot be further decomposed

Composite
> Implements the operations as applicable to composite objects, using (or accessing) a list of components kept locally and probably using the equivalent Component operations

The client deals only with the IComponent interface, which simplifies its task.

Implementation

Although our illustration referred to photos and albums, the design and implementation of the Composite pattern is completely independent from the kind of basic component being handled. We could equally well be dealing with groups of people or bank account portfolios. The composite operations, however, have to iterate through a structure of these components. To realize both the flexibility of components of any type and a connection between leaf and composite, we can use the C# *generics* feature.

C# Feature—Generics

Generics are an extension to the type system whereby structs, classes, interfaces, delegates, and methods can be parameterized with types. For example, a generic type like List<T> is a generator for constructed types like List<string> and List<Person>. All the collections in the .NET Framework library used by C# are available in generic form. They include Dictionary, Stack, Queue, and List, plus variations on them. There are also generic methods such as Sort and BinarySearch. These require the types they are working on to implement the IComparer interface so that comparisons between elements can be done correctly.

To specify a generic type or method, use the generic parameters in angle brackets, as in <T> or <T, P>. The generic type can be used to specify further generic elements, again using the <T> format, or it can be used normally as a type, as in T.

To construct an actual type or method from a generic one, supply actual types for each of the generic parameters, as in <string>.

cf. C# Language Specification Version 3.0, September 2007, Section 10.1.3

By declaring IComponent, Component, and Composite as generic types, we create an implementation of the Composite pattern that can be instantiated in a practical example.

For the Composite pattern, we will not create a *program*, but a *namespace* containing two classes, Composite and Component, and an interface, IComponent.

Starting with the IComponent interface, we declare it as a generic of type T. Then each of the anticipated operations follows:

```
public interface IComponent <T> {
   void         Add(IComponent <T> c);
   IComponent <T> Remove(T s);
   IComponent <T> Find(T s);
   string       Display(int depth);
   T            Item {get; set;}
}
```

Because the types will be in a separate namespace, they must all be declared as public.

Why do Add, Remove, and Find refer to IComponent <T> and Remove and Find refer to T as well? What is the difference between <T> and T? Recall that an object of type IComponent is either a Component or a Composite and will have state associated with being an IComponent, in addition to the actual value of the element it is storing. The element is of the type T, so in the case of Find and Remove, we pass as parameters the actual element values of type T. For example, if the interface were instantiated with T as an Image, we would pass an Image object to Find and in return get a reference to an IComponent object. The returned object would contain the Image object if the search were successful.

The last line of the interface is interesting because it introduces a new syntax for properties in classes. Before C# 3.0, this new syntax was only present in interfaces. It has now been extended to classes as well and makes programs shorter and easily readable.

C# 3.0 Feature—Properties and Accessors

A *property* gives controlled access to the private local state of an object, either directly to its fields or via some computation. Properties define one or two accessors: get and/ or set. The most common form of a property is:

```
public type Field {get; set;}
```

where Field is an identifier. This declaration creates a private field and makes it accessible for public reading and writing via the name Field.

By placing such properties in an interface, we are effectively requiring classes to supply property accessors as well as the usual methods when implementing the interface.

Properties can omit either the get or the set accessor; it is more typical to omit the set, which makes the property read-only.

Properties can also compute the result of a get or set, in which case, the expanded syntax is:

```
public type Field {
  get { statements; return expression; }
  set { statements including reference to value; }
}
```

A property typically, but not necessarily, has access to a private type Field. value is the implicit parameter of a call to set a property.

cf. C# Language Specification Version 3.0, September 2007, Section 10.7

Now, let's consider how the Component class would be implemented in accordance with the IComponent interface, as in the namespace shown in Example 3-1.

Example 3-1. Composite pattern—namespace code

```
1  using System;
2  using System.Collections.Generic;
3  using System.Text; // for StringBuilder
4
5  namespace CompositePattern {
6
7    // The Interface
8    public interface IComponent <T> {
9      void Add(IComponent <T> c);
10     IComponent <T> Remove(T s);
11     string Display(int depth);
12     IComponent <T> Find(T s);
13     T Name {get; set;}
14   }
15
16   // The Component
17   public class Component <T> : IComponent <T> {
18     public T Name {get; set;}
19
20     public Component (T name)  {
21         Name = name;
22     }
23
24     public void Add(IComponent <T> c) {
25        Console.WriteLine("Cannot add to an item");
26     }
27
28     public IComponent <T>  Remove(T s) {
29         Console.WriteLine("Cannot remove directly");
30         return this;
31     }
32
33     public string Display(int depth) {
34         return new String('-', depth) + Name+"\n";
35     }
36
37     public IComponent <T>  Find (T s) {
38       if (s.Equals(Name))
39        return this;
40       else
41         return null;
42     }
43   }
44
45   // The Composite
46   public class Composite <T> : IComponent  <T> {
47     List  <IComponent <T>> list;
48
49     public T Name {get; set;}
50
51     public Composite (T name)  {
52         Name = name;
```

Example 3-1. Composite pattern—namespace code (continued)

```
53              list = new List <IComponent <T>> ();
54          }
55
56          public void Add(IComponent  <T> c) {
57              list.Add(c);
58          }
59
60          IComponent <T> holder=null;
61
62          // Finds the item from a particular point in the structure
63          // and returns the composite from which it was removed
64          // If not found, return the point as given
65          public IComponent <T> Remove(T s) {
66            holder = this;
67            IComponent <T> p = holder.Find(s);
68            if (holder!=null) {
69              (holder as Composite<T>).list.Remove(p);
70              return holder;
71            }
72            else
73              return this;
74          }
75
76          // Recursively looks for an item
77          // Returns its reference or else null
78          public IComponent <T>  Find (T s) {
79            holder = this;
80            if (Name.Equals(s)) return this;
81            IComponent <T> found=null;
82            foreach (IComponent <T> c in list)  {
83              found = c.Find(s);
84              if (found!=null)
85                break;
86            }
87            return found;
88          }
89
90          // Displays items in a format indicating their level in the composite structure
91          public string Display(int depth) {
92            StringBuilder s = new StringBuilder(new String('-', depth));
93            s.Append("Set "+ Name +  " length :" + list.Count + "\n");
94            foreach (IComponent <T> component in list) {
95              s.Append(component.Display(depth + 2));
96            }
97            return s.ToString( );
98          }
99      }
100  }
```

The namespace starts off with the definition of the interface with its four methods and one property. Then follows the Component class. Not all of IComponent's methods are meaningful for Components. Adding and removing are done only in Composites, so a simple error message is written out (see the upcoming "Exercises" section for an extension on this point). In the Component's Find method (lines 37–42), the class relies on the actual type parameter for T having an Equals method. If it does not, the generic instantiation will fail at compile time.

The Display method (lines 33–35) also assumes that the field accessed by the Name property has a ToString method defined. In fact, only string-like types will work properly here, so it is likely that the Display method should be defined later (see the upcoming "Exercises" section.)

The Composite class also implements the IComponent interface (line 46). The Find and Remove methods of the Composite are more elaborate than those in the Component so that they can handle arbitrary structures of composites and components. Let's look at some of the more interesting statements:

- The Composite keeps as a list a local structure that consists of Components and Composites (line 47). When the contents are Composites, a new object is created, as well as a new list. The list is declared as:

  ```
  List <IComponent <T>> list;
  ```

  This shows that an open generic type can be used as a parameter to another generic type.

- The logic of Remove (lines 65–74) is that we first find the item in the structure and then, if it is there, we remove it from the list structure held locally in the Composite (line 69):

  ```
  (holder as Composite<T>).list.Remove(p);
  ```

  The holder variable is of type IComponent and needs to be cast to a Composite before the list can be accessed.

- An open generic type can still be used in a foreach loop, as in the Find and Display methods (lines 82 and 94):

  ```
  foreach (IComponent <T> c in list) {
    found = c.Find(s);
  ```

- The call to Find will go to the appropriate method, depending on the actual type of c at runtime. This supports the Composite pattern's ideal of having Components and Composites be treated the same.

That completes the theoretical Composite pattern implementation. Apart from the concern with the Display method, the three preceding types can be used together for any elements. Thus, we can put them in a namespace called CompositePattern for use in the next example.Example: Photo Library

In this example, we are concerned with collecting the filenames of digital photos into named sets. We will not use actual images in this example, just filenames as strings. The client is given a domain-specific set of commands with which to create and manipulate the library. Central to the manipulation of the library, from the user's point of view, is "where we are." We start out at an empty set called "Album." Some of the commands leave the system at the component that has just been adjusted, whereas others move it back to the first component in the set. The commands are:

AddSet
> Add a new empty set with a name and stay there.

AddPhoto
> Add a new named photo after the pointer and stay there.

Find
> Find the named component (set or photo), or return null if it is not found.

Remove
> Remove the named component (set or photo) and stay at the set from which it was removed.

Display
> Display the whole structure.

Quit
> Exit the program.

Thus, the two operations that work on either Components or Composites are Find and Remove. Consider some examples of the workings of this system, illustrated in Example 3-2. The input commands are shown in the middle, the result of Display is shown on the left, and some commentary appears on the right.

 The input file contains all the commands in the middle. The program will expect this file to be called *Composite.dat*.

Example 3-2. Composite pattern—Photo Library sample run

```
                AddSet Home
                AddPhoto Dinner.jpg
                AddSet Pets     Going down another level
                AddPhoto Dog.jpg
                AddPhoto Cat.jpg
                Find Album      Ensures Garden is at same level as Home
                AddSet Garden
                AddPhoto Spring.jpg
                AddPhoto Summer.jpg
                AddPhoto Flowers.jpg
                AddPhoto Trees.jpg
                Display         Returns to start of Album
 Set Album length :2
--Set Home length :2
----Dinner.jpg
----Set Pets length :2
------Dog.jpg
------Cat.jpg
--Set Garden length :4
----Spring.jpg
----Summer.jpg
```

Example 3-2. Composite pattern—Photo Library sample run (continued)

```
----Flowers.jpg
----Trees.jpg
            Remove Flowers.jpg        Will remain at Garden
            AddPhoto BetterFlowers.jpg   To end of Garden
            Display
 Set Album length :2
--Set Home length :2
----Dinner.jpg
----Set Pets length :2
------Dog.jpg
------Cat.jpg
--Set Garden length :4
----Spring.jpg
----Summer.jpg
----Trees.jpg
----BetterFlowers.jpg
            Find Home
            Remove Pets
            Display
 Set Album length :2
--Set Home length :1
----Dinner.jpg
--Set Garden length :4
----Spring.jpg
----Summer.jpg
----Trees.jpg
----BetterFlowers.jpg
            Quit
```

The Client class that implements these commands is shown in Example 3-3. It is a simple command interpreter that makes good use of C#'s switch on string feature.

Example 3-3. Composite pattern example code—Photo Library

```csharp
using System;
using System.Collections.Generic;
using System.IO;
using CompositePattern;

  // The Client
  class CompositePatternExample {
    static void Main () {
      IComponent <string> album = new Composite<string> ("Album");
      IComponent <string> point = album;
      string [] s;
      string command, parameter;
      // Create and manipulate a structure
      StreamReader instream = new StreamReader("Composite.dat");
      do {
        string t = instream.ReadLine( );
        Console.WriteLine("\t\t\t\t"+t);
        s = t.Split( );
```

Example 3-3. Composite pattern example code—Photo Library (continued)

```
          command = s[0];
          if (s.Length>1) parameter = s[1]; else parameter = null;
          switch (command) {
            case "AddSet" :
              IComponent <string> c = new Composite <string> (parameter);
              point.Add(c);
              point = c;
              break;
            case "AddPhoto" :
              point.Add(new Component <string> (parameter));
              break;
            case "Remove" :
              point = point.Remove(parameter);
              break;
            case "Find" :
              point = album.Find(parameter);
              break;
            case "Display" :
              Console.WriteLine(album.Display(0));
              break;
            case "Quit" :
              break;
          }
      } while (!command.Equals("Quit"));
   }
}
```

Use

The Composite pattern has wide applicability and is often used in conjunction with the Decorator, Iterator, and Visitor patterns. Its composite lists can also make use of the Flyweight pattern, discussed next. The Composite pattern looks like an ordinary data structure implementation, but it is more than that because of its ability to manipulate the different types of the elements equally.

Use the Composite pattern when…

You have:
- An irregular structure of objects and composites of the objects

You want:
- Clients to ignore all but the essential differences between individual objects and composites of objects
- To treat all objects in a composite uniformly

But consider using as well:
- The Decorator pattern to provide operations like Add, Remove, and Find
- The Flyweight pattern to share components, provided the notion of "where I am" can be disregarded and all operations start at the root of the composite
- The Visitor pattern to localize the operations that are currently distributed between the Composite and Component classes

Exercises

1. A manager is an employee who leads engineers, technicians, and support personnel, all of whom are also employees. Focusing on the operation of going on leave, model this scenario with the Composite pattern.

2. In the Composite pattern example, the Component class has two error conditions. Implement them using exceptions, and decide whether the exceptions should be part of the IComponent interface. In general, how do you think patterns should deal with exceptions?

3. The Display methods in Component and Composite assume that the type T is string-like. Create a version of the Composite pattern where T is not a type that converts to strings (use Image, for instance) and investigate whether the Display methods can be overridden by extension methods in the namespace of the Client.

4. In the Composite class, change the List to a Dictionary class. How will this affect the Find operation?

5. Although we strove to have one interface for components and composites, an alternative approach is to consider the operations that are really common and to separate out those that apply only to, for example, composites. We will then have two levels of interfaces, as in:

```
interface IComponent {
  // Name, Display
}
interface IComposite<T> IComponent where T : IComponent {
  // Add, Remove, Find
}
```

Now, there is no need for IComponent to be generic—a component is just something that has a name and can be displayed. The tension about when to use T and when to use IComponent<T> falls away, too. Reprogram the example in this manner. (Hint: the second interface above makes use of generic constraints, which are covered in Chapter 6.)

Flyweight Pattern

Role

The Flyweight pattern promotes an efficient way to share common information present in small objects that occur in a system in large numbers. It thus helps reduce storage requirements when many values are duplicated. The Flyweight pattern distinguishes between the *intrinsic* and *extrinsic* state of an object. The greatest savings in the Flyweight pattern occur when objects use both kinds of state but:

- The intrinsic state can be shared on a wide scale, minimizing storage requirements.
- The extrinsic state can be computed on the fly, trading computation for storage.

Illustration

Consider now the image aspect of the Photo Library application, as discussed with the Composite pattern. At any one time, we want to have a full page of images displayed and, with no discernable time lag, we want to be able to scroll up and down through the library. This implies that as many images as possible should be preloaded into memory and kept there while the photo application is running. For a Photo Group application, the primary function is to arrange photos in groups. Photos can belong to several different groups, so the number of images to display could increase enormously. If all of the images do not fit in memory, the fact that they can belong to different groups means that any given photo may be called up for display at irregular times, resulting in a lot of disk transfers.

Consider the illustration in Figure 3-3. With a smaller window, the first two groups could have scrolled off the window by the time the Food group appears, requiring at least three of the images to be refetched and displayed.

An object's *unshared* state is the set of groups to which it belongs. Its extrinsic state is the actual image, which is large—it occupies about 2 MB. However, there are methods in the System.Drawing namespace to convert an image to a thumbnail of about 8 KB. This will be the object's intrinsic state, which is small enough to allow all the unique images to remain in memory at any one time. Through the group information, the application can display the images in various combinations. Using disk fetches, it can also show the complete original-sized images.

Design

Consider the UML diagram in Figure 3-4. As explained in the previous section, the Flyweight pattern relies on being able to divide up the application's state into three types. The intrinsicState resides in the Flyweight objects. The Flyweight class implements an IFlyweight interface, which specifies the operations upon which the rest of the system relies. The Client maintains the unSharedState as well as a dictionary of all the Flyweights, which it gets from a FlyweightFactory whose job it is to ensure that only one of each value is created. Finally, the extrinsicState does not appear in the system as such; it is meant to be computed at runtime for each instrinsicState instance, as required.

The players in the Flyweight pattern are:

Client
: Computes and maintains the unshared state of the objects

IFlyweight
: Defines an interface through which Flyweights can receive and act on intrinsic state

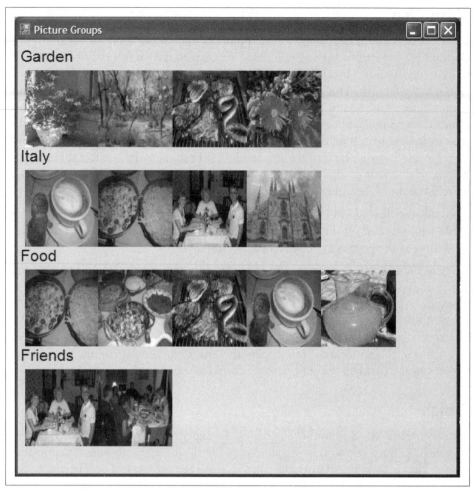

Figure 3-3. Flyweight pattern illustration—Photo Group

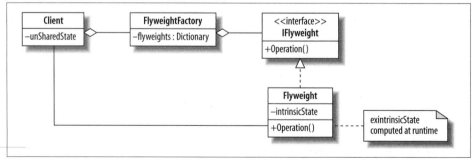

Figure 3-4. Flyweight pattern UML diagram

`FlyweightFactory`
> Creates and manages unique `Flyweight` objects

`Flyweight`
> Stores intrinsic state that is shareable among all objects

There are other design options. For example, in Figure 3-4, the `Flyweight` is shown as computing the `extrinsicState`. However, the `Client` could do the computation and pass the `extrinsicState` to the `Flyweight` as a parameter to the `Operation`. Also, we envisage the `unSharedState` as a `Dictionary` of values related to the `Flyweights`; however, the `unSharedState` could have a more complex structure, warranting its own class. In this case, it would stand alongside the `Flyweight` class and implement the `IFlyweight` interface.

QUIZ

Match the Flyweight Pattern Players with the Photo Group Illustration

To test whether you understand the Flyweight pattern, cover the lefthand column of the table below and see if you can identify the players among the items from the illustrative example (Figure 3-4), as shown in the righthand column. Then check your answers against the lefthand column.

`Client`	Photo Group Application
`xIFlyweight`	Specification of an image
`FlyweightFactory`	Register of unique images
`Flyweight`	Creator and drawer of a thumbnail
`intrinsicState`	Thumbnail
`extrinsicState`	Full image
`unSharedState`	Group information

Implementation

Our implementation of the Flyweight pattern makes use of two interesting features from C# 1.0 and three from C# 3.0. They are:

- Structs
- Indexers
- Implicit typing for local variables and arrays
- Object and collection initializers
- Anonymous types

In addition, it uses generic collections from C# 2.0, as discussed in the section on the Composite pattern. I will introduce these features in the text that follows.

This pattern encompasses three types: `IFlyweight`, `Flyweight`, and `FlyweightFactory`. As in the Composite pattern, we shall put them in a namespace and use the namespace as the theory example for the pattern.

 Because the types are in an interface, they and their constructors must be declared as `public`.

We'll start with the interface:

```
public interface IFlyweight {
  void Load (string filename);
  void Display (PaintEventArgs e, int row, int col);
}
```

The `Load` method will load into memory a thumbnail version of a given image using its filename. The `Display` method will display that thumbnail. Later, we will need to add further `Display` options for displaying the full version of the image (its extrinsic state). Now, let's consider the first of our five features: structs.

C# Feature—Structs

C# has two typing constructs that define attributes and operations: the well-known *class* and the lesser-known *struct*. Structs are similar to classes in that they represent types that can contain data members and function members. However, a variable of a struct type directly contains the data of the struct, whereas a variable of a class type contains a reference to the data. Instances of both class and structs are *objects*. However, Structs have *value semantics*—that is, the value is passed on assignment, rather than the reference, as is the case with objects instantiated from classes.

Structs are lightweight and are implemented without the overhead. They are particularly useful for small data structures. The restriction on structs is that they cannot inherit from other types; they can, however, implement interfaces.

cf. C# Language Specification Version 3.0, September 2007, Section 11

A `Flyweight` is an ideal candidate for a struct; `Flyweights` are small, and they do not inherit from anything (although the type does implement an interface). Here is our `Flyweight` struct:

```
public struct Flyweight : IFlyweight {
  // Intrinsic state
  Image pThumbnail;
```

```
public void Load (string filename) {
    pThumbnail = new Bitmap("images/"+filename).
        GetThumbnailImage(100, 100, null, new IntPtr());
}

public void Display(PaintEventArgs e, int row, int col) {
  e.Graphics.DrawImage(pThumbnail,col*100+10, row*130+40,
      pThumbnail.Width,pThumbnail.Height);
}
}
```

As desired, Load uses the image at the given filename, but it doesn't retain a copy of it in its intrinsicState; it keeps only the thumbnail. The computations done to position the thumbnails across the screen are shown in Figure 3-3. They could obviously be improved using constants. Notice, however, that the row and col information is derived from the unSharedState of the group, which is kept by the Client.

Next, let's consider the factory. We'll look further at factories in Chapter 6, but for now, I'll just say that in their simplest form, they generate objects according to specific conditions. Here, we are interested in checking whether an object exists already before we add it to a collection. Before we dive into the code, let's take a quick look at indexers (see over).

Now, we can give the FlyweightFactory class:

```
1   public class FlyweightFactory {
2     // Keeps an indexed list of IFlyweight objects in existence
3     Dictionary <string,IFlyweight> flyweights =
4         new Dictionary <string,IFlyweight> ();
5
6     public FlyweightFactory () {
7       flyweights.Clear();
8     }
9
10    public IFlyweight this[string index] {
11      get {
12        if (!flyweights.ContainsKey(index))
13            flyweights[index]=new Flyweight();
14        return flyweights[index];
15      }
16    }
17  }
```

In lines 3–4, a Dictionary is declared, mapping strings to flyweights. On lines 13–14, the Dictionary is accessed using the indexer that is part of the Dictionary definition. Line 13 is an example of the use of the set accessor, and line 14 calls a get accessor.

This is all part of the member declared in lines 10–16, where we define our own indexer for the FlyweightFactory class. Line 10 specifies the return type and the key type, and lines 12–14 give the body of the get accessor. It starts by checking whether there is already a Flyweight with this key. If not, it allocates one. In either case, it returns the element in the dictionary with the correct index.

Jumping ahead, we will see that the FlyweightFactory is instantiated as follows:

```
static FlyweightFactory album = new FlyweightFactory();
```

and accessed as follows:

```
album[filename].Load(filename);
```

Thus, the indexer provides array-like access to an object that holds a private collection.

Example: Photo Group

Now, consider the application that produced the output in Figure 3-4. Its code, preceded by the FlyweightPattern namespace developed above, is shown in Example 3-4.

 Instructions for compiling a namespace separately from the program that uses it are included in the discussion of the Façade pattern in Chapter 4.

Example 3-4. Flyweight pattern example—Photo Group including the FlyweightPattern namespace

```csharp
using System;
using System.Collections.Generic;
using System.Drawing;
using System.Windows.Forms;

namespace FlyweightPattern {

    // Flyweight Pattern          Judith Bishop  Sept 2007

    public interface IFlyweight {
      void Load (string filename);
      void Display (PaintEventArgs e, int row, int col);
    }

    public struct Flyweight : IFlyweight {
      // Intrinsic state
      Image pThumbnail;
      public void Load (string filename) {
        pThumbnail = new Bitmap("images/"+filename).
            GetThumbnailImage(100, 100, null, new IntPtr());
    }

    public void Display(PaintEventArgs e, int row, int col) {
      e.Graphics.DrawImage(pThumbnail,col*100+10, row*130+40,
          pThumbnail.Width,pThumbnail.Height);
    }
  }

  public class FlyweightFactory {
    // Keeps an indexed list of IFlyweight objects in existence
    Dictionary <string,IFlyweight> flyweights =
        new Dictionary <string,IFlyweight> ();

    public FlyweightFactory () {
       flyweights.Clear();
    }

    public IFlyweight this[string index] {
      get {
        if (!flyweights.ContainsKey(index))
        flyweights[index] = new Flyweight();
        return flyweights[index];
      }
    }
  }
}

//=============== End of namespace, start of program

using System;
using System.Collections.Generic;
using System.Drawing;
```

```
using System.Windows.Forms;
using FlyweightPattern;

class Client {
  // Shared state - the images
  static FlyweightFactory album = new FlyweightFactory( );

  // Unshared state - the groups
  static Dictionary <string,List<string>> allGroups =
      new Dictionary <string,List<string>> ( );

  public void LoadGroups ( ) {
    var myGroups = new [] {
      new  {Name = "Garden",
            Members = new [] {"pot.jpg", "spring.jpg",
            "barbeque.jpg", "flowers.jpg"}},
        new  {Name = "Italy",
            Members = new [] {"cappucino.jpg","pasta.jpg",
            "restaurant.jpg", "church.jpg"}},
        new  {Name = "Food",
            Members = new [] {"pasta.jpg", "veggies.jpg",
            "barbeque.jpg","cappucino.jpg","lemonade.jpg" }},
        new  {Name = "Friends",
            Members = new [] {"restaurant.jpg", "dinner.jpg"}}
    };

    // Load the Flyweights, saving on shared intrinsic state
    foreach (var g in myGroups) { // implicit typing
      allGroups.Add(g.Name,new List <string>( ));
      foreach (string filename in g.Members) {
        allGroups[g.Name].Add(filename);
        album[filename].Load(filename);
      }
    }
  }

  public void DisplayGroups (Object source, PaintEventArgs e) {
    // Display the Flyweights, passing the unshared state
    int row;
    foreach(string g in allGroups.Keys) {
      int col;
      e.Graphics.DrawString(g,
          new Font("Arial", 16),
          new SolidBrush(Color.Black),
          new PointF(0, row*130+10));
      foreach (string filename in allGroups[g]) {
        album[filename].Display(e, row, col);
        col++;
      }
      row++;
    }
  }
}
```

Example 3-4. Flyweight pattern example—Photo Group including the FlyweightPattern namespace (continued)

```
    }

    class Window : Form {
      Window( ) {
        this.Height = 600;
        this.Width = 600;
        this.Text = "Picture Groups";
        Client client = new Client( );
        client.LoadGroups( );
        this.Paint += new PaintEventHandler (client.DisplayGroups);
      }

      static void Main ( ) {
        Application.Run(new Window( ));
      }
    }
  }
```

The application runs in two phases: load groups and display groups. For ease of image handling, we'll use the `Application.Run` model from C#. The Windows object calls `LoadGroups` explicitly, and `DisplayGroups` is invoked implicitly through the `PaintEventHandler` once the `Form` is drawn. `LoadGroups` illustrates the use of some of the implicit typing and initializing features of C# 3.0. (See the following sidebars.)

C# 3.0 Feature—Implicit Typing

Variables can be declared as fields in classes or as locals in methods. A local variable of a method (but not a field of a class or a struct) can have its type inferred from the expression used to initialize it. This is called *implicit typing*. The syntax is to use var in place of the type. This new syntax can aid readability by reducing redundancy. In the following example, the type is now specified only once:

```
var marks = new Dictionary <string, int> ( );
```

The syntax is vital when the type is not named (an *anonymous type*, discussed in the upcoming sidebar). In this case, implicit typing enables the type to be inferred from an associated variable or type, as in:

```
foreach (var g in myGroups) { ... }
```

cf. C# Language Specification Version 3.0, September 2007, Section 8.5

`myGroups` in the `LoadGroups` method is an example of an anonymous type with a collection and an array initializer. It establishes the image filenames in each group. Of course, this data should be read from the disk, but it is interesting to see how it can be entered into the program via an anonymously typed data structure. The initializer defines the data structure members (in this case, Name and Members)—used later in the method by the foreach loop to set up the groups:

```
foreach (var g in myGroups) { // implicit typing
  allGroups.Add(g.Name,new List <string>());
  foreach (string filename in g.Members) {
    allGroups[g.Name].Add(filename);
    album[filename].Load(filename);
  }
}
```

The flyweight activity happens in the last line, where album is accessed with a given file-name and either returns an existing shared flyweight object or creates one and then returns it. The Load method is then called on this object, which is of type IFlyweight.

C# 3.0 Feature—Implicitly Typed Arrays

With respect to arrays in C# 2.0, only the length could be inferred from the simple form of array initializer. Implicit typing has since been extended to arrays so that both the element type and the length are inferred from the expression, as in:

```
var myGroups = new [] {
  new  {Name=  "Garden",
        Members = new [] {"pot.jpg", "spring.jpg"
        "barbeque.jpg", "flowers.jpg"}},
  new  {Name = "Friends",
        Members = new [] {"restaurant.jpg", "dinner.jpg"}}

};
```

This would create a new array of a type that has two rows (row 0 and row 1). Each element is an object with two fields, Name and Members. Members itself is an array with a different length in each case.

cf. C# Language Specification Version 3.0, September 2007, Section 7.5.10.4

C# 3.0 Feature—Object and Collection Initializers

Initializers specify values for fields or properties of objects or collections. Examples of initializers include:

```
Point p = new Point {X = 0, Y = 1};
List<int> digits = new List<int>
    { 0, 1, 2, 3, 4, 5, 6, 7, 8, 9 };
```

In C# 2.0, initialization syntax was valid only for arrays.

cf. C# Language Specification Version 3.0, September 2007, Section 7.5.10.1-3

Anonymous types are created from object initializers. An anonymous type is a nameless class type that inherits directly from the supertype object. The members of an anonymous type are a sequence of read-only properties inferred from the anonymous object initializer used to create an instance of the type. By nesting new declarations, an initializer can specify values for an entire collection of objects. For example, the anonymous type created by this declaration:

```
var group = new    {Name = "Italy",
    Members = new  [] {"cappuccino.jpg", "pasta.jpg",
    "restaurant.jpg", "church.jpg"}},
```

would have two properties, Name and Members, with Members being an array of strings. The types would have internal names and would be compatible with any other type of the same structure. So, for example, group could be assigned to an element of myGroups, as in:

```
myGroups[0] = group;
```

Automatic get properties are created for the listed members, so we can access the value of group.Name. There is no set property.

cf. C# Language Specification Version 3.0, September 2007, Section 7.5.10.6

Use

The Flyweight pattern is specifically designed to be used when all the following conditions are in place:

- There is a very large number of objects (thousands) that may not fit in memory.
- Most of the state can be kept on disk or calculated at runtime.
- The remaining state can be factored into a much smaller number of objects with shared state.

Many examples of the Flyweight pattern refer to text processing, where the flyweight objects are characters. However, the previous example using images is more convincing in this day and age.

Use the Flyweight pattern when...

There are:
- Many objects to deal with in memory
- Different kinds of state, which can be handled differently to achieve space savings
- Groups of objects that share state
- Ways of computing some of the state at runtime

You want to:
- Implement a system despite severe memory constraints

Exercises

1. Implement the final stage of the Photo Group application, which involves fetching and displaying an image (extrinsic state) when its thumbnail (intrinsic state) is clicked.

2. Integrate the Photo Library and Photo Group applications so that commands can be issued as well as photos displayed. Keep track of the two patterns (Composite and Flyweight) and report at the end of the exercise how they fit together.

3. In the earlier Composite pattern example (Example 3-3), the specification of the Photo Library was read from a file. As an exercise in object initialization, specify the initial state of the library in the program using the same data:

    ```
    AddSet Home
    AddPhoto Dinner.jpg
    AddSet Pets      Going down another level
    AddPhoto Dog.jpg
    AddPhoto Cat.jpg
    Find Album       Ensures Garden is at same level as Home
    AddSet Garden
    AddPhoto Spring.jpg
    AddPhoto Summer.jpg
    AddPhoto Flowers.jpg
    AddPhoto Trees.jpg
    ```

    (Hint: take these lines out of the data file. The program won't have to change otherwise, as the loop will start processing from the first command it finds in the file, which will be `Display`.)

Pattern Comparison

I grouped the Composite and Flyweight patterns in this chapter because they both deal with structures of multiple objects. The Composite pattern is concerned with reacting to commands for accessing and altering a data structure in a uniform way, whereas the Flyweight pattern is a clever way of saving space when there are multiple identical objects. They both have the property that the types making up the pattern can be packaged into a namespace and then used by a client.

In our examples, the `CompositePattern` namespace was programmed generically, giving any client the built-in flexibility of instantiating the pattern to suit its needs. The constraints that I mentioned at the time were that a type used for instantiating `Component` needed to have `Equals` and `ToString` methods defined. The `Equals` method is essential for the correct working of the `Find` method, but the `ToString` requirement can be dispensed with if different output is arranged. The `FlyweightPattern` namespace, on the other hand, contains the `IFlyweight` and `Flyweight` types, which are very specific to the photo application used for illustration. (It also contains the `FlyweightFactory` class, which is not dependent on any class from the client.)

Flyweight is a server pattern in the sense that it can be useful to many other patterns to keep data compact. Examples we will encounter later are the Interpreter, State, and Strategy patterns. The Composite pattern is also useful in combination with other patterns that need to manage data structures. More typically, the Composite pattern will use the Flyweight pattern, rather than the other way around.

The division of intrinsic versus extrinsic state in the Flyweight pattern has a parallel with the virtual Proxy pattern. The original intent of the Flyweight pattern was that the extrinsic state would be computed from the intrinsic state. In our example of the Photo Group application, we did not so much compute the extrinsic state as use the name of the photo to fetch it from disk. The Proxy pattern has a similar feel to it in that, given a starting point, we can go to the disk and fetch the full item required. One difference is that the Proxy pattern deals with an object individually, whereas the Flyweight pattern from the start works with a dictionary of objects. These observations are summarized in Table 3-1.

Table 3-1. Comparison of Composite and Flyweight patterns

	Composite	Flyweight
Fixed types	IComponent <T> Component <T> Composite <T>	IFlyweight Flyweight FlyweightFactory
Generic	Yes	FlyweightFactory is type-independent
Constraints	T implements Equals and ToString	Structure and relationship of intrinsic and extrinsic state built into Flyweight type
Companion patterns	Decorator, Builder, Iterator, Visitor	Composite, Interpreter, State, Strategy, Proxy

CHAPTER 4

Structural Patterns: Adapter and Façade

The main pattern we will consider in this chapter is the Adapter pattern. It is a versatile pattern that joins together types that were not designed to work with each other. It is one of those patterns that comes in useful when dealing with legacy code—i.e., code that was written a while ago and to which one might not have access. There are different kinds of adapters, including class, object, two-way, and pluggable. We'll explore the differences here. The second pattern we will look at in this chapter—the Façade pattern—is a simple one that rounds out the structural group. The aim of this pattern is to provide a simplified interface to a set of complex systems.

Adapter Pattern

Role

The Adapter pattern enables a system to use classes whose interfaces don't quite match its requirements. It is especially useful for off-the-shelf code, for toolkits, and for libraries. Many examples of the Adapter pattern involve input/output because that is one domain that is constantly changing. For example, programs written in the 1980s will have very different user interfaces from those written in the 2000s. Being able to adapt those parts of the system to new hardware facilities would be much more cost effective than rewriting them.

Toolkits also need adapters. Although they are designed for reuse, not all applications will want to use the interfaces that toolkits provide; some might prefer to stick to a well-known, domain-specific interface. In such cases, the adapter can accept calls from the application and transform them into calls on toolkit methods.

Illustration

Our illustration of the Adapter pattern is a very real one—it involves hardware instruction sets, not input/output. From 1996 to 2006, Apple Macintosh computers ran on the PowerPC processor. The operating system was Mac OS X. But in April 2006, Apple started releasing all new Apple computers—iMacs, Minis, and Mac-Books—with Intel Core Duo processors. Mac OS X was rewritten to target the new processor, and users of the new computers mostly accessed existing Intel-based software via other operating systems, such as Linux and Windows. Figure 4-1 shows iMacs made in 1998 and 2006.

Figure 4-1. Adapter pattern illustration—migration of Mac OS X from a 1998 PowerPC-based iMac to a 2007 Intel-based iMac

Mac OS X was originally designed to take advantage of the AltiVec floating-point and integer SIMD instruction set that is part of the PowerPC processor. When the Intel processor replaced this processor, calls to AltiVec instructions from Mac OS X had to be retargeted to the Intel x86 SSE extensions, which provide similar functionality to AltiVec.

For something as important as an operating system, the code could be rewritten to replace the calls to AltiVec with calls to SSE. However, Apple recognized that application developers might not want to do this, or might not have access to the source of old AltiVec-based code, so they recommended the use of the *Accelerate* framework. The Accelerate framework is a set of high-performance vector-accelerated libraries. It provides a layer of abstraction for accessing vector-based code without needing to use vector instructions or knowing the architecture of the target machine. (This is the important point for us here.) The framework automatically invokes the appropriate instruction set, be it PowerPC or Intel (in these processors' various versions).

Thus, the Accelerate framework is an example of the Adapter pattern. It takes an existing situation and adapts it to a new one, thus solving the problem of migrating existing code to a new environment. No alterations to the original code are required.*

Design

The Adapter pattern's important contribution is that it promotes programming to interfaces. The Client works to a domain-specific standard, which is specified in the ITarget interface. An Adaptee class provides the required functionality, but with a different interface. The Adapter implements the ITarget interface and routes calls from the Client through to the Adaptee, making whatever changes to parameters and return types are necessary to meet the requirements. A Target class that implements the ITarget interface directly could exist, but this is not a necessary part of the pattern. In any case, the Client is aware only of the ITarget interface, and it relies on that for its correct operation.

The adapter shown in Figure 4-2 is a *class adapter* because it *implements* an interface and *inherits* a class. The alternative to inheriting a class is to *aggregate* the Adaptee. This creates an *object adapter*. The design differences are primarily that *overriding* Adaptee behavior can be done more easily with a class adapter, whereas *adding* behavior to Adaptees can be done more easily with an object adapter. As we go along, I will point out different instances.

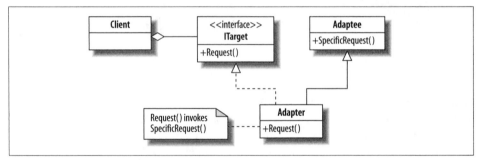

Figure 4-2. Adapter pattern UML diagram

The purpose of the ITarget interface is to enable objects of adaptee types to be interchangeable with any other objects that might implement the same interface. However, the adaptees might not conform to the operation names and signatures of ITarget, so an interface alone is not a sufficiently powerful mechanism. That is why we need the Adapter pattern. An Adaptee offers similar functionality to Request, but under a different name and with possibly different parameters. The Adaptee is

---

* For more about this migration, read the "Introduction to AltiVec/SSE Migration Guide" at *http://developer. apple.com*.

completely independent of the other classes and is oblivious to any naming conventions or signatures that they have. Now, let's consider the roles in the pattern:

ITarget
>The interface that the Client wants to use

Adaptee
>An implementation that needs adapting

Adapter
>The class that implements the ITarget interface in terms of the Adaptee

Request
>An operation that the Client wants

SpecificRequest
>The implementation of Request's functionality in the Adaptee

 The pattern applies to a single computer, which would only have either the PowerPC or the Intel chip. In this case, it has the Intel chip—hence the need for the adapter. There is no Target class present, just the ITarget interface.

QUIZ

Match the Adapter Pattern Players with the Mac OS X Migration Illustration

To test whether you understand the Adapter pattern, cover the lefthand column of the table below and see if you can identify its players among the items from the illustrative example (Figure 4-1), as shown in the righthand column. Then check your answers against the lefthand column.

Client	Mac OS X (or any Mac application)
ITarget	The specification of the AltiVec instruction set
Request	A call to an AltiVec instruction
Adapter	The Accelerate framework
Adaptee	An Intel processor with an SSE instruction set
DifferentRequest	A Call to an SSE instruction

Implementation

It is best to illustrate the structure of the adapter with a small example, even at the theory code level. Suppose that technical readings are being collected and reported at a high level of precision, but the client can only make use of rough estimates.

The signatures for the interface would be couched in terms of integers, and for the actual implementation in terms of double-precision numbers. Thus, an adapter is needed, as shown in Example 4-1.

Example 4-1. Adapter pattern theory code

```
1    using System;
2
3    // Adapter Pattern - Simple         Judith Bishop  Oct 2007
4    // Simplest adapter using interfaces and inheritance
5
6    // Existing way requests are implemented
7    class Adaptee {
8      // Provide full precision
9      public double SpecificRequest (double a, double b) {
10       return a/b;
11     }
12   }
13
14   // Required standard for requests
15   interface ITarget {
16     // Rough estimate required
17     string Request (int i);
18   }
19
20   // Implementing the required standard via Adaptee
21   class Adapter : Adaptee, ITarget {
22     public string Request (int i) {
23       return "Rough estimate is " + (int) Math.Round(SpecificRequest (i,3));
24     }
25   }
26
27   class Client {
28
29     static void  Main () {
30       // Showing the Adapteee in standalone mode
31       Adaptee first = new Adaptee();
32       Console.Write("Before the new standard\nPrecise reading: ");
33       Console.WriteLine(first.SpecificRequest(5,3));
34
35       // What the client really wants
36       ITarget second = new Adapter();
37       Console.WriteLine("\nMoving to the new standard");
38       Console.WriteLine(second.Request(5));
39     }
40   }
41   /* Output
42   Before the new standard
43   Precise reading: 1.66666666666667
44
45   Moving to the new standard
46   Rough estimate is 2
47   */
```

The main program in the client shows two scenarios. First, there is an example of how the Adaptee could be called directly (line 33)—its output is shown in line 43. However, the client wants to work to a different interface for requests (lines 17 and 38). The Adapter implements the ITarget interface and inherits the Adaptee (line 21). Therefore, it can accept Request calls with a string-int signature and route them to the Adaptee with a double-double-double signature (line 23). The new output is shown on line 46.

A feature of adapters is that they can insert additional behavior between the ITarget interface and the Adaptee. In other words, they do not have to be invisible to the Client. In this case, the Adapter adds the words "Rough estimate is" to indicate that the Request has been adapted before it calls the SpecificRequest (line 23).

Adapters can put in varying amounts of work to adapt an Adaptee's implementation to the Target's interface. The simplest adaptation is just to reroute a method call to one of a different name, as in the preceding example. However, it may be necessary to support a completely different set of operations. For example, the Accelerate framework mentioned in the "Illustration" section will need to do considerable work to convert AltiVec instructions to those of the Intel Core Duo processor. To summarize, we have the following options when matching adapter and adaptee interfaces:

Adapter interface and adaptee interface have same signature
This is the trivial case, with not much work to do.

Many examples of the Adapter pattern operate at this level and are not illustrative or helpful in explaining its real power. Beware of them.

Adapter interface has fewer parameters than adaptee interface
The adapter calls the adaptee with some dummy input.

This case is shown in Example 4-1, where the second parameter is defaulted to 3.

Adapter interface has more parameters than adaptee interface
The adapter adds the missing functionality, making it half an adapter and half a component in its own right.

Adapter interface has other types than adaptee interface
The adapter performs some type conversion (casting).

This case is shown in Example 4-1, where the first double parameter is created from an integer and the double return type is cast back to a string.

Of course, combinations of these basic cases are also possible.

Two-Way Adapters

Adapters provide access to some behavior in the Adaptee (the behavior required in the ITarget interface), but Adapter objects are not interchangeable with Adaptee objects. They cannot be used where Adaptee objects can because they work on the implementation of the Adaptee, not its interface. Sometimes we need to have objects that can be transparently ITarget or Adaptee objects. This could be easily achieved if the Adapter inherited both interfaces; however, such multiple inheritance is not possible in C#, so we must look at other solutions.

The two-way adapter addresses the problem of two systems where the characteristics of one system have to be used in the other, and vice versa. An Adapter class is set up to absorb the important common methods of both and to provide adaptations to both. The resulting adapter objects will be acceptable to both sides. Theoretically, this idea can be extended to more than two systems, so we can have multiway adapters, but there are some implementation limitations: without multiple inheritance, we have to insert an interface between each original class and the adapter.

Our Macintosh example has a follow-up that illustrates this point nicely. With an Intel processor on board, a Mac can run the Windows operating system.* Windows, of course, is targeted directly for the Intel processor and will make use of its SSE instructions where necessary. In such a situation, we can view Windows and Mac OS X as two clients wanting to get access to the Adaptee (the Intel processor). The Adapter catches both types of instruction calls and translates them if required. For an instruction issued by an application, the situation on the different operating systems running on a Mac with an Intel processor can be summed up using pseudocode as follows:

Mac OS X
```
    ExecuteAltiVec(instruction);
```
Windows
```
    ExecuteSEE(instruction);
```
Adapter
```
    void ExecuteAltiVec(instruction) {
      ExecuteSSE(ConvertToSSE(instruction));
    }
    void ExecuteSSE(instruction) {
      Intel.ExecuteSSE(instruction);
    }
```

---

* Windows runs on a Mac with the help of the Parallels or BootCamp virtual machines.

A key point with a two-way adapter is that it can be used in place of both ITarget and the Adaptee. When called to execute AltiVec instructions, the adapter behaves as a PowerPC processor (the Target), and when called to execute SSE instructions, it behaves as an Intel processor (the Adaptee).

Example: The Seabird

We have already looked at some theory code and discussed an interesting application of the Adapter pattern concept. It is now time for an example. That illustrates a two-way adapter but sticks closely to the structure of Example 4-1.

Suppose an inventor has an embedded control system for a revolutionary water plane called the *Seabird*. The plane derives from both aircraft and seacraft design: specifically, the Seabird has the body of a plane but the controls and engine of a ship. Both parts are being assembled as-is. The inventor of the Seabird is adapting as much as he can so that it is possible to control the craft via the interfaces provided by both parts.

In pattern terms, the Seabird will be a two-way adapter between the Aircraft and Seacraft classes. When running the experiments on the Seabird, the inventor will use an adapter and will be able to access methods and data in both classes. In other words, Seabird will behave as both an Aircraft and a Seacraft. We could get a simple adapter to behave as an Aircraft, say, and use the features of a Seacraft, but we could not do this the other way as well. With a two-way adapter, however, this is possible.

The ITarget interface, IAircraft, has two properties, Airborne and Height, and one method, TakeOff. The Aircraft class implements the interface in the manner of an aircraft. The IAdaptee interface, ISeacraft (new in this version of the pattern), has two methods—Speed and IncreaseRevs—that are implemented by the Seacraft class. The Adapter inherits from the Adaptee (Seacraft) and implements the ITarget (IAircraft) in the normal way. The adapter then has to do some work to match these two different interfaces to each other. Table 4-1 makes it easier to see how one would approach such an adapter.

Table 4-1. Adapter pattern Seabird example—methods and properties

Aircraft (Target)	Seacraft (Adaptee)	Seabird (Adapter)	Experiment (Client)
		Inherits Seabird, implements Aircraft	Instantiates seabird
Methods			
TakeOff—sets Airborne and Height to 200		TakeOff—involves Seacraft, IsFlying, and IncreaseRevs	seabird.TakeOff—goes to Seabird
	IncreaseRevs— changes speed by 10	IncreaseRevs—calls Seacraft IncreaseRevs and Seacraft IsFlying and sets the height	(seabird as ISeacraft) IncreaseRevs—goes to Seabird

Table 4-1. Adapter pattern Seabird example—methods and properties (continued)

Aircraft (Target)	Seacraft (Adaptee)	Seabird (Adapter)	Experiment (Client)
Variables			
Airborne—is true after takeoff		Airborne—is true if Height > 50	seabird.Airborne—goes to Seabird
	Speed—returns the speed		(seabird as Seacraft) Speed—goes to Seacraft
Height—returns the height		Height—returns the stored height	seabird.Height—goes to Seabird

The classes representing each part of the invention offer different methods: TakeOff for an aircraft and IncreaseRevs for a seacraft. In the simple adapter, only TakeOff would work. In the two-way adapter, we also capture the method from the Adaptee (IncreaseRevs) and adapt it to include information that otherwise would be supplied by the Target (the height, here).

Two-way adapters also handle variables—in this case, Airborne, Speed, and Height. Those from the Aircraft (the Target) are trapped and adapted to return locally held information. The one in the Seacraft (Adaptee) is routed through.

The result of all of the above, when translated into C# classes, is that the Client can conduct experiments on the Seabird as follows:

```
1  Console.WriteLine("\nExperiment 3: Increase the speed of the Seabird:");
2  (seabird as ISeacraft).IncreaseRevs();
3  (seabird as ISeacraft).IncreaseRevs();
4  if (seabird.Airborne)
5    Console.WriteLine("Seabird flying at height "
6        + seabird.Height +
7        " meters and speed "+(seabird as ISeacraft).Speed + " knots");
8  Console.WriteLine("Experiments successful; the Seabird flies!");
```

The calls to seabird.Airborne and seabird.Height (lines 4 and 6) are regular adapter methods that adapt as described in Table 4-1. However, the ability to treat the Seabird as a Seacraft as well (lines 2, 3, and 7) is peculiar to the two-way adapter. The full program is given in Example 4-2.

Example 4-2. Two-way Adapter pattern example code—Seabird

```
using System;

    // Two-Way Adapter Pattern  Pierre-Henri Kuate and Judith Bishop  Aug 2007
    // Embedded system for a Seabird flying plane

// ITarget interface
public interface IAircraft {
  bool Airborne {get;}
  void TakeOff();
  int Height {get;}
}
```

Example 4-2. Two-way Adapter pattern example code—Seabird (continued)

```
  // Target
  public sealed class Aircraft : IAircraft {
    int height;
    bool airborne;
    public Aircraft() {
      height = 0;
      airborne = false;
  }
  public void TakeOff () {
    Console.WriteLine("Aircraft engine takeoff");
    airborne = true;
    height = 200; // Meters
  }
  public bool Airborne {
    get {return airborne;}
  }
  public int Height {
    get {return height;}
  }
}

// Adaptee interface
public interface ISeacraft {
  int Speed {get;}
  void IncreaseRevs();
}
// Adaptee implementation
public class Seacraft : ISeacraft {
  int speed = 0;

  public virtual void IncreaseRevs() {
    speed += 10;
    Console.WriteLine("Seacraft engine increases revs to " + speed + " knots");
  }
  public int Speed {
    get {return speed;}
  }
}

  // Adapter
  public class Seabird : Seacraft, IAircraft {
    int height = 0;
    // A two-way adapter hides and routes the Target's methods
    // Use Seacraft instructions to implement this one
    public void TakeOff() {
      while (!Airborne)
        IncreaseRevs();
    }

    // Routes this straight back to the Aircraft
    public int Height {
      get {return height;}
    }
```

Example 4-2. Two-way Adapter pattern example code—Seabird (continued)

```
    // This method is common to both Target and Adaptee
    public override void IncreaseRevs() {
      base.IncreaseRevs();
      if(Speed > 40)
          height += 100;
    }

    public bool Airborne {
      get {return height > 50;}
    }
  }

class Experiment_MakeSeaBirdFly {
  static void Main () {
    // No adapter
    Console.WriteLine("Experiment 1: test the aircraft engine");
    IAircraft aircraft = new Aircraft();
    aircraft.TakeOff();
    if (aircraft.Airborne) Console.WriteLine(
        "The aircraft engine is fine, flying at "
        +aircraft.Height+"meters");

    // Classic usage of an adapter
    Console.WriteLine("\nExperiment 2: Use the engine in the Seabird");
    IAircraft seabird = new Seabird();
    seabird.TakeOff(); // And automatically increases speed
    Console.WriteLine("The Seabird took off");

    // Two-way adapter: using seacraft instructions on an IAircraft object
    // (where they are not in the IAircraft interface)
    Console.WriteLine("\nExperiment 3: Increase the speed of the Seabird:");
    (seabird as ISeacraft).IncreaseRevs();
    (seabird as ISeacraft).IncreaseRevs();
    if (seabird.Airborne)
      Console.WriteLine("Seabird flying at height "+ seabird.Height +
          " meters and speed "+(seabird as ISeacraft).Speed + " knots");
    Console.WriteLine("Experiments successful; the Seabird flies!");
  }
}

/* Output
Experiment 1: test the aircraft engine
Aircraft engine takeoff
The aircraft engine is fine, flying at 200 meters

Experiment 2: Use the engine in the Seabird
Seacraft engine increases revs to 10 knots
Seacraft engine increases revs to 20 knots
Seacraft engine increases revs to 30 knots
Seacraft engine increases revs to 40 knots
Seacraft engine increases revs to 50 knots
The Seabird took off
```

Example 4-2. Two-way Adapter pattern example code—Seabird (continued)

```
Experiment 3: Increase the speed of the Seabird:
Seacraft engine increases revs to 60 knots
Seacraft engine increases revs to 70 knots
Seabird flying at height 300 meters and speed 70 knots
Experiments successful; the Seabird flies!
*/
```

Pluggable Adapters

Developers who recognize that their systems will need to work with other components can increase their chances of adaptation. Identifying in advance the parts of the system that might change makes it easier to plug in adapters for a variety of new situations. Keeping down the size of an interface also increases the opportunities for new systems to be plugged in. Although not technically different from ordinary adapters, this feature of small interfaces gives them the name *pluggable* adapters.

A distinguishing feature of pluggable adapters is that the name of a method called by the client and that existing in the ITarget interface can be different. The adapter must be able to handle the name change. In the previous adapter variations, this was true for all Adaptee methods, but the client had to use the names in the ITarget interface. Suppose the client wants to use its own names, or that there is more than one client and they have different terminologies. To achieve these name changes in a very dynamic way, we can use delegates (see later sidebar).

Now, consider Example 4-3, which shows how to write pluggable adapters with delegates.

Example 4-3. Pluggable Adapter pattern theory code

```
1     using System;
2
3     // Adapter Pattern - Pluggable            Judith Bishop  Oct 2007
4     // Adapter can accept any number of pluggable adaptees and targets
5     // and route the requests via a delegate, in some cases using the
6     // anonymous delegate construct
7
8     // Existing way requests are implemented
9     class Adaptee {
10      public double Precise (double a, double b) {
11        return a/b;
12      }
13    }
14
15    // New standard for requests
16    class Target {
17      public string Estimate (int i) {
18        return "Estimate is " + (int) Math.Round(i/3.0);
19      }
20    }
21
```

Example 4-3. Pluggable Adapter pattern theory code (continued)

```
22        // Implementing new requests via old
23        class Adapter : Adaptee {
24          public Func <int,string> Request;
25
26          // Different constructors for the expected targets/adaptees
27
28          // Adapter-Adaptee
29          public Adapter (Adaptee adaptee) {
30          // Set the delegate to the new standard
31          Request = delegate(int i) {
32              return "Estimate based on precision is " +
33              (int) Math.Round(Precise (i,3));
34          };
35          }
36
37          // Adapter-Target
38          public Adapter (Target target) {
39            // Set the delegate to the existing standard
40            Request = target.Estimate;
41          }
42        }
43
44    class Client {
45
46      static void Main ( ) {
47
48          Adapter adapter1 = new Adapter (new Adaptee( ));
49          Console.WriteLine(adapter1.Request(5));
50
51          Adapter adapter2 = new Adapter (new Target( ));
52          Console.WriteLine(adapter2.Request(5));
53
54      }
55    }
56    /* Output
57    Estimate based on precision is 2
58    Estimate is 2
59    */
```

The delegate is contained in the Adapter and is instantiated on line 24, from one of the standard generic delegates. On lines 33 and 40, it is assigned to the methods Precise and Estimate, which are in the Adaptee and Target, respectively. Lines 31–34 show the use of an anonymous function to augment the results from the Adaptee. Notice that the Client (the Main method) refers only to its chosen method name, Request (see sidebar).

The pluggable adapter sorts out which object is being plugged in at the time. Once a service has been plugged in and its methods have been assigned to the delegate objects, the association lasts until another set of methods is assigned. What characterizes a pluggable adapter is that it will have constructors for each of the types that it adapts. In each of them, it does the delegate assignments (one, or more than one if there are further methods for rerouting).

C# Feature—Delegates

A method that is specified in an interface is implemented with the same name in the base class. However, such close coupling is not always appropriate. The delegate construct can be used to break the coupling for this purpose. A *delegate* is a type that defines a method signature. A *delegate instance* is then able to accept a method of that signature, regardless of its method name or the type that encapsulates it.

The delegate syntax in C# evolved considerably from Versions 1.0 to 2.0 to 3.0. We shall concentrate on the 3.0 version, which is the simplest to code. The language has predefined *standard generic delegate types*, as follows:

```
delegate R Func<R>();
delegate R Func<A1, R>(A1 a1);
delegate R Func<A1, A2, R>(A1 a1, A2 a2);
// ... and up to many arguments
```

where R is the return type and the As and as represent the argument types and names, respectively. Thus, declaring a delegate instance is now straightforward. For example, we can define a Request delegate that takes an integer parameter and returns a string:

```
public Func <int,string> Request;
```

Next, we can assign an actual method to Request, as in:

```
Request = Target.Estimate;
```

The delegate can then be invoked just as any other method would be:

```
string s = Request(5);
```

This statement would invoke the Estimate method in the Target class, returning a string.

cf. C# Language Specification Version 3.0, September 2007, Section 10.8

Example: CoolBook

Our last Adapter pattern example picks up on an earlier example that we explored with the Proxy and Bridge patterns: SpaceBook. Recall that Example 2-4 introduced the SpaceBook class and its authentication frontend, MySpaceBook. Then, Example 2-6 showed how we could create a Bridge to an alternative version of MySpaceBook called MyOpenBook, which did not have authentication. Now, we are going to consider going GUI. The input and output of SpaceBook (wall writing, pokes, etc.) will be done via Windows forms. There will be a separate form for each user, and users will be able to write on each other's pages as before. However, now the input will be interactive, as well as being simulated by method calls in the program. Thus, we will have a prototype of a much more realistic system.

Creating a GUI and handling its events is a specialized function, and it is best to isolate it as much as possible from the ordinary logic of the system. In setting up Cool-Book, we wrote a minimal GUI system called Interact. All Interact does is set up a window with a TextBox and a Button called "Poke," and pass any click events on the Button to a delegate (see sidebar). Separately from this, we wrote MyCoolBook, which mimics the functionality of MyOpenBook and, for reasons of simplicity at this stage, maintains its own community of users. Given the following client program, the output will be as shown in Figure 4-3.

```
static void Main( ) {

    MyCoolBook judith = new MyCoolBook("Judith");
    judith.Add("Hello world");

    MyCoolBook tom = new MyCoolBook("Tom");
    tom.Poke("Judith");
    tom.Add("Hey, We are on CoolBook");
    judith.Poke("Tom");
    Console.ReadLine( );
}
```

The second "Tom : Poked you" was created interactively by Tom typing in "Judith" on his wall, selecting it, and clicking the Poke button. Judith then wrote on her own wall, and was getting ready to poke Tom when the snapshot was taken.

MyCoolBook builds on top of Interact and acts as the adapter class. As can be seen in the Client, MyOpenBook and MySpaceBook have been completely plugged out and replaced by MyCoolBook. We can just change the instantiations back, and everything will revert to the old system. This is what a pluggable adapter achieves. Consider the insides of the adapter in Example 4-4. It inherits from MyOpenBook and, through inheritance, it makes use of the MySpaceBook object stored there, as well as the Name property. It reimplements the three important methods—Poke and the two Add methods—and has two methods that connect it to Interact via a form object called visuals.

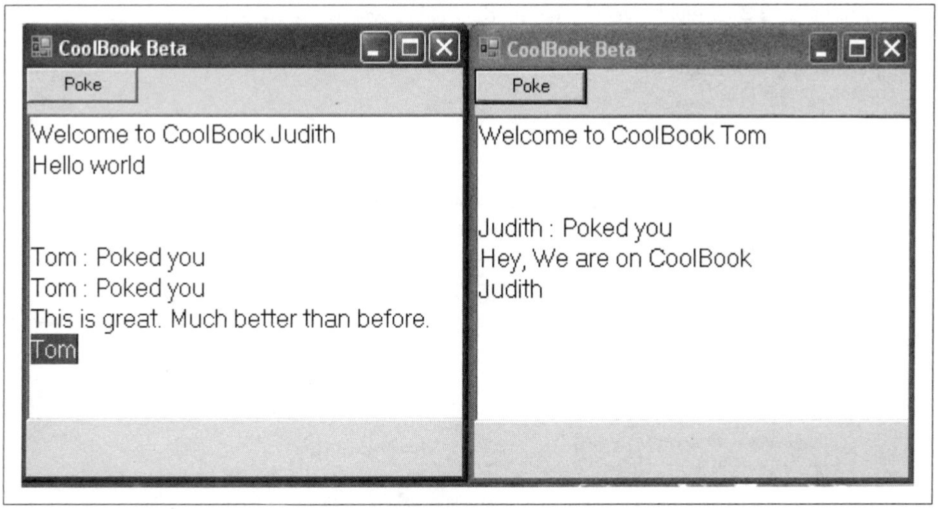

Figure 4-3. Adapter pattern—output from CoolBook

Example 4-4. Pluggable Adapter pattern example code—MyCoolBook

```
// Adapter
public class MyCoolBook : MyOpenBook {
  static SortedList<string, MyCoolBook> community =
      new SortedList<string, MyCoolBook>(100);
  Interact visuals;

  // Constructor starts the GUI
  public MyCoolBook(string name) : base(name) {
    // Create the Interact GUI on the relevant thread, and start it
    new Thread(delegate( ) {
      visuals = new Interact("CoolBook Beta");
      visuals.InputEvent += new InputEventHandler(OnInput);
      visuals.FormClosed += new FormClosedEventHandler(OnFormClosed);
      Application.Run(visuals);
    }).Start( );
    community[name] = this;

    while (visuals == null) {
      Application.DoEvents( );
      Thread.Sleep(100);
    }

    Add("Welcome to CoolBook " + Name);
  }

  // Closing the GUI
  private void OnFormClosed(object sender, FormClosedEventArgs e) {
```

```
        community.Remove(Name);
    }

    // A handler for input events, which then calls Add to
    // write on the GUI
    private void OnInput(object sender, EventArgs e, string s) {
        Add("\r\n");
        Add(s, "Poked you");
    }

    // This method can be called directly or from the other
    // Add and Poke methods. It adapts the calls by routing them
    // to the Interact GUI.
    public new void Add(string message) {
    visuals.Output(message);
    }

  public new void Poke(string who) {
    Add("\r\n");
    if (community.ContainsKey(who))
        community[who].Add(Name, "Poked you");
    else
      Add("Friend " + who + " is not part of the community");
  }

  public new void Add(string friend, string message) {
    if (community.ContainsKey(friend))
        community[friend].Add(Name + " : " + message);
    else
      Add("Friend " + friend + " is not part of the community");
  }
}
```

Of the three reimplemented methods, only the behavior of the first Add is specific to
MyCoolBook. The other two methods are very much like those in MyOpenBook. However, the problem is that given the closed nature of SpaceBook, MyCoolBook cannot
access the dictionary there and has to keep its own community. This sometimes happens with adapters. If it were possible to rewrite parts of the Target in a more collab-
orative way, the adapter could do less work. This idea is addressed in the upcoming
"Exercises" section. The code for the full CoolBook system is shown in the Appendix.

One point to note is the anonymous function that is passed to the Thread class in the
CoolBook constructor. This is a very quick way of creating an object in a new thread.
The last statement is Application.Run( ), which starts drawing the form and opens
up a message "pump" for the interactive input/output on it. Finally, Start is called
on the thread.

C# Feature—Events

Delegates are used extensively in Windows GUI event-driven programming, where they reflect the need to call back into the user's code when some *event* happens. Mostly, existing code of this type will use an older syntax. Also, because the new Func delegates must have return types, void delegates must use the original syntax too. Consider a simple example of wanting to inform one object that input has occurred in another object (this is part of Example 4-4). We first declare a delegate visible to both classes:

```
public delegate void InputEventHandler(object sender,
    EventArgs e, string s);
```

Then, in the class where the event is handled, we create an instance of the delegate and add it to the event object of the class that will receive the event. When creating the delegate, we indicate the method that it will call (in this case, OnInput):

```
visuals.InputEvent += new InputEventHandler(OnInput);

void OnInput(object sender, EventArgs e, string s) {
  // Do something
}
```

The signature of OnInput must match that of InputEventHandler, which it does. Now, in the class where event occurs, we declare the event:

```
public event InputEventHandler InputEvent;
```

and in some method we invoke it:

```
public void Input(object source, EventArgs e) {
  InputEvent(this, EventArgs.Empty, who);
}
```

The action of invoking the InputEvent delegate causes the method currently assigned to it (here, OnInput) to be invoked. Thus, the callback from one class to the other is achieved.

More than one method can be associated with a delegate; when such a delegate is invoked, all its methods are called. Thus, if another object needed to know about input in the preceding example, it could add its own handler method on to InputEvent using +=. Event handlers can be removed using -=.

cf. C# Language Specification Version 3.0, September 2007, Section 10.8

Use

The Adapter pattern is found wherever there is code to be wrapped up and redirected to a different implementation. In 2002, Nigel Horspool and I developed a system called *Views* that enabled an XML specification of a Windows GUI to run on the cross-platform version of Windows called Rotor. The Views engine ran with the GUI program and adapted Views method calls to Windows calls. That benefited the clients (students) because they could use a simpler interface to GUI programming.

A subsequent advantage was that Vista, the successor to Windows XP, used the same approach.

At the time, it was a long way around to get Windows forms, but the adaptation paid off later. In 2004, the backend of the Views engine was ported by Basil Worrall to QT4, a graphics toolkit running on Linux. Immediately, all applications that were using Views for GUI programming became independent of Windows and could run with the Mono .NET Framework on Linux. The Views engine was therefore a pluggable adapter. (Our paper describing the approach is referenced in the Bibliography at the end of the book.)

Use the Adapter pattern when...

You have:
- A domain-specific interface.
- A class to connect to with a mismatching interface.

You want to:
- Create a reusable class to cooperate with yet-to-be-built classes.
- Change the names of methods as called and as implemented.
- Support different sets of methods for different purposes.

Choose the Adapter you need...

Class adapter
  Simple and versatile, invisible to the client.
Object adapter
  Extensible to subclasses of the adapter.
Two-way adapter
  Enables different clients to view an object differently.
Pluggable adapter
  Presence of adapter is transparent; it can be put in and taken out
  Several adapters can be active.

Exercises

1. Consider the Seabird program. Would it be possible to instantiate an `Aircraft` object instead of a `Seacraft` object and change the methods inside `Seabird` accordingly? If so, make the changes. If not, explain how the present program would need to be altered to enable this and then make the changes.

2. Add a "SuperPoke" button to CoolBook, enabling one user to send a message to another.

3. Having two different communities for SpaceBook and CoolBook is clearly a disadvantage. Assume you can make minor changes to the `SpaceBook`, `MySpaceBook`, and `MyOpenBook` classes, and see whether you can remove the community collection from `MyCoolBook`, routing all accesses back through `MyOpenBook` to `SpaceBook`.

Façade Pattern

Role

The role of the Façade pattern is to provide different high-level views of subsystems whose details are hidden from users. In general, the operations that might be desirable from a user's perspective could be made up of different selections of parts of the subsystems.

Illustration

Simple interfaces to complex subsystems abound in real life. They can be created to make frequent use of a system faster, or to differentiate between novices and power users. A good illustration is Amazon.com's 1-Click® system (Figure 4-4), which simplifies the process of ordering items for well-known customers. Normally, after selecting an item to purchase, an Amazon customer has to enter delivery and bank account details before the order is accepted. If these details are stored and the customer verifies her identity in some way, 1-Click takes that customer straight to the checkout. The customer's stored bank account details and selected delivery address are used for the purchase, thus considerably speeding up (and simplifying) the ordering process. Thus, the 1-Click option forms a façade to the fuller system underneath.

Figure 4-4. Façade pattern illustration—1-Click®

Design

Hiding detail is a key programming concept. What makes the Façade pattern different from, say, the Decorator or Adapter patterns is that the interface it builds up can be entirely new. It is not coupled to existing requirements, nor must it conform to existing interfaces. There can also be several façades built up around an existing set of subsystems. The term "subsystem" is used here deliberately; we are talking at a higher level than classes. See the UML diagram in Figure 4-5; it considers the subsystems to be grouped together, so they can interact in agreed ways to form the top-level operations.

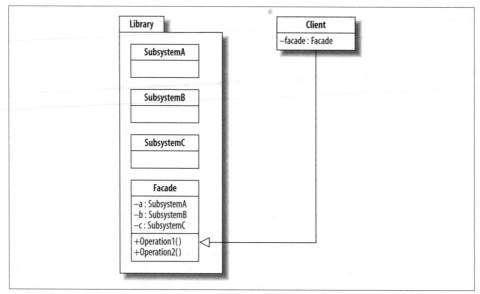

Figure 4-5. Façade pattern UML diagram

The roles are:

Namespace 1
> A library of subsystems

Subsystem
> A class offering detailed operations

Façade
> A class offering a few high-level operations as selections from the subsystems

Namespace 2
> Where the client resides

Client
> Calls the high-level operations in the Façade in Namespace 1

As shown in the UML diagram, the client's code does not make reference to the classes of the names of the subsystems; it only gets access to their operations via the Façade.

Implementation

The Façade pattern is simple to implement. It uses the C# concept of namespaces. Classes in namespaces have the facility to define accessibility as internal or public. If accessibility is defined as internal, the member is visible only in the assembly in which the namespace is compiled. In a very large system, the client's GUI will be in a different namespace from the library, so we can enforce the Façade. (Alternative implementations of the Façade pattern will be discussed shortly.)

In Example 4-5, the theory code comes from two files: *Façade-Main.cs* and *Façade-Library.cs*. Both have to be compiled with special directives so that *library* in *Façade-Library.cs* is recognized as a *lib* file and the client in *Façade-Main.cs* can reference it. These commands are:

```
// Compile the library
csc /t:library /out:FaçadeLib.dll Façade-Library.cs

// Compile the main program
csc /r:FaçadeLib.dll Façade-Main.cs
```

 This process of compiling and using libraries is facilitated in environments such as Visual Studio.

The example mirrors the diagram in Figure 4-5. Three subsystems, implemented as classes, are inserted into the library. Façade is a static class that instantiates the three subsystems under the façade as objects called a, b, and c. Operations 1 and 2 then select combinations of methods from a, b, and c. For example, Operation1 will call two methods in a, one in b, and none in c. Thus, the Façade is a means of providing an interface to operations that should, on their own, remain hidden.

The client starts with a using statement that indicates it wants access to the public members in the FacadeLib namespace. Then it calls the Façade's two high-level operations. The output is shown below in Example 4-5.

Example 4-5. Façade pattern theory code

```csharp
using System;

    // Facade Pattern                    Judith Bishop  Dec 2006
    // Sets up a library of three systems, accessed through a
    // Facade of two operations
    // Compile with
    // csc /t:library /out:FacadeLib.dll Facade-Library.cs

namespace Library {

    internal class SubsystemA {
      internal string A1() {
          return "Subsystem A, Method A1\n";
      }
      internal string A2() {
          return "Subsystem A, Method A2\n";
      }
    }

    internal class SubsystemB {
      internal string B1() {
        return "Subsystem B, Method B1\n";
      }
    }

    internal class SubsystemC {
      internal string C1() {
        return "Subsystem C, Method C1\n";
      }
    }
  }

public static class Facade {
  static SubsystemA a = new SubsystemA();
  static SubsystemB b = new SubsystemB();
  static SubsystemC c = new SubsystemC();

  public static void Operation1() {
    Console.WriteLine("Operation 1\n" +
        a.A1() +
        a.A2() +
        b.B1());
  }

  public static void Operation2() {
    Console.WriteLine("Operation 2\n" +
        b.B1() +
        c.C1());
  }
}
```

Example 4-5. Façade pattern theory code (continued)

```
    // ============= Different compilation

    using System;
    using FacadeLib;

    // Compile with csc /r:FacadeLib.dll Facade-Main.cs

    class Client {
      static void Main ( ) {
        Facade.Operation1( );
        Facade.Operation2( );
      }
    }
  }
/* Output

Operation 1
Subsystem A, Method A1
Subsystem A, Method A2
Subsystem B, Method B1

Operation 2
Subsystem B, Method B1
Subsystem C, Method C1
*/
```

Everything in the façade has to be public so that the Client, which is compiled into a different assembly, can access it. The classes all have the default internal visibility, limiting access to them to the assembly in which they were compiled (*excluding* the Client). As a test, if we try to let the Client instantiate any of the subsystems directly, we will get an error like the following:

```
SubsystemC x = new SubsystemC( );
x.C1( );
Façade2Main.cs(12,3): error CS0122: 'FaçadeLib.SubsystemC' is inaccessible due to its
protection level
```

Façade Alternatives

Some alternative implementations of the Façade pattern are:

Transparent façades

> The façade described in the preceding example is *opaque*, in that the subsystems cannot be accessed except via the Façade object. This requirement might be too stringent. Suppose some users want to get at the individual operations of particular subsystems. We can change all the internal modifiers to public, which will make the façade optional, or *transparent*. That is, as well as being able to go through the Façade, the client will be able to instantiate SubsystemA directly, for example, and then call A1.

Static façades

In most cases, there will only be one instance of a façade in the client for a set of subsystems, so its operations could more appropriately be called on the user's side as members of the class itself, as in:

```
public void ClientMain () {
  Façade.Operation1( );
  Façade.Operation2( );
}
```

This implies that Façade is a static class. No instantiation is necessary; the user interfaces with the Façade class directly. In fact, the Singleton pattern (Chapter 5) would be the preferred way of achieving this effect.

Example: Novice Photo Library

Consider the Composite pattern example in Chapter 3 that showed how photos could be loaded into directories of arbitrary configurations. The instructions for using the six commands relied on the current place ("where I am"), which was a powerful, but perhaps confusing, concept. For novices, it might be a good idea to abstract from the power of the Photo Library and just let them load sets of photos, all at the same level, and immediately display them (as Flickr does). The commands could simply be:

```
Upload setname
photoname1 photoname2 ...
```

ending with a blank line or some other indicator. These instructions would translate into the following existing ones:

```
Find album
AddSet setname
AddPhoto photoname1
AddPhoto photoname2
...
Display
```

Instead of going in and altering the code to have a new command, we can have a completely separate Façade that makes the calls as described above. The more complex and rich commands might be available to expert users, but not to novices. (See the preceding discussion on opaque and transparent façades.)

Use

Façades can be useful in different circumstances. There are many instances where a computer system is built up out of a set of largely independent subsystems. One well-known case is a compiler: it consists of clearly identifiable subsystems called a lexical analyzer, a syntax analyzer, semantic analyzers, a code generator, and several optimizers. In modern compilers, each subsystem has many subtasks. The different tasks and subtasks are called in a sequence, but sometimes they are not all needed.

For example, if an error occurs in one of the analysis tasks, the compiler might not go onto a later phase. (The .NET compilers follow this approach.) Hiding this detail behind a façade enables a program to call tasks within subsystems in a logical order, passing the necessary data structures between them.

Use the Façade pattern when...

A system has several identifiable subsystems and:
- The abstractions and implementations of a subsystem are tightly coupled.
- The system evolves and gets more complex, but early adopters might want to retain their simple views.
- You want to provide alternative novice, intermediate, and "power user" interfaces.
- There is a need for an entry point to each level of layered software.

But consider using instead:
- The Abstract Factory pattern for designs where subsystems create objects on behalf of the client.

Choose the Façade you need...

Opaque
Subsystem operations can only be called through the Façade.

Transparent
Subsystem operations can be called directly as well as through the Façade.

Singleton
Only one instance of the Façade is meaningful.

Exercises

1. Program the suggested extension for novices to the Photo Library program.
2. Consider large systems that you use on the Internet, and come up with more examples of Façades.
3. If you have access to source code for a compiler, find the part where the subsystems are called and examine how the data structures are passed between them.

Pattern Comparison

The Adapter pattern has much in common with the patterns discussed in Chapter 2. The differences are in the *intents* of the patterns. A bridge, for example, separates an interface and its implementation so that they can vary independently, whereas an adapter changes the interface of an existing object. The Adapter pattern is more useful for one-off changes, whereas the Bridge pattern anticipates that change might happen continuously.

A decorator enhances an object without changing its interface and should be transparent to the application. An adapter is not transparent, as it is the named implementation of the interface the client sees. The Proxy pattern does not change any interfaces; it defines substitute objects for other objects.

From a certain point of view, the Façade pattern is also adapting requests: it transforms high-level requests into a sequence of lower-level requests. The Façade's intent is to hide complexity, and the Façade subsystems are not intended to be accessible by the client.

To complete the picture, we can classify the Adapter and Façade patterns according to the mechanisms shown in Table 4-2.

Table 4-2. Comparison of Adapter and Façade patterns

Mechanism	Adapter	Façade
Original	Adaptee	SubsystemA, B, and C
Interface	ITarget	Façade
New	Adapter	Operation1 and 2
Client	Aggregates ITarget	Accesses Façade
Client activates	New	New
Original changed by	No change	No change
New classes/subsystems	Adapter provides adaptations to their methods	Façade supplies high-level operations
Operation routed	From new to original	From new to original

CHAPTER 5

Creational Patterns: Prototype, Factory Method, and Singleton

The creational patterns aim to separate a system from how its objects are created, composed, and represented. They increase the system's flexibility in terms of the *what*, *who*, *how*, and *when* of object creation. Creational patterns encapsulate the knowledge about which classes a system uses, but they hide the details of how the instances of these classes are created and put together. Programmers have come to realize that composing systems with inheritance makes those systems too rigid. The creational patterns are designed to break this close coupling. In this and the following chapter, we shall make further use of some C# features that help to abstract the instantiation process—generics and delegates (introduced in Chapters 3 and 4, respectively) are two of these.

We'll start by looking at three small patterns that are helpful in combination with many others. The Prototype pattern ensures that when copies of complex objects are made, they are true copies. The Factory Method pattern is a means of creating objects without knowing the exact subclass being used. Finally, the Singleton pattern ensures that only one of a class can be built and that all users are directed to it.

Prototype Pattern

Role

The Prototype pattern creates new objects by cloning one of a few stored prototypes. The Prototype pattern has two advantages: it speeds up the instantiation of very large, dynamically loaded classes (when copying objects is faster), and it keeps a record of identifiable parts of a large data structure that can be copied without knowing the subclass from which they were created.

Illustration

Let's again consider the Photo Group application discussed in Chapter 3, which held groups of photographs (see Figure 3-3). At some stage, we might like to archive one of the groups by copying it to another album. Then, later, we can bring it back again (perhaps if the original is deleted by mistake). In this case, the archive becomes a holder of prototypes that can be copied whenever required. We shall call the updated version of the application with this added functionality *Photo Archive*.

Design

Objects are usually instantiated from classes that are part of the program. The Prototype pattern presents an alternative route by creating objects from existing prototypes. The UML for the Prototype pattern is given in Figure 5-1.

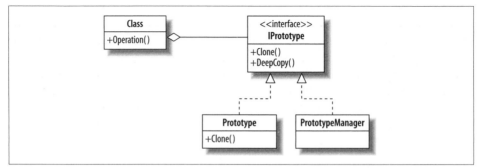

Figure 5-1. Prototype pattern UML diagram

Given a key, the program creates an object of the required type, not by instantiation, but by copying a clean instance of the class. This process of copying, or *cloning*, can be repeated over and over again. The copies, or clones, are objects in their own right, and the intention of the pattern is that their state can be altered at will without affecting the prototype. During the run of the program new prototypes can be added, either from new classes or from variations on existing prototypes. Although there are other designs, the most flexible is to keep a prototype manager that maintains an indexed list of prototypes that can be cloned. The main players in the pattern are:

IPrototype
    Defines the interface that says prototypes must be cloneable

Prototype
    A class with cloning capabilities

PrototypeManager
    Maintains a list of clone types and their keys

Client
    Adds prototypes to the list and requests clones

Match the Prototype Pattern Players with the Photo Archive Illustration

To test whether you understand the Prototype pattern, cover the lefthand column of the table below and see if you can identify its players among the items from the illustrative example (using the picture in Figure 3-3), as shown in the righthand column. Then check your answers against the lefthand column.

IPrototype	Facility for archiving
Prototype	An archived photo set
PrototypeManager	The Photo Library
Client	The user

C# Features—Cloning and Serialization

MemberwiseClone is a method that is available on all objects. It copies the values of all fields and any references, and returns a reference to this copy. However, it does not copy what the references in the object point to. That is, it performs what is known as a *shallow copy*. Many objects are simple, without references to other objects, and therefore shallow copies are adequate. To preserve the complete value of the object, including all its subobjects use a *deep copy*.

It is not easy to write a general algorithm to follow every link in a structure and recreate the arrangement elsewhere. However, algorithms do exist, and in the .NET Framework they are encapsulated in a process called *serialization*. Objects are copied to a given destination and can be brought back again at will. The options for serialization destinations are several, including disks and the Internet, but the easiest one for serializing smallish objects is memory itself. Thus a deep copy consists of serializing and deserializing in one method.

A generic method that will work for all types that are marked as serializable (such as lists and so on) is shown in Example 5-1. Note that there are two Serialization namespaces that must be imported. Marking a type as serializable is done with the [Serializable()] attribute.

Serialization is part of the .NET Framework, not the C# language. The following reference is to the .NET library online.

cf. *http://msdn2.microsoft.com/en-us/library/ system.runtime.serialization(VS.71).aspx*

Serializing an object structure is possible only if all referenced objects are serializable. Avoid serializing an object that has a reference to a "resource," such as an open file handler or a database connection.

Part of the Prototype pattern then relies on a namespace with two methods: Clone and DeepCopy. In fact, Clone is merely a synonym for MemberwiseClone and can be omitted. The namespace is shown in Example 5-1.

Example 5-1. Prototype pattern theory code—namespace

```
1  using System;
2  using System.Collections.Generic;
3  using System.Runtime.Serialization;
4  using System.Runtime.Serialization.Formatters.Binary;
5
6  namespace PrototypePattern {
7    // Prototype Pattern        Judith Bishop  Nov 2007
8    // Serialization is used for the deep copy option
9    // The type T must be marked with the attribute [Serializable()]
10
11   [Serializable()]
12   public abstract class IPrototype <T> {
13
14     // Shallow copy
15     public T Clone() {
16       return (T) this.MemberwiseClone();
17     }
18
19     // Deep Copy
20     public T DeepCopy() {
21       MemoryStream stream = new MemoryStream();
22       BinaryFormatter formatter = new BinaryFormatter();
23       formatter.Serialize(stream, this);
24       stream.Seek(0, SeekOrigin.Begin);
25       T copy = (T) formatter.Deserialize(stream);
26       stream.Close();
27       return copy;
28     }
29   }
30 }
```

Implementation

The implementation of the Prototype pattern in C# is greatly assisted by two facilities in the .NET Framework: cloning and serialization. Both of these are provided as interfaces in the System namespace.

Now, consider the program to test the namespace, as in Example 5-2. It is a small example that sets up three prototypes, each consisting of a country, a capital, and a language (lines 26–28). The last of these, Language, refers to another class called DeeperData. The purpose of this class is to create a reference in the prototype. The example will show that for this deeper data item, there is a difference between shallow copying and deep copying.

Example 5-2. Prototype pattern theory code

```
1  using System;
2  using System.Collections.Generic;
3  using System.Runtime.Serialization;
4  using PrototypePattern;
5
6    // Prototype Pattern        Judith Bishop  Dec 2006, Nov 2007
7    // Serializable is used for the deep copy option
8
9    [Serializable()]
10   // Helper class used to create a second level data structure
11   class DeeperData {
12     public string Data {get; set;}
13
14     public DeeperData(string s) {
15       Data = s;
16     }
17     public override string ToString () {
18       return Data;
19     }
20   }
21
22   [Serializable()]
23   class  Prototype : IPrototype <Prototype>  {
24
25     // Content members
26     public string Country {get; set;}
27     public string Capital {get; set;}
28     public DeeperData Language {get; set;}
29
30     public Prototype (string country, string capital, string language) {
31       Country = country;
32       Capital = capital;
33       Language = new DeeperData(language);
34     }
35
36     public override string ToString() {
37       return Country+"\t\t"+Capital+"\t\t->"+Language;
38     }
39
40   }
41   [Serializable()]
42   class PrototypeManager : IPrototype <Prototype>  {
43     public Dictionary <string, Prototype> prototypes
44       = new Dictionary <string, Prototype> {
45       {"Germany",
46        new Prototype ("Germany", "Berlin", "German")},
47       {"Italy",
48        new Prototype ("Italy", "Rome", "Italian")},
```

Example 5-2. Prototype pattern theory code (continued)

```
49          {"Australia",
50            new Prototype ("Australia", "Canberra", "English")}
51       };
52    }
53
54    class PrototypeClient : IPrototype <Prototype> {
55
56      static void Report (string s, Prototype a, Prototype b) {
57        Console.WriteLine("\n"+s);
58        Console.WriteLine("Prototype "+a+"\nClone        "+b);
59      }
60
61      static void Main () {
62
63        PrototypeManager manager = new PrototypeManager();
64        Prototype  c2, c3;
65
66        // Make a copy of Australia's data
67        c2  = manager.prototypes["Australia"].Clone();
68        Report("Shallow cloning Australia\n===============",
69            manager.prototypes["Australia"], c2);
70
71        // Change the capital of Australia to Sydney
72        c2.Capital = "Sydney";
73        Report("Àltered Clone's shallow state, prototype unaffected",
74            manager.prototypes["Australia"], c2);
75
76        // Change the language of Australia (deep data)
77        c2.Language.Data = "Chinese";
78        Report("Altering Clone deep state: prototype affected *****",
79             manager.prototypes["Australia"], c2);
80
81        // Make a copy of Germany's data
82        c3  = manager.prototypes["Germany"].DeepCopy();
83        Report("Deep cloning Germany\n============",
84             manager.prototypes["Germany"], c3);
85
86        // Change the capital of Germany
87        c3.Capital = "Munich";
88        Report("Altering Clone shallow state, prototype unaffected",
89             manager.prototypes["Germany"], c3);
90
91        // Change the language of Germany (deep data)
92        c3.Language.Data = "Turkish";
93        Report("Altering Clone deep state, prototype unaffected",
94            manager.prototypes["Germany"], c3);
95      }
96    }
97    /* Output
98    Shallow cloning Australia
99    ===============
```

Example 5-2. Prototype pattern theory code (continued)

```
100 Prototype Australia       Canberra              ->English
101 Clone     Australia       Canberra               ->English
102
103 Altered Clone's shallow state, prototype unaffected
104 Prototype Australia       Canberra              ->English
105 Clone     Australia       Sydney                 ->English
106
107 Altering Clone deep state: prototype affected *****
108 Prototype Australia       Canberra              ->Chinese
109 Clone     Australia       Sydney                 ->Chinese
110
111 Deep cloning Germany
112 ============
113 Prototype Germany         Berlin      ->German
114 Clone     Germany         Berlin       ->German
115
116 Altering Clone shallow state, prototype unaffected
117 Prototype Germany         Berlin      ->German
118 Clone     Germany         Munich       ->German
119
120 Altering Clone deep state, prototype unaffected
121 Prototype Germany         Berlin      ->German
122 Clone     Germany         Munich       ->Turkish
123 */
```

The main program consists of a series of experiments demonstrating the effects of cloning and deep copying. In the first group, Australia is shallow copied. Lines 104–105 show the changing of Australia's clone. The capital is Canberra in the prototype and Sydney in the clone. The statement responsible is on line 72; however, changing the language to Chinese (as is done on line 77) also changes the prototype's language (line 108). That is not what we wanted. We got the error because we did a shallow copy and the language in the prototype and in the clone reference the same DeeperData object.

In the next experiment, we clone Germany using a deep copy (line 82). The output on line 118 shows that altering the clone's shallow state—its capital (line 87)—works correctly, as does altering the deep state—its language to Turkish (line 92). Line 121 shows the prototype after the changes; it is unaffected.

 Remember that all classes involved in the prototype must add the Serializable( ) attribute.

Example: Photo Archive

As an example of the Prototype pattern, we'll extend the Photo Group application from Chapter 3 to include archiving using the following new commands:

```
Archive set
Retrieve set
Display Archive
```

The archive is an additional component at the same level as the album. The action associated with the two new commands is very simple:

```
case "Archive" : archive = point.Share(parameter,archive); break;
case "Retrieve" : point = archive.Share(parameter,album); break;
```

and this is the Share method in the Composite class:

```
public IComponent <T> Share (T set, IComponent <T> toHere) {
  IPrototype <IComponent <T>> prototype=
  this.Find (set) as IPrototype <IComponent <T>>;
  toHere.Add(copy);
  return toHere;
  }
```

Of course, the Prototype Pattern is added as a used namespace as well. Given these changes to the program, the output can look like this (starting from the Display of the constructed composite):

```
 1  Set Album length :2
 2  --Set Home length :2
 3  ----Dinner.jpg
 4  ----Set Pets length :2
 5  ------Dog.jpg
 6  ------Cat.jpg
 7  --Set Garden length :4
 8  ----Spring.jpg
 9  ----Summer.jpg
10  ----Flowers.jpg
11  ----Trees.jpg
12
13              Find Pets
14              Archive Pets
15              Display Archive
16  Set Archive length :1
17  --Set Pets length :2
18  ----Dog.jpg
19  ----Cat.jpg
20
21              Find Album
22              Remove Home
23              Find Album
24              Remove Garden
25              Display
26  Set Album length :0
27
```

```
28              Retrieve Pets
29                Display
30  Set Album length :1
31  --Set Pets length :2
32  ----Dog.jpg
33  ----Cat.jpg
```

Lines 14 and 15 show that the Pets set is archived. In lines 21–24, we remove everything from the album; we then copy the contents back from the archive in lines 28–33. Because we used a deep copy, we could copy Pets repeatedly, or, as the name of the method suggests, aim to share it with other programs. The full listing of the Photo Archive program is in the Appendix.

Use

The Prototype pattern co-opts one instance of a class and uses it as a "breeder" for all future instances. Designs that make heavy use of the Composite and Decorator patterns often can benefit from the Prototype pattern as well. Prototypes are useful when object initialization is expensive and you anticipate few variations on the initialization parameters. In this context, the Prototype pattern can avoid expensive "creation from scratch," supporting cheap cloning of a preinitialized prototype. However, cloning via serialization is not particularly cheap itself, so it is worth considering shallow cloning if you are absolutely sure you have a flat, single-level data structure.

There are different situations where the Prototype pattern would be used:

- Say you have loaded a set of objects into memory and choose to copy by means of user input. When implementing user input, typically there are only a few choices of objects. These are known as the prototypes, and they are identified within the program by matching them up with the admissible input keys (such as strings, integers, or characters). The reason for using prototyping and not instantiation is to reduce the overhead when creating objects that have heavyweight constructors.

- There are composite structures in the program and parts of them need to be copied, perhaps for archiving. Which part to copy will normally be identified by user input. The parts will all be the same (or within the same hierarchy, as in the Composite pattern), and the copy will become the prototype, which should not be altered. An example of this scenario is the Photo Archive application.

Use the Prototype pattern when...

You want to:
- Hide concrete classes from the client.
- Add and remove new classes (via prototypes) at runtime.
- Keep the number of classes in the system to a minimum.
- Adapt to changing structures of data at runtime.

Exercises

1. Community networking systems such as Facebook support *groups* that people can join. Each group has a title, administrative members, a group type (open/closed), and a list of related groups. Otherwise, a group operates just like an ordinary page. Reorganize the SpaceBook application (Example 2-3) so that SpaceBooks and different sorts of SpaceGroups are prototypes.

2. Write a simple system that manages external courses offered by the Department of Tourism Management (e.g., Scenic Spots, Historic Sites, Local Cuisine, Meeting the People, and so on). Identify the attributes that each course should have—length, price, topics, etc.—and set them all up as prototypes with a manager. Then, create a little test program that enables users to select a course, get a copy of it, and fill in details to enroll for the course.

Factory Method Pattern

Role

The Factory Method pattern is a way of creating objects, but letting subclasses decide exactly which class to instantiate. Various subclasses might implement the interface; the Factory Method instantiates the appropriate subclass based on information supplied by the client or extracted from the current state.

Illustration

Consider a high-class grocery store in London that stocks avocados all year round. It relies on a buyer to ensure that avocados arrive regularly, no matter what the time of year. The buyer sources the best avocados and supplies them to the store. The buyer is operating as a Factory Method, returning Kenyan, South African, or Spanish avocados depending on the time of year. Although the produce is labeled, the store-keeper is not particularly interested in the source of the products. Figure 5-2 shows what might happen at different times of the year.

Figure 5-2. Factory Method pattern illustration—avocado sourcing

Design

The client declares a Product variable but calls a FactoryMethod to instantiate it. This defers the decision as to which particular product to create. In the UML diagram in Figure 5-3, there are two choices: ProductA and ProductB.

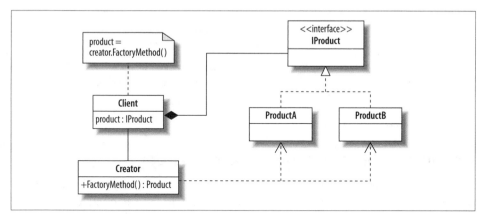

Figure 5-3. Factory Method pattern UML diagram

The list of players is:

IProduct
    The interface for products

ProductA *and* ProductB
    Classes that implement IProduct

Creator
    Provides the FactoryMethod

FactoryMethod
    Decides which class to instantiate

The design of this pattern enables the decision-making about which product to be instantiated to be handled in one place. If the client knew about all the options, the decisions would be dispersed in its code. As it is, the client need only be concerned with getting products; it does not even have to bind in all the different subclasses of products. Of course, the client can have more than one creator, for different types of products.

QUIZ

Match the Factory Method Pattern Players with the Avocado Illustration

To test whether you understand the Factory Method pattern, cover the lefthand column of the table below and see if you can identify its players among the items from the illustrative example (Figure 5-2), as shown in the righthand column. Then check your answers against the lefthand column.

Client	Shoekeeper
Creator	Buyer
ProductA	Supplier of avocados from Spain
ProductB	Supplier of avocados from South Africa
IProduct	Supplying avocados

Implementation and Example: Avocado Sourcing

A simple program implementing the avocado supplier example is shown in Example 5-3. Each of the avocado-producing countries has a class, and they all implement IProduct so that they can ship avocados to the buyer. Depending on the month, the FactoryMethod (lines 31–38) will choose to supply either ProductA (avocados from South Africa) or ProductB (avocados from Spain). There is also a third option, a DefaultProduct, which is selected when avocados are not available (in this case, in month 3). The important line is line 46, which shows a product being created from a factory (the buyer) without the client knowing the product's class.

Example 5-3. Factory Method pattern example code

```
1    using System;
2    using System.Collections;
3
4    class FactoryPattern {
5
6        // Factory Method Pattern           Judith Bishop   2006
7
8        interface IProduct {
9          string ShipFrom( );
10       }
11
12       class ProductA : IProduct {
13         public String ShipFrom ( ) {
14           return " from South Africa";
15         }
16       }
17
18       class ProductB : IProduct {
19         public String ShipFrom ( ) {
20           return "from Spain";
21         }
22       }
23
24       class DefaultProduct : IProduct {
25         public String ShipFrom ( ) {
26           return "not available";
27         }
28       }
29
30       class Creator {
31         public IProduct FactoryMethod(int month) {
32           if (month >= 4 && month <=11)
33               return new ProductA( );
34           else
35           if (month == 1 || month == 2 || month == 12)
36               return new ProductB( );
37           else return new DefaultProduct( );
38         }
39       }
40
41       static void Main( ) {
42         Creator c = new Creator( );
43         IProduct product;
44
45         for (int i=1; i<=12; i++) {
46           product = c.FactoryMethod(i);
47           Console.WriteLine("Avocados "+product.ShipFrom( ));
48         }
49       }
50    }
51
```

Example 5-3. Factory Method pattern example code (continued)

```
52  /* Output
53  Avocados from Spain
54  Avocados from Spain
55  Avocados not available
56  Avocados  from South Africa
57  Avocados  from South Africa
58  Avocados  from South Africa
59  Avocados  from South Africa
60  Avocados  from South Africa
61  Avocados  from South Africa
62  Avocados  from South Africa
63  Avocados  from South Africa
64  Avocados from Spain
65  */
```

Use

The Factory Method pattern is a lightweight pattern that achieves independence from application-specific classes. The client programs to the interface (in this case, IProduct) and lets the pattern sort out the rest.

A particular advantage of the Factory Method pattern is that it can connect parallel class hierarchies. If each hierarchy contains a FactoryMethod, it can be used to create instances of subclasses in a sensible way.

Use the Factory Method pattern when...

- Flexibility is important.
- Objects can be extended in subclasses
- There is a specific reason why one subclass would be chosen over another—this logic forms part of the Factory Method.
- A client delegates responsibilities to subclasses in parallel hierarchies.

Consider using instead....

- The Abstract Factory, Prototype, or Builder patterns, which are more flexible (though also more complex).
- The Prototype pattern to store a set of objects to clone from the abstract factory.

Exercises

1. Extend the avocado sourcing example to source different seasonal products such as artichokes, asparagus, and grapes. Create them as prototypes and extend the Factory Method to work with more than one class.

2. Set up a system to draw circles, squares, and lines. Create a Factory Method that instantiates one of these classes at random and uses it to draw a shape of random size on the screen. Run the program to see what interesting shapes you get.

3. A company has a web site to display test results from a plain text file. The company recently purchased a new computer that produces a binary data file,

and it has another new machine on the way that will possibly produce a different data file. The company is also considering switching to an XML format. Write a system to deal with such changes. The web site just needs data to display; your job is to provide the specified data format for the web site.

Singleton Pattern

Role

The purpose of the Singleton pattern is to ensure that there is only one instance of a class, and that there is a global access point to that object. The pattern ensures that the class is instantiated only once and that all requests are directed to that one and only object. Moreover, the object should not be created until it is actually needed. In the Singleton pattern, it is the class itself that is responsible for ensuring this constraint, not the clients of the class.

Illustration

Any class or subsystem that defines a data bank or provides access to applications, devices, or windows would benefit from the Singleton pattern. Take for example the Mac OS X Dock, shown in Figure 5-4. The Dock shows all the applications that a user accesses regularly. Those that are open have a little black arrow (Tiger) or white dot (Leopard) under them. In this case, reading from the left, Mac OS X, Preferences, Thunderbird, Firefox, Flickr Upload, Parallels for Windows, and Microsoft Word are open. Skype, Seamonkey, iPhoto, and VPUML are closed; they will be opened only when needed.

Figure 5-4. Singleton pattern illustration—the Mac Dock

In most cases, when an open application's icon is clicked, Mac OS X will immediately pass control to that application and make its window visible on the screen. This is an example of the Singleton pattern: there is one instance of the application, and all accesses go there. The applications themselves then take care of opening different windows or documents. Not all applications implement the Singleton pattern, however. For example, the Parallels virtual machine will start a new virtual machine when its icon is clicked, regardless of whether it is currently open or closed.

This behavior is justified in that Parallels can support several operating systems at once, each in its own virtual machine. In contrast, Word, for example, can have many documents open, but they are all attended to by the same instance of the Word application.

 The concept of a Dock does not exist in Windows Vista itself, but there are third-party applications that mimic it.[*]

Design

The Singleton pattern adds functionality by modifying an existing class. The modifications required are:

- Make the constructor private and add a private static constructor as well.
- Add a private static read-only object that is internally instantiated using the private constructor.
- Add a public static property that accesses the private object.

It is the public property (3) that is now visible to the world. All constructor requests for the class go to the property. The property accesses the private static object and will instantiate it if it does not already exist. The UML diagram in Figure 5-5 sums all this up.

Figure 5-5. Singleton pattern UML diagram

The visible players in the Singleton pattern are:

Singleton
> The class containing the mechanism for a unique instance of itself

Instance
> A property for making and accessing an instance of the Singleton class

---

[*] See *http://www.stardock.com/products/objectdock/*.

Match the Singleton Pattern Players with the Dock Illustration

To test whether you understand the Singleton pattern, cover the lefthand column of the table below and see if you can identify its players among the items from the illustrative example (Figure 5-4), as shown in the righthand column. Then check your answers against the lefthand column.

Singleton	An application icon in the Dock
Instance	An application

Implementation

A good implementation of the Singleton pattern in C# relies on the precise interpretation of language rules regarding construction.* Given the plan outlined in the previous section, a correct and elegant implementation is presented in Example 5-4.

Example 5-4. Singleton pattern theory code

```
1  public sealed class Singleton {
2     // Private Constructor
3     Singleton( ) { }
4
5     // Private object instantiated with private constructor
6     static readonly Singleton instance = new Singleton( );
7
8     // Public static property to get the object
9     public static Singleton UniqueInstance {
10       get { return instance;}
11    }
12 }
```

The constructor in line 3 is private by default. To create an object, the client calls the UniqueInstance property defined in lines 9–11, as in:

```
Singleton s1 = Singleton.UniqueInstance;
```

As soon as a class is accessed by the first call on any of its methods, properties, or constructors (and in this case, only the property is callable), its fields are set up. Here, this involves initializing the field called uniqueInstance by invoking the constructor on line 3. For illustrative purposes, we can test that the following two instantiations will refer to the same object:

```
Singleton s1 = Singleton.Instance;
Singleton s2 = Singleton.Instance;
```

---

* See Jon Skeets's article at *http://www.csharphelp.com/archives4/archive670.html*.

As with all static fields, the initialization is not repeated, and therefore the second call on the Instance property, for s2, returns the same object reference.

The Singleton pattern would also like to offer lazy instantiation—i.e., that the object is not initialized until its first invocation.

 Be aware that in a multithreaded program, different threads could try to instantiate a class simultaneously. For this reason, a Singleton implementation that relies on an if statement to check whether the instance is null will not be thread-safe. Do not use code like that!

To do this, we put the instantiation of the Singleton object in a nested class, SingletonCreator, as in Example 5-5 in lines 6–11. The static constructor then falls away.

Example 5-5. Singleton pattern—lazy instantiation

```
 1  public class Singleton {
 2    // Private constructor
 3    Singleton () { }
 4
 5    // Nested class for lazy instantiation
 6    class SingletonCreator {
 7      static SingletonCreator () {}
 8      // Private object instantiated with private constructor
 9      internal static readonly
10        Singleton uniqueInstance = new Singleton();
11    }
12
13    // Public static property to get the object
14    public static Singleton UniqueInstance {
15      get {return SingletonCreator.uniqueInstance;}
16    }
17  }
```

Instantiation of the object will be triggered by the first reference to the static member of the nested class, which occurs in the UniqueInstance property (lines 14–16). This implementation is fully lazy but has all the performance benefits of the previous one. Note that although nested classes have access to the enclosing class's private members, the reverse is not true (hence the need for Instance to be internal here). That doesn't raise any other problems, though, as the class itself is private by default.

An important part of the Singleton pattern is the initializing of resources in the Singleton constructor. In fact, if no resources are being initialized in the constructor, it usually means that a normal static class should be used rather than a Singleton. An example of such initialization is shown in the next section.

Example: Singleton Façade

There are several patterns that make the implicit assumption that only one instance of a class will be created. The Façade pattern is one of these—there should be only one instance of each Façade. The Singleton pattern can enforce this requirement.

To integrate the Singleton into an existing pattern, we again follow the steps outlined earlier. The revised constructor for the Façade is as follows:

```
// start Singleton pattern
// private constructors
Façade( ) {
  a = new SubsystemA( );
  b = new SubsystemB( );
  c = new SubsystemC( );
}
static Façade( ) {}

// private object
static readonly Façade uniqueInstance = new Façade( );

// public static property
public static Façade Instance {
  get {return uniqueInstance;}
}
// end Singleton pattern
```

Then, in the client, instead of:

```
Façade façade = new Façade( );
```

(which would not compile because the constructor is private now), we use:

```
Façade façade = Façade.Instance;
```

If we need to refer to the Façade again from another place in the system, we can declare a new variable and create a new Façade object, but it will still access the same instance.

Use

Many other patterns—for example, the Builder, Prototype, and Abstract Factory patterns—can make use of the Singleton pattern to ensure that only one copy of a class is created. However, the effectiveness of the Singleton pattern relies entirely on developers all using the same rules. Even though implementing a singleton as outlined in this chapter doesn't require much coding effort, it would be nice to be able to *reuse* the implementation. But if the standard rules are not followed, one developer may use an Instance property and another a Create method, for example, or one may use the nested class while the other doesn't. Even if two developers use the same nested class, they might give the class different names. The result could be a complete mess, even for a simple singleton! A solution to this issue is proposed in the "Pattern Comparison" section, later in this chapter.

- You need to ensure there is only one instance of a class.
- Controlled access to that instance is essential.
- You might need more than one instance at a later stage.
- The control should be localized in the instantiated class, not in some other mechanism.

Exercises

1. The community in the SpaceBook application (Example 2-4) was created as static. Rework SpaceBook as a Singleton class.

2. Consider an international airline with a number of servers situated all over the world that are used to process reservations. At different times of the 24-hour clock, some will be heavily loaded and some lightly loaded. Each server can apply to a load balancer to be added to or removed from the system temporarily as time goes by. Model this system with the load balancer as a singleton.

Pattern Comparison

There is a symbiosis between patterns and languages, and it is dynamic. As this book has shown, the new features of C# 3.0 have made implementing patterns easier. (A quick comparison of the code in this book with standard C# pattern code will confirm this statement.) Two of the patterns discussed in this chapter—the Prototype and Singleton patterns—raise some interesting points about pattern language features.

Implementing the Prototype pattern was quite a challenge 10 years ago, when obtaining a deep copy of an arbitrary data structure meant creating a graph traversal algorithm from scratch. Now, it can all be done with one method call to Serialize, plus some associated setup of streams. This facility is available to all languages in .NET, and Java has a similar mechanism. Thus, the implementation of the pattern as it was originally envisaged has almost disappeared. Nevertheless, its intent remains, and managing prototypes is still very much part of the developer's task.

Considering the Singleton pattern, is there any way in which the language might help to make it *reusable?** One solution for achieving reusability is to use C# generics, as shown in Example 5-6.

Example 5-6. Singleton pattern generic code

```
1 using System;
2
3  // Singleton Pattern     Judith Bishop Nov 2007
4  // Generic version
5
6 public class Singleton <T> where T : class, new(){
```

---

* Thanks to Alastair van Leeuwen for initiating this discussion and for the generic example.

Example 5-6. Singleton pattern generic code (continued)

```
7    Singleton( ) { }
8
9    class SingletonCreator {
10     static SingletonCreator ( ) {}
11     // Private object instantiated with private constructor
12     internal static readonly T instance = new T( );
13   }
14
15   public static T UniqueInstance {
16     get {return SingletonCreator.instance;}
17   }
18 }
19
20 class Test1 {}
21 class Test2 {}
22
23 class Client {
24
25   static void Main ( ) {
26     Test1 t1a = Singleton<Test1>.UniqueInstance;
27     Test1 t1b = Singleton<Test1>.UniqueInstance;
28     Test2 t2 = Singleton<Test2>.UniqueInstance;
29
30     if (t1a == t1b) {
31       Console.WriteLine("Objects are the same instance");
32     }
33   }
34 }
```

The Singleton class corresponds to that in Example 5-5, with the addition of two generic constraints (see Chapter 6) to ensure that the type used for the generic instantiation is a class and has a constructor (line 6). Variables of any class can be created with the same Singleton class, as shown in lines 25–27. Given how neat and tidy this class is, it would be useful to draw it into the language. Perhaps we can look ahead to a new version of C#, where a new language construct—singleton—will define that a class is in fact a singleton. In theory, the language will make sure that the singleton implementation has an Instance property, and the developer will not have to state whether the constructor of the singleton is private—the language will *force* the constructor to be private. The process of language and pattern convergence is not at an end, so the Singleton construct may well come into the language one day.

CHAPTER 6

Creational Patterns: Abstract Factory and Builder

The creational patterns introduce a very popular concept in design patterns: factories. Factories are classes that handle the instantiation of related objects without subclassing. We saw in Chapter 5 how the Factory Method pattern can hide the class name from the place where an object is instantiated. The Abstract Factory pattern takes this one step further, creating families of related or dependent objects. The Builder pattern offers additional flexibility in terms of the combination of objects being built.

Abstract Factory Pattern

Role

This pattern supports the creation of products that exist in families and are designed to be produced together. The abstract factory can be refined to concrete factories, each of which can create different products of different types and in different combinations. The pattern isolates the product definitions and their class names from the client so that the only way to get one of them is through a factory. For this reason, product families can easily be interchanged or updated without upsetting the structure of the client.

Illustration

A scourge of modern society is the huge number of fakes on the market. The products of many famous brands are copied and presented for sale, often as the real thing. Sometimes the copies are identified up front as replicas, so the customer is aware of what he is buying. However, often the customer is unaware (or maybe does not care) from which factory the goods actually originated. Figure 6-1 shows some replica handbags—they look like Guccis but could have come from a factory such as Poochy (a made-up name).

Figure 6-1. Abstract Factory pattern illustration—replica Gucci handbags (Poochies)

The Abstract Factory pattern creates a similar layer of opacity by actually hiding the factory name from the client. In computer terms, this makes it possible to swap the factory, while still providing the goods according to an agreed interface.

Design

The Abstract Factory pattern has a lot of players, as illustrated in the following UML diagram (Figure 6-2), but the design is actually quite simple. The client has a concrete factory conforming to the AbstractFactory interface. Through that, it asks for product objects (here, of type A and B). However, these are abstract product types; the concrete factories sort out exactly which products the client gets. This enables the system to be independent of how the products are created, composed, and implemented. The client is not concerned about the details of the products, nor even about their actual class names; it just knows that an A type object and a B type object are provided.

Formally, the players in the pattern are:

AbstractFactory
> An interface with Create operations for each of the abstract products

Factory1, Factory2
> Implementations of all the AbstractFactory creation operations

AbstractProduct
> An interface for a kind of product with its own operations

ProductA1, ProductA2, ProductB1, ProductB2
> Classes that implement the AbstractProduct interface and define product objects to be created by the corresponding factories

Client
> A class that accesses only the AbstractFactory and AbstractProduct interfaces

An interesting aspect of the Abstract Factory pattern is that the whole product family can be changed while the application is running. For example, if the client is using the family of objects created by FactoryA, it can instantiate FactoryB and switch to that. Because the products implement the same abstract interface, any operations it may contain will be the same, although their implementations will differ.

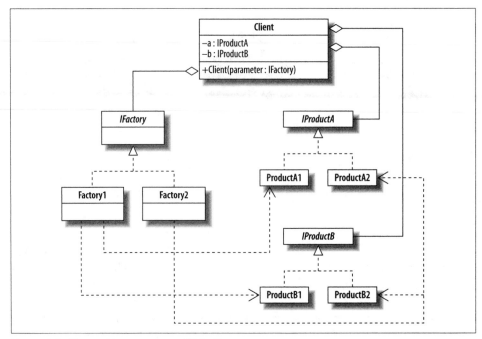

Figure 6-2. Abstract Factory pattern UML diagram

QUIZ

Match the Abstract Factory Pattern Players with the Replica Handbag Illustration

To test whether you understand the Abstract Factory pattern, cover the lefthand column of the table below and see if you can match the players in the righthand column to the items in the illustrative example (Figure 6-1). Then check your answers against the lefthand column.

Client	Customer buying a handbag
AbstractFactory	Returns a handbag
FactoryA	Gucci
FactoryB	Poochy
AbstractProduct	Handbags
ProductA1	Genuine bags
ProductB1	Replica bags

Implementation and Example: Gucci and Poochy

The code that we shall develop here is based on the preceding illustration. The implementation we have chosen for the Abstract Factory pattern is not the usual inheritance-based one—it also makes use of generics to simplify the creation of the factories. Instead of several factory subclasses, we have only one, and it is generic. A factory and its interface look like this:

```
interface IFactory<Brand>
  where Brand : IBrand {
    IBag CreateBag();
    IShoes CreateShoes();
}

// Factories (both in the same one)
class Factory<Brand> : IFactory<Brand>
    where Brand : IBrand, new() {

  public IBag CreateBag() {
    return new Bag<Brand>();
  }
  public IShoes CreateShoes() {
    return new Shoes<Brand>();
  }
}
```

Our factory is going to make bags and shoes. The structure of the factories is always the same, so we create a generic one based on brand. The generic specification for Factory includes some *constraints*.

C# Feature—Generic Constraints

Generic type and method declarations can optionally specify *constraints* on the types that can be used to instantiate them. Constraints can indicate which interfaces the type should implement. For example:

```
class SortedList<T> where T: IComparable<T> {...}
```

Here, a type T used to instantiate SortedList must implement IComparable.

new() as a constraint indicates that the type must have a constructor.

cf. C# Language Specification Version 3.0, September 2007, Section 10.1.5

In our example, the two Products are bags and shoes. Bags indicate what they are made of, and shoes indicate their price. Once again, we declare the products as generic:

```
// Product 1
interface IBags {
  string Material { get; }
}
// Concrete Product 1
 class Bag<Brand> : IBag
     where Brand : IBrand, new() {
   private Brand myBrand;
   public Bag() {
       myBrand = new Brand();
   }

   public string Material { get { return myBrand.Material; } }
 }
```

When the Factory to be used is instantiated, as in:

```
IFactory<Brand> factory = new Factory<Brand>();
```

one of the small brand specifications, such as:

```
class Gucci : IBrand {
  public int Price { get { return 1000; } }
  public string Material { get { return "Crocodile skin"; } }
}
```

is passed through to the Factory. Then, when a product is to be made, as in:

```
IBag bag = factory.CreateBag();
IShoes shoes = factory.CreateShoes();
```

the Factory uses the same brand to instantiate the generic Bag and Shoe classes. The full example code is in Example 6-1.

Example 6-1. Abstract Factory pattern example code

```
1        using System;
2
3          namespace AbstractFactoryPattern {
4            // Abstract Factory      D-J Miller and Judith Bishop  Sept 2007
5            // Uses generics to simplify the creation of factories
6
7            interface IFactory<Brand>
8                where Brand : IBrand {
9              IBag CreateBag();
10             IShoes CreateShoes();
11           }
12
13           // Concrete Factories (both in the same one)
14           class Factory<Brand> : IFactory<Brand>
15               where Brand : IBrand, new() {
16             public IBag CreateBag() {
17               return new Bag<Brand>();
18             }
19
20             public IShoes CreateShoes() {
21               return new Shoes<Brand>();
```

Example 6-1. Abstract Factory pattern example code (continued)

```
22              }
23          }
24
25              // Interface IProductA
26          interface IBag {
27            string Material { get; }
28          }
29
30          // Interface IProductB
31          interface IShoes {
32            int Price { get; }
33          }
34
35          // All concrete ProductA's
36          class Bag<Brand> : IBag
37              where Brand : IBrand, new( ) {
38            private Brand myBrand;
39            public Bag( ) {
40              myBrand = new Brand( );
41            }
42
43            public string Material { get { return myBrand.Material; } }
44          }
45
46          // All concrete ProductB's
47          class Shoes<Brand> : IShoes
48              where Brand : IBrand, new( ) {
49           private Brand myBrand;
50           public Shoes( ) {
51             myBrand = new Brand( );
52           }
53
54           public int Price { get { return myBrand.Price; } }
55          }
56
57          // An interface for all Brands
58          interface IBrand {
59            int Price { get; }
60            string Material { get; }
61          }
62
63          class Gucci : IBrand {
64            public int Price { get { return 1000; } }
65            public string Material { get { return "Crocodile skin"; } }
66          }
67
68          class Poochy : IBrand {
69            public int Price { get { return new Gucci( ).Price / 3; } }
70            public string Material { get { return "Plastic"; } }
71          }
72
```

Example 6-1. Abstract Factory pattern example code (continued)

```
73    class Groundcover : IBrand {
74      public int Price { get { return 2000; } }
75      public string Material { get { return "South african leather"; } }
76    }
77
78    class Client<Brand>
79        where Brand : IBrand, new( ) {
80      public void ClientMain( ) //IFactory<Brand> factory) {
81        IFactory<Brand> factory = new Factory<Brand>( );
82
83        IBag bag = factory.CreateBag( );
84        IShoes shoes = factory.CreateShoes( );
85
86        Console.WriteLine("I bought a Bag which is made from " + bag.Material);
87        Console.WriteLine("I bought some shoes which cost " + shoes.Price);
88      }
89    }
90
91    static class Program {
92      static void Main( ) {
93        // Call Client twice
94        new Client<Poochy>( ).ClientMain( );
95        new Client<Gucci>( ).ClientMain( );
96        new Client<Groundcover>( ).ClientMain( );
97      }
98    }
99  }
100 /* Output
101 I bought a Bag which is made from Plastic
102 I bought some shoes which cost 333
103 I bought a Bag which is made from Crocodile skin
104 I bought some shoes which cost 1000
105 I bought a Bag which is made from South african leather
106 I bought some shoes which cost 2000
107 */
```

The IBrand interface is not a part of the original Abstract Factory pattern, but it does simplify adding new factories. Three different factories are included in this example to show that the generic implementation makes it very easy to add essential information about production without the need to write another Factory class. In this case, all that was needed to add Groundcover as a factory were lines 73–76. The output from running with all three factories in succession is shown in lines 101–106.

Use

As we have seen, the Abstract Factory pattern handles families of products and keeps their details independent from the clients. As such, it is ideal for generating different layouts and multiple-look-and-feel user interfaces. It can also be successfully applied for portability across operating systems, where the sense of what is required is the same—open file, close window, etc.—but the events and consequences differ.

An oft-quoted limitation of the Abstract Factory pattern is that it is not easy to add new kinds of products. The number and names of the abstract products are coded directly into the abstract factory (see lines 9–10 in Example 6-1). Therefore, adding a new product requires the factory interface and all its subclassed concrete factories to be updated. Even the client needs to change to take advantage of the new addition. The Builder pattern, which we will discuss next, emphasizes extensibility over flexibility.

Use the Abstract Factory pattern when...

• A system should be independent of how its products are created, composed, and represented.
• A system can be configured with one of multiple families of products.
• The constraint requiring products from the same factory to be used together must be enforced.
• The emphasis is on revealing interfaces, not implementations.

Exercises

1. Add belts to the products that are to be made by the factories in the example.

2. Under what conditions would the example in Figure 5-3 (sourcing avocados) become a candidate for the Abstract Factory pattern? Program it up as such.

3. Just for the experience, program Example 6-1 without generics, using separate classes for each of the factories. Comment on the differences between the implementations.

Builder Pattern

Role

The Builder pattern separates the specification of a complex object from its actual construction. The same construction process can create different representations.

Illustration

Following on from the replica bag example introduced in the previous section, suppose that an online order company offers bags and shoes—both real and replica—on a bespoke basis (i.e., with the products made to order). We would expect that the time taken to make one of the genuine articles would be longer. In addition, we would notice other differences between the products. Each bag (Product) is made up of several parts, including the outside material, the lining, the label, the handle, and so on. The genuine, more expensive bags will have more parts usually. Certainly, there can be differences in the part lists for different makes of bags. For example, apart from being plastic (not leather), a replica bag might not have a nice lining.

The Builder pattern goes into the details of how the products are actually made, and some of this information can be transmitted back to the customer. For example, the time taken to deliver will be obvious, but the country of origin as specified on the label might also be important.

Design

The Builder pattern is based on Directors and Builders. Any number of Builder classes can conform to an IBuilder interface, and they can be called by a director to produce a product according to specification. The builders supply parts that the Product objects accumulate until the director is finished with the job. Suppose a Director wants two of one kind of part and one of another. It would request them from a Builder and pass them on to be added to the product's list. The point about the Builder pattern is that different builders can supply different (though conforming) parts. Consider the UML for the Builder pattern in Figure 6-3.

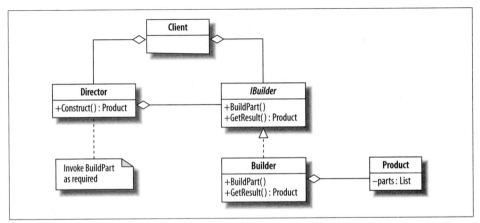

Figure 6-3. Builder pattern UML diagram

There can be several Directors and Builders. The client calls Construct for a particular Director with a particular Builder. The Director has an individual way of putting together parts on offer from the Builder interface. The Product maintains a running list of the parts as they are created, and this list is the result of the construction process. Here are the main players:

IBuilder
 An interface defining what can be built

Director
 A sequence of operations that can be followed to create a Product

Builder
 A class that is called by a Director to make Product parts

Product
 The object under construction, by parts

A specific advantage of the Builder/Director partnership is that the products do not all necessarily turn out the same. The Builder can redefine the way it works and, even with the same Director, produce a different product. Furthermore, the Builder pattern constructs the product step by step under the director's control. Only when the construction is complete is the product returned to the director for the director to work with.

Implementation

In the theory code shown in Example 6-2, the Client creates a director and two builders. The director wants to make products as follows:

```
class Director {
    // Build a Product from several parts
    public void Construct(IBuilder builder) {
        builder.BuildPartA();
        builder.BuildPartB();
        builder.BuildPartB();
    }
}
```

In other words, a part A followed by two part Bs. This makes up a product. However, depending on the builder supplied, the output will be different. Builder1 does indeed make these parts, but Builder2 makes PartX's and PartY's. Though different, they conform to the IBuilder interface. Thus output from two calls to the Director could be:

```
    Product Parts -------
    PartA PartB PartB

    Product Parts -------
    PartX PartY PartY
```

The full program is shown in Example 6-2.

Example 6-2. Builder pattern theory code

```
 1  using System;
 2  using System.Collections.Generic;
 3
 4    // Builder Pattern              Judith Bishop November 2007
 5    // Simple theory code with one director and two builders
 6
 7      class Director {
 8          // Build a Product from several parts
 9          public void Construct(IBuilder builder) {
10              builder.BuildPartA();
11              builder.BuildPartB();
12              builder.BuildPartB();
13          }
14      }
15
16      interface IBuilder {
17          void BuildPartA();
18          void BuildPartB();
19          Product GetResult();
20      }
21
22      class Builder1 : IBuilder {
23          private Product product = new Product();
24          public  void BuildPartA() {
25              product.Add("PartA ");
26          }
27
28          public void BuildPartB() {
29              product.Add("PartB ");
30          }
31
32          public Product GetResult() {
33              return product;
34          }
35      }
36
37      class Builder2 : IBuilder {
38          private Product product = new Product();
39          public void BuildPartA() {
40              product.Add("PartX ");
41          }
42
43          public void BuildPartB() {
```

Example 6-2. Builder pattern theory code (continued)

```
44                   product.Add("PartY ");
45              }
46
47          public Product GetResult() {
48              return product;
49          }
50      }
51
52      class Product {
53          List <string> parts = new List <string> ();
54          public void Add(string part) {
55              parts.Add(part);
56          }
57
58          public void Display() {
59              Console.WriteLine("\nProduct Parts -------");
60              foreach (string part in parts)
61                  Console.Write(part);
62              Console.WriteLine();
63          }
64      }
65
66      public class Client {
67
68          public static void Main() {
69              // Create one director and two builders
70              Director director = new Director();
71
72              IBuilder b1 = new Builder1();
73              IBuilder b2 = new Builder2();
74
75              // Construct two products
76              director.Construct(b1);
77              Product p1 = b1.GetResult();
78              p1.Display();
79
80              director.Construct(b2);
81              Product p2 = b2.GetResult();
82              p2.Display();
83          }
84      }
85  /* Output
86  Product Parts -------
87  PartA PartB PartB
88
89  Product Parts -------
90  PartX PartY PartY
91  */
```

Example

The example is very similar to that of the Abstract Factory pattern. The crucial difference is that the Director contains more functionality than the factories were required to. To illustrate, here is one of the two Directors from the code in Example 6-2:

```
class Gucci : IBrand {
 public IBag CreateBag() {
   Bag b = new Bag();
   Program.DoWork("Cut Leather", 250);
   Program.DoWork("Sew leather", 1000);
   b.Properties += "Leather";
   Program.DoWork("Create Lining", 500);
   Program.DoWork("Attach Lining", 1000);
   b.Properties += " lined";
   Program.DoWork("Add Label", 250);
   b.Properties += " with label";
   return b;
 }
}
```

The DoWork method simulates the passing of time so that we can see that some products take longer than others to make. In lines 61–72 of Example 6-2, the Director for replica bags (lines 61–72) has fewer steps than that for Gucci bags (lines 46–49). Ultimately, as shown in the output, they are also produced faster. Example 6-3 shows the full example code.

Example 6-3. Builder pattern example code

```
1  using System;
2  using System.Diagnostics;
3  using System.IO;
4  using System.Threading;
5
6   namespace BuilderPattern {
7     // Builder Pattern     D-J Miller and Judith Bishop   Sept 2007
8
9     // Abstract Factory : Builder Implementation
10    interface IBuilder<Brand>
11        where Brand : IBrand {
12      IBag CreateBag();
13    }
14
15    // Abstract Factory now the Builder
16    class Builder<Brand> : IBuilder<Brand>
17        where Brand : IBrand, new() {
18
19      Brand myBrand;
20      public Builder() {
21        myBrand = new Brand();
22      }
23
24      public IBag CreateBag() {
25        return myBrand.CreateBag();
```

Example 6-3. Builder pattern example code (continued)

```
26        }
27    }
28
29    // Product 1
30    interface IBag {
31      string Properties { get; set; }
32    }
33
34    // Concrete Product 1
35    class Bag : IBag
36    {
37      public string Properties { get; set; }
38    }
39
40
41    // Directors
42    interface IBrand {
43      IBag CreateBag( );
44    }
45
46    class Gucci : IBrand {
47      public IBag CreateBag( ) {
48        Bag b = new Bag( );
49        Program.DoWork("Cut Leather", 250);
50        Program.DoWork("Sew leather", 1000);
51        b.Properties += "Leather";
52        Program.DoWork("Create Lining", 500);
53        Program.DoWork("Attach Lining", 1000);
54        b.Properties += " lined";
55        Program.DoWork("Add Label", 250);
56        b.Properties += " with label";
57        return b;
58      }
59    }
60
61    class Poochy : IBrand {
62      public IBag CreateBag( ) {
63        Bag b = new Bag( );
64        Program.DoWork("Hire cheap labour", 200);
65        Program.DoWork("Cut Plastic", 125);
66        Program.DoWork("Sew Plastic", 500);
67        b.Properties += "Plastic";
68        Program.DoWork("Add Label", 100);
69        b.Properties += " with label";
70        return b;
71      }
72    }
73
74    class Client<Brand>
75        where Brand : IBrand, new( ) {
76      public void ClientMain( ) //IFactory<Brand> factory) {
77        IBuilder<Brand> factory = new Builder<Brand>( );
78
```

Example 6-3. Builder pattern example code (continued)

```
79          DateTime date = DateTime.Now;
80          Console.WriteLine("I want to buy a bag!");
81          IBag bag = factory.CreateBag( );
82
83          Console.WriteLine("I got my Bag which took " +
84              DateTime.Now.Subtract(date).TotalSeconds * 5 + " days");
85          Console.WriteLine("  with the following properties " +
86              bag.Properties+"\n");
87      }
88    }
89
90    static class Program {
91
92      static void Main( ) {
93        // Call Client twice
94        new Client<Poochy>().ClientMain( );
95        new Client<Gucci>().ClientMain( );
96      }
97
98      public static void DoWork(string workitem, int time) {
99        Console.Write("" + workitem + ": 0%");
100       Thread.Sleep(time);
101       Console.Write("....25%");
102       Thread.Sleep(time);
103       Console.Write("....50%");
104       Thread.Sleep(time);
105       Console.WriteLine("....100%");
106     }
107   }
108 }
109
110 /* Output
111 I want to buy a bag!
112 Hire cheap labour: 0%....25%....50%....100%
113 Cut Plastic: 0%....25%....50%....100%
114 Sew Plastic: 0%....25%....50%....100%
115 Add Label: 0%....25%....50%....100%
116 I got my Bag which took 14.02016 days
117   with the following properties Plastic with label
118
119 I want to buy a bag!
120 Cut Leather: 0%....25%....50%....100%
121 Sew leather: 0%....25%....50%....100%
122 Create Lining: 0%....25%....50%....100%
123 Attach Lining: 0%....25%....50%....100%
124 Add Label: 0%....25%....50%....100%
125 I got my Bag which took 45.0648 days
126   with the following properties Leather lined with label
127 */
```

Use

Builders can be found in applications that create complex structures. The result of a builder is often a composite.

Exercises

1. A popular example of the Builder pattern is supplying a car with given characteristics. Suppose there is one car company that offers three models: economy, medium, and luxury. Write a nongeneric program that illustrates the pattern in this domain. The program should be able to handle different car models (products), and each model should offer different options for things such as wheels, upholstery, color, and air conditioning.

2. Use the Builder pattern to create a maze. The IBuilder interface should have methods such as BuildMaze, BuildRoom, BuildDoor, and GetMaze. Then create a StandardMazeBuilder and a DifficultMazeBuilder that implement the operations differently; for example, in the BuildRoom method, the StandardMaze could have two doors and the DifficultMaze between one and four doors. The client asks a director to create a maze builder of a given kind, and then to build the maze.

Pattern Comparison

The Builder and Abstract Factory patterns are similar in that they both look at construction at an abstract level. However, the Builder pattern is concerned with *how* a single object is made up by the different factories, whereas the Abstract Factory pattern is concerned with *what* products are made. The Builder pattern abstracts the algorithm for construction by including the concept of a director. The director is responsible for itemizing the steps and calls on builders to fulfill them. Directors do not have to conform to an interface.

A further elaboration on the theme of creating products is that instead of the client explicitly declaring fields of type ProductA and ProductB, say, the Product object the builder returns is actually a list of parts, which can have different lengths and contents depending on the director that was in charge at its creation.

A comparison of the two patterns is given in Table 6-1.

Table 6-1. Comparison of Abstract Factory and Builder patterns

Criteria	Abstract Factory	Builder
Client aggregates	A Factory and Products	A Director, Builders, and a Product
Product creation is via	A factory	A director
Product creation invokes	CreateProductA	Construct(builder)
Factory/Builder returns	A specific product	A part of a product
Product has	Specific properties	A list of parts

CHAPTER 7

Behavioral Patterns: Strategy, State, and Template Method

Behavioral patterns are concerned with algorithms and communication between them. The operations that make up a single algorithm might be split up between different classes, making a complex arrangement that is difficult to manage and maintain. The behavioral patterns capture ways of expressing the division of operations between classes and optimize how the communication should be handled. In this first chapter on behavioral patterns, we'll look at three simple but very useful patterns: the Strategy, State, and Template Methods.

Strategy Pattern

Role

The Strategy pattern involves removing an algorithm from its host class and putting it in a separate class. There may be different algorithms (strategies) that are applicable for a given problem. If the algorithms are all kept in the host, messy code with lots of conditional statements will result. The Strategy pattern enables a client to choose which algorithm to use from a family of algorithms and gives it a simple way to access it. The algorithms can also be expressed independently of the data they are using.

Illustration

A classic illustration of the Strategy pattern is found in the choice of algorithms for sorting. There are many sorting algorithms, and although some, such as Quicksort, are generally very fast, there are situations when this would be a poor choice and another algorithm, such as Mergesort, would perform better. Even the linear sorts, such as Shellsort, can perform very well under certain conditions. When studying sorting, one learns about the different conditions to consider and how to optimize the choice of algorithms. This is a strategy that can be captured in the Strategy pattern.

Sorting lends itself to animation, as shown in Figure 7-1. The graph plots the index against the value at successive stages in the sort. Thus, initially the box shows a scatter of points. As the algorithm progresses, the points start to converge on the diagonal, indicating that the values are in the correct positions in the list. The lefthand window shows Mergesort in action, and the righthand window shows Quicksort.

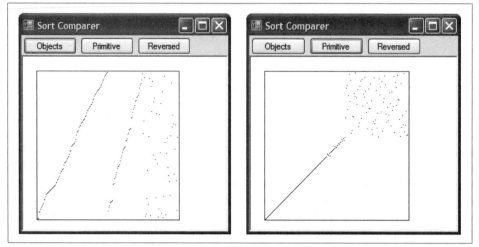

Figure 7-1. Strategy pattern illustration—sorting objects with Mergesort and sorting primitive types with Quicksort

In terms of strategy, the animator is set up so that the user indicates the type of items being sorted (at a very rough level in this example). The underlying Strategy pattern then selects an appropriate sort method. In this case, larger values (objects) that have costly compare operations are sent to Mergesort, which uses the lowest number of comparisons of all popular sorts. On the other hand, Quicksort can go very fast with primitive items (where the comparisons are cheap), so it is preferred for those types of values. The third button is there because of a limitation of Quicksort: without careful programming, it is very slow with reversed data. This button can be used to activate Mergesort. The Strategy pattern makes it easy to add other criteria and sorts to the animator as needed.

Design

The design of the Strategy pattern is encapsulated in the UML diagram in Figure 7-2. Within a given Context, an appropriate strategy is chosen from an available family of strategies. The algorithm in the strategy is then followed through to a conclusion.

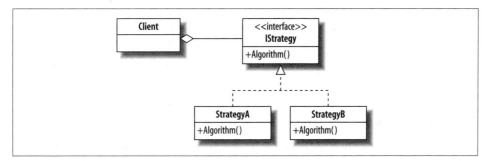

Figure 7-2. Strategy pattern UML diagram

The roles for the players in this pattern are as follows:

Context
 A class that maintains contextual information for an IStrategy object's algorithm to work on

IStrategy
 Defines an interface common to all the strategies

StrategyA, StrategyB
 Classes that include algorithms that implement the IStrategy interface

---

QUIZ

Match the Strategy Pattern Players with the Sorting Animator Illustration

To test whether you understand the Strategy pattern, cover the lefthand column of the table below and see if you can identify its players among the items from the illustrative example (Figure 7-2), as shown in the righthand column. Then check your answers against the lefthand column.

Context	The GUI, the list generator, and the selection of the Strategy
Strategy	Class containing the methods used for a particular sort
IStrategy	Sorting interface (e.g., specifying the list and its item type)
Algorithm	Mergesort or Quicksort

As defined, the Context aggregates an object of the chosen Strategy type. Generally, it will only have access to the main method that the algorithm requires. If it needs more information from the Strategy, this should be included in the IStrategy interface. On the other hand, the Strategy will need to work within the Context and access its state.

Implementation

The theory code for the Strategy pattern (Example 7-1) does not need any new C# 3.0 features. It relies on aggregation of the IStrategy interface in the Context (line 13). The client calls the Algorithm method on the Context (line 59), and it is routed through to the method of the strategy applicable at the time. In this example, the strategies have Move methods that count up and down. A random number generated in the client determines when to switch from counting up to counting down. The resulting output is shown in line 65.

Example 7-1. Strategy pattern theory code

```
1    using System;
2
3    // Strategy Pattern              Judith Bishop  Oct 2007
4    // Shows two strategies and a random switch between them
5
6    // The Context
7    class Context {
8        // Context state
9        public const int start = 5;
10       public int Counter = 5;
11
12       // Strategy aggregation
13       IStrategy strategy = new Strategy1();
14
15       // Algorithm invokes a strategy method
16       public int Algorithm() {
17         return strategy.Move(this);
18       }
19
20       // Changing strategies
21       public void SwitchStrategy() {
22         if (strategy is Strategy1)
23             strategy = new Strategy2();
24         else
25             strategy = new Strategy1();
26       }
27    }
28
29    // Strategy interface
30    interface IStrategy {
31       int Move (Context c);
32    }
33
```

Example 7-1. Strategy pattern theory code (continued)

```
34    // Strategy 1
35    class Strategy1 : IStrategy {
36      public int Move (Context c) {
37        return ++c.Counter;
38      }
39    }
40
41    // Strategy 2
42    class Strategy2 : IStrategy {
43      public int Move (Context c) {
44        return --c.Counter ;
45      }
46    }
47
48    // Client
49    static class Program {
50      static void Main ( ) {
51        Context context = new Context();
52        context.SwitchStrategy();
53        Random r = new Random(37);
54        for (int i=Context.start; i<=Context.start+15; i++) {
55          if (r.Next(3) == 2) {
56            Console.Write("|| ");
57            context.SwitchStrategy();
58          }
59          Console.Write(context.Algorithm() +"  ");
60        }
61        Console.WriteLine();
62      }
63    }
64 /* Output
65 4  || 5  6  7  || 6  || 7  8  9  10  || 9  8  7  6  || 7  || 6  5
66 */
```

Some key points about the implementation of the Strategy pattern are:

- The Context will often contain a switch statement or a cascading if statement, where information is processed to reach a decision on which Strategy to adopt.

- If the strategies are simple methods, they can be implemented without enclosing classes, and the delegate mechanism can be used to hook the chosen Strategy into the Context at runtime.

- Extension methods can be used to define new strategies independently of the original classes that they support.

Example: Sorting Animator

The program that produces the animations in Figure 7-1 is shown in Example 7-2. Consider first the Context (lines 61–86). ButtonClick is activated from the GUI and, based on the button clicked, will decide on a strategy to follow. In other words, it will select one of the available strategy classes and instantiate it. After generating data from the class at line 15 (not shown in full here), it activates the GUI window and starts the sort. We don't show the full sorting algorithms here, only the interaction with the Context (see lines 96–112 for Mergesort). Input is the list that is being sorted, and the algorithms contain strategic calls to update the user interface through the UpdateUI event.

Example 7-2. Strategy pattern example code—Sorting Animator

```
1     using System;
2     using System.Collections.Generic;
3     using System.Linq;
4     using System.Windows.Forms;
5     using System.Drawing;
6     using System.Threading;
7
8     namespace Strategy {
9
10        // Strategy Pattern       Judith Bishop and D-J Miller   Sept 2007
11        // Gives a choice of sort routines to display
12        // Algorithms and GUI adapted from a Java system at
13        // http://www.geocities.com/SiliconValley/Network/1854/Sort1.html
14
15        static class StartSetGenerator {
16          private static List<int> myList;
17
18          public static IEnumerable<int> GetStartSet( ) {
19            // omitted
20          }
21
22      class StrategyView<T> : Form
23          where T : IComparable<T> {
24        PictureBox pb;
25        Func<IEnumerable<T>> Generator;
26
27        // Constructor to set up the GUI
28        public StrategyView(Func<IEnumerable<T>> generator) {
29          // omitted
30
31        public void DrawGraph(IEnumerable<T> list) {
32          if (pb.Image == null)
33              pb.Image = new Bitmap(pb.Width, pb.Height);
34          Graphics g = Graphics.FromImage(pb.Image);
35          g.Clear(Color.White);
36          g.DrawRectangle(Pens.Blue, 19, 19, 202, 202);
37          g.Dispose( );
38          Bitmap b = pb.Image as Bitmap;
39
```

Example 7-2. Strategy pattern example code—Sorting Animator (continued)

```
40        // Plots the index x against the value val of all elements in the list
41        // IEnumerable<T>.Count is an extension
42        int listSize = list.Count();
43        int x = 0;
44        foreach (T item in list) {
45          // val must be a nullable integer. The as operator will return null
46          // if it cannot convert the item to int
47          int? val = item as int?;
48          if (!val.HasValue)
49            val = 0;
50          // Drawing methods do not handle nullable types
51          b.SetPixel(x + 20, 20 + 200 - ((int)val), Color.Black);
52          x++;
53        }
54
55      this.Refresh();
56      Thread.Sleep(100);
57      Application.DoEvents();
58    }
59
60    // The Context
61    void ButtonClick(object sender, EventArgs e) {
62      Button control = sender as Button;
63      SortStrategy<T> strategy = null;
64
65      switch (control.Name) {
66        case "LargeItems":
67          strategy = new MergeSorter<T>();
68          break;
69        case "SmallItems":
70          strategy = new QuickSorter<T>();
71          break;
72        case "ReversedList":
73          strategy = new MergeSorter<T>();
74          break;
75      }
76
77      IEnumerable<T> newlist = Generator();
78      DrawGraph(newlist);
79      if (strategy == null)
80          return;
81
82      // DrawGraph will be invoked during sorting when
83      // the UpdateUI event is triggered
84      strategy.UpdateUI += new Action<IEnumerable<T>>(DrawGraph);
85      strategy.Sort(newlist);
86    }
87  }
88
89  // Strategy interface
90  interface SortStrategy<T> where T : IComparable<T> {
91    event Action<IEnumerable<T>> UpdateUI;
```

Example 7-2. Strategy pattern example code—Sorting Animator (continued)

```
92       void Sort(IEnumerable<T> input);
93     }
94
95     // Strategy 1
96     class MergeSorter<T> : SortStrategy<T>
97         where T : IComparable<T> {
98
99       public event Action<IEnumerable<T>> UpdateUI;
100
101      List<T> aux;
102      int opCount = 0;
103      public void Sort(IEnumerable<T> input) {
104        UpdateUI(input);
105        opCount++;
106        List<T> sorteditems = new List<T>(input);
107        aux = new List<T>(sorteditems.Count);
108        for (int i = 0; i < sorteditems.Count; i++)
109          aux.Add(default(T));
110        MergeSort(ref sorteditems, 0, sorteditems.Count - 1);
111        UpdateUI(sorteditems);
112      }
113
114      private void Merge(ref List<T> a, int l, int m, int r) {
115        // omitted
116
117      private void MergeSort(ref List<T> a, int l, int r) {
118        // omitted
119    }
120
121    // Strategy 2
122    class QuickSorter<T> : SortStrategy<T>
123        where T : IComparable<T> {
124
125      public event Action<IEnumerable<T>> UpdateUI;
126
127      int opCount = 0;
128      public void Sort(IEnumerable<T> input) {
129        UpdateUI(input);
130        opCount++;
131        List<T> sorteditems = new List<T>(input);
132
133        QuickSort(ref sorteditems, 0, sorteditems.Count - 1);
134        UpdateUI(sorteditems);
135      }
136
137      private int Partition(ref List<T> a, int l, int r) {
138        // omitted
139
140      private void QuickSort(ref List<T> a, int l, int r) {
141        // omitted
142    }
143
144    static class Program {
```

Example 7-2. Strategy pattern example code—Sorting Animator (continued)

```
145      static void Main( ) {
146          Application.EnableVisualStyles( );
147          Application.SetCompatibleTextRenderingDefault(false);
148          Application.Run(new StrategyView<int>(StartSetGenerator.GetStartSet));
149      }
150   }
151 }
```

UpdateUI is an event that is set in line 84 (in the Context) to refer to DrawGraph. This is a more transparent way of the Strategy getting back to the animator than having it call DrawGraph directly. Notice that DrawGraph (lines 31–58) has an interesting loop that uses a new feature in C# 2.0: *nullable types*.

C# Feature—Nullable Types

Nullable types add to primitive types and structs the ability to include an "undefined value." In keeping with objects, the value is called null, and it can be assigned and checked for.

In programs, all primitive types are assigned default values on instantiation. Therefore, the ability to assign null to numeric and Boolean types is particularly useful when dealing with databases and other data types containing elements that may not be assigned a value. For example, a Boolean field in a database can store the values true or false, or it may be undefined.

In C#, a nullable type is declared with the addition of a question mark (e.g., int? x). An extra property—HasValue—can then be used to check whether a value is non-null. To convert back to a non-nullable type, use the as operator. as will return null if it cannot convert the value. For example, int? val = DateTime.Now as int?;

cf. C# Language Specification Version 3.0, September 2007, Section 4.1.10

Consider the loop in question. The items in the list are of type T, and it is possible that they might not have values. The cast to int on line 47 will therefore be trapped unless null is included as a possibility for val. In the next line, we can convert any possible nulls to zeros. Then, on line 51, we see that we have to convert the int? type to int so that it can be used in arithmetic:

```
44          foreach (T item in list) {
45              // val must be an integer. The as conversion needs it
46              // also to be a non-nullable, which is checked by the ?
47              int? val = item as int?;
48              if (!val.HasValue)
49                  val = 0;
50              // Drawing methods do not handle nullable types
51              b.SetPixel(x + 20, 20 + 200 - ((int)val), Color.Black);
52              x++;
53          }
```

Use

There are many examples where a different algorithm can be passed to an active method or class. Dialog boxes, for example, can have different validating strategies depending on the kind of data required, whereas graph-drawing programs can accept algorithms for drawing pie charts, histograms, or bar charts. The C# 3.0 LINQ support libraries (for database queries) use this kind of separation between data and algorithm extensively.

Use the Strategy pattern when...

- Many related classes differ only in their behavior.
- There are different algorithms for a given purpose, and the selection criteria can be codified.
- The algorithm uses data to which the client should not have access.

Exercises

1. One of the criteria for choosing a sorting algorithm is whether the data is initially presorted, reverse-sorted, or in random order. Add to the Generator class in the Sorting Animator so that different arrangements of data in the list can be created. Then, add some more buttons to make the user's description of the problem at least two-dimensional (i.e., size of elements and arrangement of data). Change the strategy selection accordingly.

2. Add to the animator a linear sort like Shellsort, and define its criteria so that it can also be selected when appropriate. (Hint: Shellsort is good enough for short lists.)

3. In the proxy-protected version of MySpaceBook (Chapter 2), the registration process does not check whether the input is valid. Decide on more rich input (such as email addresses and requirements for passwords), and implement the input of each field using the Strategy pattern.

State Pattern

Role

The next pattern in this group, the State pattern, can be seen as a dynamic version of the Strategy pattern. When the state inside an object changes, it can change its behavior by switching to a set of different operations. This is achieved by an object variable changing its subclass, within a hierarchy.

Illustration

Consider a frequent flyer program run by an airline. A traveler starts out at, say, Blue level; then, as miles are accumulated by flying, she moves up to Silver or Gold level. At these levels, travelers can access lounges, get an extra baggage allowance, and also earn miles at a faster rate. For example, at the Silver tier, for every 1000 miles flown, a credit for 1250 miles is earned; at the Gold level, the credit is for 1500 miles. Other benefits also apply, as shown in the sample from South African Airways in Figure 7-3.

Dedicated contact centre	●	●	●
Voyager newsletter	●	●	●
Sector Tiering	●	●	●
Appreciation Bonus Miles		●	●
Threshold Bonus Miles		●	●
Tier Activity Bonus Miles		●	●
Priority Check-in		●	●
Lounge access		●	●
Preferential seating if booked on eligible fare		●	●
Excess Baggage		●	●

Figure 7-3. State pattern illustration—frequent flyer program

A frequent flyer program works in annual cycles: at the end of each year, a member's activity is calculated for the year and she is assigned to a tier. In the case of our hypothetical program, one of the requirements is to fly 25,000 miles in one year to attain Silver status and keep it for the next year; for Gold status a member must fly 50,000 miles.

So, in this illustration, the State is the member's level in the program. When the State for a traveler changes, the behavior with respect to lounge access, baggage allowances, and so on also changes.

Design

The State pattern presents an interesting interplay between a Context and a State. The Context represents information that is mostly fixed, whereas the State can change between the available options as the program progresses. The UML diagram for this pattern is shown in Figure 7-4.

From the diagram, we can identify the players in the pattern as:

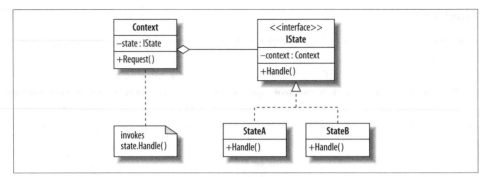

Figure 7-4. State pattern UML diagram

Context
> A class that maintains an instance of a State that defines the current context and the interface of interest to clients

IState
> Defines an interface for a particular state of the Context

StateA *and* StateB
> Classes that implement behavior associated with a state of the Context

The Context has a variable of type IState that starts out with a reference to a particular State object (say, StateA). All Requests are passed through to the Handle operation in that State. As shown in the diagram, the State has full access to the data in the Context. Thus, at any point, either the Context or the active State can decide that it is time to switch states. This is accomplished by assigning the state attribute of the Context object to an object of the other state. Immediately, all requests begin going to the new state, where they can elicit quite different behaviors than before.

Q U I Z

Match the State Pattern Players with the Frequent Flyer Illustration

To test whether you understand the State pattern, cover the lefthand column of the table below and see if you can identify its players among the items from the illustrative example (Figure 7-3), as shown in the righthand column. Then check your answers against the lefthand column.

Context	A member's account details
Request	An activity such as flying and earning miles, spending miles, or accessing a lounge
IState	The list of different policies that can change according to the tier
StateA, StateB, etc.	Particular policies applying to each tier (specific Blue, Silver, or Gold tier status rules and benefits)
Handle	An activity in a particular tier policy

So, for example, part of the member's details (the Context) will be her membership tier. Suppose it is Silver. This information will be stored in the state variable in the Context, and when she flies, a 25 percent bonus will be added to the miles she accumulates.

Implementation

Like the Strategy pattern, the State pattern relies on simple mechanisms: interfaces and aggregation. In Example 7-3, there are two state classes, NormalState and FastState, which act at different rates on a counter in the Context class. Both states implement the IState interface with the same two operations: MoveUp and MoveDown. The states themselves decide when it is time to switch to a different state. In this example, the decision is based on a comparison of the numeric value of the counter to a set limit in the Context. The test program simulates the operation of the state for 15 turns. The output is shown in line 74. The double bar (||) indicates a change of state.

Example 7-3. State pattern theory code

```
1     using System;
2     using System.Collections.Generic;
3
4       // State Pattern                              Judith Bishop  Oct 2007
5       // Shows two states with two operations, which themselves change the state
6       // Increments and decrements a counter in the context
7
8     interface IState {
9       int MoveUp(Context context);
10      int MoveDown(Context context);
11    }
12
13    // State 1
14    class NormalState : IState {
15      public int MoveUp(Context context) {
16        context.Counter+=2;
17        return context.Counter;
18      }
19
20      public int MoveDown(Context context) {
21        if (context.Counter < Context.limit) {
22          context.State = new FastState();
23          Console.Write("|| ");
24        }
25        context.Counter-=2;
26        return context.Counter;
27      }
28    }
29
30    // State 2
31    class FastState : IState {
32      public int MoveUp(Context context) {
33        context.Counter+=5;
34        return context.Counter;
```

Example 7-3. State pattern theory code (continued)

```
35        }
36
37        public int MoveDown(Context context) {
38          if (context.Counter < Context.limit) {
39            context.State = new NormalState();
40            Console.Write("||");
41          }
42          context.Counter-=5;
43          return context.Counter;
44        }
45      }
46
47      // Context
48      class Context {
49        public const int limit = 10;
50        public IState State {get; set; }
51        public int Counter = limit;
52        public int Request(int n) {
53          if (n==2)
54              return State.MoveUp(this);
55          else
56              return State.MoveDown(this);
57        }
58      }
59
60      static class Program {
61        // The user interface
62        static void Main () {
63          Context context = new Context();
64          context.State = new NormalState();
65          Random r = new Random(37);
66          for (int i = 5; i<=25; i++) {
67            int command = r.Next(3);
68            Console.Write(context.Request(command)+" ");
69          }
70          Console.WriteLine();
71        }
72      }
73    /* Output
74    8 10 8 || 6 11 16 11 6 ||1 3 || 1 ||-4 || -6 -1 4 ||-1 || -3 2 7 ||2 4
75    */
```

The different States can be classes, or if they are quite simple—without much data—
they can be implemented as delegates. This difference was explored in the discussion of the Adapter pattern. In both cases, states are switched by assigning objects,
and all calls to Requests are done via the currently active State object in the Context.

An advantage of the State pattern is that the transition between states is explicit; we
can see when one state hands over to another. Moreover, the state change is accomplished in one go (by assigning a reference), so there cannot be inconsistencies in the
internals of the Context.

When implementing the State pattern, we need to consider whether to create all the State objects at once and keep them, or create them as needed. The choice will depend upon the frequency with which states' changes are made and the size of the states' data. In the Frequent Flyer example, state changes will be infrequent, so creating the State objects as needed is the appropriate choice. In the next example, we'll consider a game, in which the states have only methods and are passed the context each time.

Example: RPC Game

Games inherently exhibit strategy. Our next example demonstrates how the State pattern can handle a very simple game called *RPC* (which stands for Run, Panic, Calm Down). In this single-person game, the player can be in one of four states:

- Resting
- Attacking
- Panicking
- Moving

The context of the game consists of the state the player is in at present. Even slightly more complex games have other attributes, such as the number of points scored for and against. The Requests that can be put through (in terms of the State pattern) are the moves the player can make, which are the ones to which the states must react. These are specified in the State abstract class as follows:

```
abstract class State {
    public virtual string Move(Context context) {return " ";}
    public virtual string Attack(Context context) {return " ";}
    public virtual string Stop(Context context) {return " ";}
    public virtual string Run(Context context) {return " ";}
    public virtual string Panic(Context context) {return " ";}
    public virtual string CalmDown(Context context) {return " ";}
}
```

The code for the RPC game example is presented in Example 7-4. Considering this code, we can see that each of the four states implements the six actions in completely different ways. They all return a string saying what happened, but some of them also change the state, as shown in lines 20–23. The RestingState's Move method is called with a given context. The response is to switch to MovingState for the same context and to return a message accordingly.

Example 7-4. State pattern example code—RPC game

```
1     using System;
2     using System.Collections.Generic;
3
4       namespace StatePattern {
5
```

Example 7-4. State pattern example code—RPC game (continued)

```
6        // State Pattern                    D-J Miller and Judith Bishop  Sept 2007
7        // Simple game where the context changes the state based on user input
8        // Has four states, each with six operations
9
10       abstract class IState {
11         public virtual string Move(Context context) {return "";}
12         public virtual string Attack(Context context) {return "";}
13         public virtual string Stop(Context context) {return "";}
14         public virtual string Run(Context context) {return "";}
15         public virtual string Panic(Context context) {return "";}
16         public virtual string CalmDown(Context context) {return "";}
17       }
18
19         // There are four States
20         class RestingState : IState {
21           public override string Move(Context context) {
22             context.State = new MovingState( );
23             return "You start moving";}
24           public override string Attack(Context context) {
25             context.State = new AttackingState( );
26             return "You start attacking the darkness"; }
27           public override string Stop(Context context) {
28             return "You are already stopped!"; }
29           public override string Run(Context context) {
30             return "You cannot run unless you are moving"; }
31           public override string Panic(Context context) {
32             context.State = new PanickingState( );
33             return "You start Panicking and begin seeing things"; }
34           public override string CalmDown(Context context) {
35             return "You are already relaxed"; }
36         }
37
38         class AttackingState : IState {
39           public override string Move(Context context) {
40             return "You need to stop attacking first"; }
41           public override string Attack(Context context) {
42             return "You attack the darkness for " +
43                 (new Random( ).Next(20) + 1) + " damage"; }
44           public override string Stop(Context context) {
45             context.State = new RestingState( );
46             return "You are calm down and come to rest"; }
47           public override string Run(Context context) {
48             context.State = new MovingState( );
49             return "You Run away from the fray"; }
50           public override string Panic(Context context) {
51             context.State = new PanickingState( );
52             return "You start Panicking and begin seeing things"; }
53           public override string CalmDown(Context context) {
54             context.State = new RestingState( );
55             return "You fall down and sleep"; }
56         }
57
58         class PanickingState : IState {
```

Example 7-4. State pattern example code—RPC game (continued)

```
59          public override string Move(Context context) {
60             return "You move around randomly in a blind panic"; }
61          public override string Attack(Context context) {
62             return "You start attacking the darkness, but keep on missing"; }
63          public override string Stop(Context context) {
64             context.State = new MovingState();
65             return "You are start relaxing, but keep on moving"; }
66          public override string Run(Context context) {
67             return "You run around in your panic"; }
68          public override string Panic(Context context) {
69             return "You are already in a panic"; }
70          public override string CalmDown(Context context) {
71             context.State = new RestingState();
72             return "You relax and calm down"; }
73       }
74
75       class MovingState : IState {
76          public override string Move(Context context) {
77             return"You move around randomly"; }
78          public override string Attack(Context context) {
79             return"You need to stop moving first"; }
80          public override string Stop(Context context) {
81             context.State = new RestingState();
82             return"You stand still in a dark room"; }
83          public override string Run(Context context) {
84             return"You run around in cirles"; }
85          public override string Panic(Context context) {
86             context.State = new PanickingState();
87             return"You start Panicking and begin seeing things"; }
88          public override string CalmDown(Context context) {
89            context.State = new RestingState();
90            return"You stand still and relax"; }
91       }
92
93       class Context {
94          public IState State { get; set; }
95
96          public void Request(char c) {
97             string result;
98             switch (char.ToLower(c)) {
99               case 'm' : result = State.Move(this); break;
100              case 'a' : result = State.Attack(this); break;
101              case 's' : result = State.Stop(this); break;
102              case 'r' : result = State.Run(this); break;
103              case 'p' : result = State.Panic(this); break;
104              case 'c' : result = State.CalmDown(this); break;
105              case 'e' : result = "Thank you for playing \"The RPC Game\""; break;
106              default : result = "Error, try again"; break;
107            }
108            Console.WriteLine(result);
109         }
110      }
111
```

Example 7-4. State pattern example code—RPC game (continued)

```
112    static class Program {
113        // The user interface
114        static void Main () {
115            // context.s are States
116            // Decide on a starting state and hold onto the Context thus established
117            Context context = new Context();
118            context.State = new RestingState();
119
120            char command = ' ';
121            Console.WriteLine("Welcome to \"The State Game\"!");
122            Console.WriteLine("You are standing here looking relaxed!");
123            while (command != 'e') {
124                Console.WriteLine("\nWhat would you like to do now?");
125                Console.Write("  Move    Attack    Stop    Run    Panic    CalmDown
126                          Exit the game: ==>");
127                string choice;
128                do
129                    choice = Console.ReadLine();
130                while (choice==null);
131                command = choice[0];
132                context.Request(command);
133            }
134        }
135    }
136 }
137 /* Output
138    Welcome to "The State Game"!
139 You are standing here looking hesitant!
140
141 What would you like to do now?
142    Move    Attack    Stop    Run    Panic    CalmDown    Exit the game: ==>m
143 You start moving
144
145 What would you like to do now?
146    Move    Attack    Stop    Run    Panic    CalmDown    Exit the game: ==>a
147 You need to stop moving first
148
149 What would you like to do now?
150    Move    Attack    Stop    Run    Panic    CalmDown    Exit the game: ==>s
151 You stand still in a dark room
152
153 What would you like to do now?
154    Move    Attack    Stop    Run    Panic    CalmDown    Exit the game: ==>p
155 You start Panicking and begin seeing things
156
157 What would you like to do now?
158    Move    Attack    Stop    Run    Panic    CalmDown    Exit the game: ==>r
159 You run around in your panic
160
161 What would you like to do now?
162    Move    Attack    Stop    Run    Panic    CalmDown    Exit the game: ==>a
```

Example 7-4. State pattern example code—RPC game (continued)

```
163    You start attacking the darkness, but keep on missing
164
165    What would you like to do now?
166      Move    Attack    Stop    Run    Panic    CalmDown    Exit the game: ==>c
167    You relax and calm down
168
169    What would you like to do now?
170      Move    Attack    Stop    Run    Panic    CalmDown    Exit the game: ==>e
171    Thank you for playing "The State Game"
172    */
```

The Context is called by the GUI (the main program) and extends over lines 93–110. Once a Context is constructed, the state is set, as from line 118. Thereafter, changes are made from within the other states.

Use

This is another pattern that can be used effectively in the implementation of graphics tools. Essentially, a tool editor can be "handed" a tool to use by the user and, when necessary, be "given" a different tool. The tool's behavior and capabilities are known to the editor, but the user controls the tool selection, based on the current context.

Use the State pattern when…

You have objects that:
  • Will change their behavior at runtime, based on some context
  • Are becoming complex, with many conditional branches

You want to:
  • Vary the set of handlers for an object request dynamically
  • Retain flexibility in assigning requests to handlers

Exercises

1. The RPC game has a good set of state changes, but the context switching is rather simple—based entirely on the previous state. Add some characteristics to the player (e.g., strength, stamina) that become part of the context and can make the state changes more interesting.

2. Investigate whether the IState class and the rest of the State classes could have been programmed as an interface and classes, without virtual methods. Explain the difference between the two techniques.

3. Program up the frequent flyer example mentioned in the illustration. Decide in advance what falls into the Context and what are the States.

Template Method Pattern

Role

The Template Method pattern enables algorithms to defer certain steps to sub-classes. The structure of the algorithm does not change, but small well-defined parts of its operation are handled elsewhere.

Illustration

Consider the sorting algorithms discussed under the Strategy pattern. Each sort has a certain structure that is independent of the kind of items being sorted—except for one operation. At some point, the sort will need to compare two items. The comparison will depend on the types of the items themselves. For example, comparing two integers could be done with a simple i==j, but if the items are, say, People objects, there could be many ways in which they could be compared. If the comparison is done on a Surname field, the sort will yield a list sorted by surname. However, the comparison could also be done on another field, such as Town, which would produce a list of people sorted by the town in which they live. Thus, we can see a clear distinction between the sorting algorithm and some subsidiary operation that is dependent on the data. The same distinction exists for other algorithms, such as searching. Sorting and searching are therefore Template Methods, as some parts of their operation are deferred to other classes.

Design

The UML diagram for the Template Method pattern is given in Figure 7-5. It shows an algorithm class that uses an IPrimitives interface to connect with methods defined in any class. This class would typically handle data (as in the earlier sorting and searching example), but it could be purely behavioral itself.

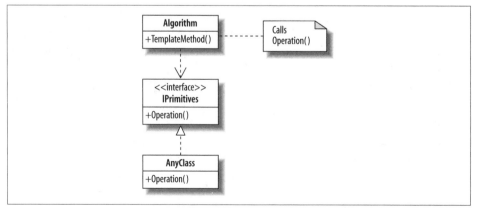

Figure 7-5. Template Method pattern UML diagram

The players are:

Algorithm
> A class that includes a TemplateMethod

TemplateMethod
> A method that defers some parts of its operation to other classes

IPrimitives
> The interface defining the operation(s) that TemplateMethod defers to other classes

AnyClass
> Any class that implements the IPrimitives interface

Operation
> One of the methods that TemplateMethod needs to complete its operation

---

QUIZ

Match the Template Method Pattern Players with the Sorting Animator Illustration

To test whether you understand the Template Method pattern, cover the lefthand column of the table below and see if you can identify its players among the items from the illustrative example (Figure 7-1), as shown in the righthand column. Then check your answers against the lefthand column.

Algorithm	Sorting visualizer
TemplateMethod	Mergesort
IPrimitives	Specification of a compare operation
AnyClass	Person
Operation	Compare two people

In this example, there is only one primitive method. There could obviously be more, either in the same interface or in other interfaces.

Implementation

The implementation of a simple Template Method program is shown in Example 7-5. It follows the UML of Figure 7-5, with the Algorithm containing the TemplateMethod and going through the IPrimitives interface to the two classes that implement it. In the main method, the Algorithm's Template Method is called with objects of ClassA and ClassB in turn, with different results. The TemplateMethod knows that it must call Operations on an object of type IPrimitives, but it does not have to know which class exactly.

Example 7-5. Template Method pattern theory code

```
1  using System;
2
3  // Template Method Pattern      Judith Bishop November 2007
4  //  Shows two versions of the same algorithm
5
6    interface IPrimitives {
7      string Operation1();
8      string Operation2();
9    }
10
11   class Algorithm {
12     public void TemplateMethod(IPrimitives a) {
13       string s =
14         a.Operation1() +
15         a.Operation2();
16         Console.WriteLine(s);
17     }
18   }
19
20   class ClassA : IPrimitives {
21     public string Operation1() {
22       return "ClassA:Op1 ";
23     }
24     public string Operation2() {
25       return "ClassA:Op2 ";
26     }
27   }
28
29   class ClassB : IPrimitives {
30     public string Operation1() {
31       return "ClassB:Op1 ";
32     }
33     public string Operation2() {
34       return "ClassB.Op2 ";
35     }
36   }
37
38   class TemplateMethodPattern {
39
40     static void Main() {
41       Algorithm m = new Algorithm();
42
43       m.TemplateMethod(new ClassA());
44       m.TemplateMethod(new ClassB());
45     }
46   }
47  /* Output
48  ClassA:Op1 ClassA:Op2
49  ClassB:Op1 ClassB.Op2
50  */
51
```

Example

Example 7-2 sorts integers for the Sorting Animator, but this is not built into the implementation. In the sort methods, the compare operations do not use the == operator, but rather the primitive operation CompareTo, as in:

```
if (aux[j].CompareTo(aux[i]) == -1) {
```

CompareTo is a method that returns 1 if a>b, 0 if a==b, and -1 if a<b. It is defined in the IComparable interface, which many predefined C# types already implement. For example, CompareTo is available for integers and strings. Because our sort methods are meant to be general, we declare that the item types must implement the interface using:

```
class MergeSorter<T> : SortStrategy<T>
    where T : IComparable<T> {
```

The where clause puts a constraint on the type <T> by saying it must implement IComparable. Any class can do so if it provides a CompareTo method. For example, inside a Person class, we might have:

```
// Comparison based on surnames
public int CompareTo(object obj) {
  if(obj is Person) {
    Person p = (Person) obj;
    return Surname.CompareTo(p.Surname);
  }
  throw new ArgumentException("object is not a Person");
}
```

But how is CompareTo defined in terms of CompareTo? Well, we are looking at names, so Surname will presumably be a string. CompareTo is defined for strings so that is what will be called. The check for the type of the object is necessary because the implementation of CompareTo must match its interface, which is defined on the object.

When a Template Method uses an interface for specifying the primitive operations, the classes must implement those operations. It is also possible to define IPrimitives as an abstract class and to provide default behavior for any of the operations, leaving the subclass to override as many operations as it wishes. Methods that have defaults are called *hook* operations, and they often do nothing by default.

Use

Template Methods are, as we have seen, very useful in conjunction with the Strategy pattern. Any system that wishes to defer primitive operations to other classes will benefit from this pattern. In C#, it is used extensively through predefined interfaces such as IComparable.

A key quality of the Template Method pattern is the ability to handle a sequence of multiple method calls, where some of the method implementations are deferred to subclasses (or other class hierarchies via a Strategy). The programmer decides which steps of an algorithm are fixed and which are customizable. The invariant steps are implemented in a base class, whereas the variant steps are either given a default implementation or no implementation at all. The programmer decides which are the required steps of an algorithm, and the order of the steps, but allows the client to extend or replace some number of these steps. For this reason, the Template Method is used prominently in frameworks. Each framework implements the fixed parts a domain's architecture and defines "placeholders" for all necessary or interesting client customization options.

> **Use the Template Method pattern when...**
> • Common behavior can be factored out of an algorithm.
> • The behavior varies according to the type of a subclass.

Exercises

1. Take one of the sorting methods and implement it for a Person class. Supply the CompareTo method as a primitive operation, implementing IComparable.
2. Investigate other similar interfaces in the .NET Framework.

Pattern Comparison

Pattern Comparison

There are considerable similarities between the Strategy and State patterns, but the main difference is one of intent:

• A Strategy object encapsulates an algorithm

• A State object encapsulates a state-dependent behavior (and possibly state transitions)

Both patterns are concerned with polymorphism. Both patterns define a parent interface or abstract class and a series of subclasses that implement the methods therein. And both patterns have a context that they maintain and use to decide on state transitions. So, the biggest difference between the patterns is that we encapsulate an algorithm into strategy classes in the Strategy pattern, but we encapsulate state into state classes in the State pattern.

The Template Method pattern is more like the Strategy pattern in that it is algorithm based. The steps of the algorithm are specified in the Template Method and some are deferred to domain classes.

These similarities and differences are illustrated in the simple theory code in Examples 7-1, 7-3, and 7-5. Table 7-1 summarizes them.

Table 7-1. Comparison of Strategy, State, and Template Method patterns

	Strategy	State	Template Method
Action achieved by	Context invokes Strategy	Client invokes Context	Algorithm invoking Operations
Switching modes based on	Client inspecting Context	State inspecting Context	Instantiation of classes in Client
Context/IPrimitives contains	Current Strategy	Current State	Operational interface

CHAPTER 8

Behavioral Patterns: Chain of Responsibility and Command

The two behavioral patterns we will explore in this chapter—Chain of Responsibility and Command—are concerned with passing requests for action to appropriate objects. The respective patterns choose the objects to pass the requests to in different ways.

Chain of Responsibility Pattern

Role

The Chain of Responsibility pattern works with a list of Handler objects that have limitations on the nature of the requests they can deal with. If an object cannot handle a request, it passes it on to the next object in the chain. At the end of the chain, there can be either default or exceptional behavior.

Illustration

The Chain of Responsibility pattern is encountered frequently in real life. Imagine members of the public (such as you and me) approaching a bank, a government office, a hospital, or a similar institution with a request. In the case of a bank, we know that a first level of clerks will handle straightforward requests. Those requests requiring more inspection will be sent up to a supervisor, and ultimately the manager might have to authorize or rule on a request. The clerk, supervisor, and manager together are an example of a chain of responsibility. Of course, sometimes clerks can deal with matters quite well on their own, as illustrated in Figure 8-1.[*]

Within the bank illustration, we can immediately see that it is the levels that form the chain (clerk, supervisor, manager), and there could well be more than one individual at each level. In human terms, such chains do not generally get very long (or else

---

[*] From S. Francis, H. Dugmore, and Rico, *www.madamandeve.co.za*, printed with permission.

Figure 8-1. Chain of Responsibility pattern illustration—a bank clerk deals with a request

customers would get very frustrated), but theoretically there is no limit. Typically, clerks will stagger their tea and lunch breaks so that there is always someone on duty; they join and leave the chain dynamically, and at different times.

Design

Imagine a client that has a request for a handler. The Chain of Responsibility pattern distances the handler from the client by passing the request along a hidden chain of handlers until one that will handle it is found.

To handle a request, the handler must have the appropriate resources, knowledge, and permissions. The handlers themselves decide whether to handle a request and can do so on the basis of workload, resource limitations, policy issues, or any other good reason.

The Chain of Responsibility pattern is a simple pattern in that it consists of a single, uniform interface that is implemented by multiple handlers (as many as are necessary or available). Each handler is linked in some way to a successor so that requests can be passed on if necessary. Depending on the language, the link to the successor is either internal or external to the handler itself. The UML for the Chain of Responsibility pattern is shown in Figure 8-2.

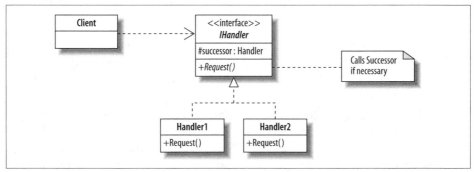

Figure 8-2. Chain of Responsibility pattern UML diagram

The roles assumed by the players in the pattern are as follows:

Client
> A class that initiates a Request

IHandler
> The interface for different Handlers

Handler1, Handler2, *etc.*
> The classes that are available as Handlers

Successor
> The link to the next Handler object

Request
> The request from the Client

Match the Chain of Responsibility Pattern Players with the Bank Illustration

To test whether you understand the Chain of Responsibility pattern, cover the lefthand column of the table below and see if you can identify its players among the items from the illustrative example (Figure 8-1), as shown in the righthand column. Then check your answers against the lefthand column.

Client	The customer
Handlers	Clerks, supervisors, managersn
Successor	The next most senior handler
Request	The customer's request, query, or problem

As we'll see next, the most efficient implementation of the Chain of Responsibility pattern depersonalizes the Handlers, reducing them to the operations that they perform.

In terms of the design, there can be variations on Figure 8-2:

- The handlers may differ only in terms of the values of the state they store (e.g., a limit on an amount), or in the behavior of the Request method. In this case, the IHandler interface can be dispensed with, and the Handlers can still be instantiated in sufficient variety.

- The UML diagram implies only one instantiation of each Handler, resulting in one handler at each level in the chain. Practically speaking, there might be several identical handlers at certain levels (e.g., clerks in a bank). A different design is required to accommodate the latter case. This design is shown in the upcoming example code.

- What happens when a request reaches the end of the chain without finding a valid handler is an important design decision. The last object may handle the request in a default manner, or an exception may be thrown without the request being handled.

- However they are implemented, Handlers need to have a means for deciding whether they can rightly handle a request. There are several ways of implementing this decision, as we shall see.

Implementation

The simple theory code for the Chain of Responsibility pattern is shown in Example 8-1. The program creates five handlers that can deal with amounts up to 1,000 times their handler IDs. Each handler links to the one that can handle a higher amount. The handlers are created from highest to lowest in the loop at lines 28–31. The links point backward, and we get the structure shown in Figure 8-3.

Example 8-1. Chain of Responsibility pattern theory code

```
1     using System;
2
3     class ChainwithStatePattern {
4
5       // Chain of Responsibility Pattern    Judith Bishop   June 2007
6
7       class Handler {
8         Handler next;
9         int id;
10        public int Limit {get; set;}
11        public Handler (int id, Handler handler) {
12          this.id = id;
13          Limit = id*1000;
14          next = handler;
15        }
16        public string HandleRequest(int data) {
17          if (data < Limit)
18              return "Request for " +data+" handled at level "+id;
19          else if (next!=null)
20              return next.HandleRequest(data);
21          else return ("Request for " +data+" handled BY DEFAULT at level "+id);
22        }
23      }
24
25      static void Main () {
26
27        Handler start = null;
28        for (int i=5; i>0; i--) {
29          Console.WriteLine("Handler "+i+" deals up to a limit of "+i*1000);
30          start = new Handler(i,  start);
31        }
32
33        int [] a = {50,2000,1500,10000,175,4500};
34        foreach (int i in a)
```

Example 8-1. Chain of Responsibility pattern theory code (continued)

```
35              Console.WriteLine(start.HandleRequest(i));
36      }
37
38   }
39   /* Output
40   Handler 5 deals up to a limit of 5000
41   Handler 4 deals up to a limit of 4000
42   Handler 3 deals up to a limit of 3000
43   Handler 2 deals up to a limit of 2000
44   Handler 1 deals up to a limit of 1000
45   Request for 50 handled at level 1
46   Request for 2000 handled at level 3
47   Request for 1500 handled at level 2
48   Request for 10000 handled BY DEFAULT at level 5
49   Request for 175 handled at level 1
50   Request for 4500 handled at level 5
51   */
```

Figure 8-3. Chain of handlers

We'll start by exploring the implementation from the client's point of view. The client wants to call a handler with some data. For example:

```
handler(2000);
```

The crux of the Chain of Responsibility pattern is in lines 35 and then 20. Line 35 calls a handler, and line 20 can pass the request on to the next in line. The handler makes this decision based on conditions it can evaluate. Lines 18 and 21 show the other two outcomes: handling the request and handling it by default if the handler is the last in the chain.

The Chain of Responsibility pattern has an inherent limitation in that the request can get lost if the chain is not set up properly or if no handler is appropriate for the passed-in data. For this reason, the last handler has a default action. An alternative implementation, as mentioned earlier, would be to define a ChainException that the Handler can throw and the Client can catch. This approach is shown in the following example.

Example: Trusty Bank

To further explore the Chain of Responsibility pattern, we'll model the action of a bank that is careful about allowing withdrawals of large amounts. Trusty Bank's business rules for handling withdrawals are:

- Clerks can handle withdrawals of up to $1,000.
- Supervisors can handle withdrawals of up to $4,000.
- The bank manager can handle withdrawals of up to $9,000.

Any amount larger than $9,000 has to be divided into several withdrawals. The bank has several clerks on duty at any one time (up to 10), and usually 3 supervisors; there is only one manager.

In this example of the Chain of Responsibility pattern, we distinguish between levels in the chain and the number of object instances at each of those levels. The organizational structure we want is shown in Figure 8-4.

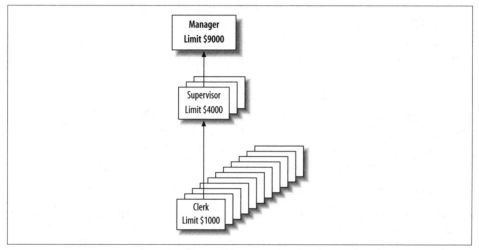

Figure 8-4. Trusty Bank organizational structure

We reflect this structure in two C# collections: one for the information about the limits and the number of positions, and one for the actual Handler objects used at runtime. The collections are:

```
static Dictionary <Levels,Structure> structure =
    new Dictionary <Levels, Structure> {
      {Levels.Manager, new Structure {Limit = 9000, Positions =1}},
      {Levels.Supervisor, new Structure {Limit = 4000, Positions =3}},
      {Levels.Clerk, new Structure {Limit = 1000, Positions =10}}};

static Dictionary <Levels, List<Handler>> handlersAtLevel =
    new Dictionary <Levels, List<Handler>> {
      {Levels.Manager, new List <Handler>()},
      {Levels.Supervisor, new List <Handler>()},
      {Levels.Clerk, new List <Handler>()}};
```

This excerpt uses two interesting C# features: *initializing* and *enumerated types*. We looked at initializing in Chapter 3, but I'll repeat the information here, more specifically for collections.

C# 3.0 Feature—Initializing Collections

In initializing a collection, we match the values with the required structure. If the items in any dimension of the structure are objects, new is required, and we open another set of brackets. If values are available, they can be inserted, as in:

```
{Levels.Clerk, new Structure {Limit = 500,
                              Positions =10}},
```

Otherwise, an object constructor will do, as in:

```
{Levels.Clerk, new List <Handler>( )},
```

If the structure is local to a method, its type can be inferred from the initialization and the var declaration is permitted, as in:

```
var structure = new Dictionary <Levels, Structure> {
```

cf. C# Language Specification Version 3.0, September 2007, Section 7.5.10.1-3

Both of the collections use an enumerated type: Levels. It is declared as:

```
enum Levels {Manager, Supervisor, Clerk}
```

Because enum constants can be associated with values, we could include the limits for the handler types with them, as in:

```
enum Levels (Manager = 9000, Supervisor = 4000, Clerk = 1000}
```

We'll revisit this idea in the upcoming "Exercises"section.

Having set up the structure, we then create a collection of three lists called handlersAtLevel. Each list contains the people who are at the level indicated, exactly as in Figure 8-4. The loop to create the handlers (requiring less writing) is:

```
foreach (Levels level in Enum.GetValues(typeof(Levels))) {
  for (int i=0; i<structure[level].Positions; i++) {
    handlersAtLevel[level].Add(new Handler(i, level));
  }
}
```

Thus, for each level, we pick up from the structure chart the number of positions required and instantiate that number of handlers, passing through an identifier and the level. Notice that this way of setting up the handlers differs from the theory code in Example 8-1 because there is no direct link to another handler; the link is deduced from the level plus a random number and found in the lists of handlersAtLevel.

The next step is to run the bank, accepting various requests, as in the theory example. Here's the loop:

---

[a] See Marc Clifton's article "The Enumerable Enumerator" (November 2, 2006), available at *http://www.codeproject.com/csharp/EnumerableEnumerator.asp*.

```
int [] amounts = {50,2000,1500,10000,175,4500};
foreach (int amount in amounts) {
  try {
    int which = choice.Next(structure[Levels.Clerk].Positions);
    Console.WriteLine(handlersAtLevel
        [Levels.Clerk][which].HandleRequest(amount));
    AdjustChain( );
  } catch (ChainException e) {
    Console.WriteLine("\nNo facility to handle a request of "+
        e.Data["Limit"]+
        "\nTry breaking it down into smaller requests\n");
  }
}
```

Here, we use a random number generator to pick a clerk and then call the chosen handler at the clerk level. Inside the chosen handler, the limit is checked. If the handler cannot deal with the amount, it uses the same technique to pick a supervisor, generating a number between 0 and 2. Given all this, the output from the program is:

```
1  Trusty Bank opens with
2  1 Manager(s) who deal up to a limit of 9000
3  3 Supervisor(s) who deal up to a limit of 4000
4  10 Clerk(s) who deal up to a limit of 1000
5
6  Approached Clerk 4. Request for 50 handled by Clerk 4
7  Approached Clerk 0. Request for 2000 handled by Supervisor 1
```

```
8    Approached Clerk 9. Request for 1500 handled by Supervisor 0
9    Approached Clerk 1.
10   No facility to handle a request of 10000
11   Try breaking it down into smaller requests
12
13   Approached Clerk 3. Request for 175 handled by Clerk 3
14   Approached Clerk 3. Request for 4500 handled by Manager 0
15   Approached Clerk 1. Request for 2000 handled by Supervisor 1
```

As this output shows, Clerks handled requests for $50 and $175 (lines 6 and 13), and three requests were sent up to Supervisors (not always the same one) on lines 7, 8, and 15. The Manager authorized one request (line 14) and rejected another (lines 9–11). When even the Manager cannot handle the request, the Handler interacts with the Client via an exception.

C# Feature—Exception Properties

C# exceptions are objects that can be created, thrown, and caught. Exceptions are caught in try/catch blocks; different catch clauses can catch different exceptions. Exceptions can carry information from the throwing object to the catching one. The following properties are useful in user programming:

Message
    A string property

Data
    An IDictionary that can hold key/value pairs

cf. C# Language Specification Version 3.0, September 2007, Section 16, and C# Class Library, the Exception Class

---

The full code for the Trusty Bank program is presented in Example 8-2.

Example 8-2. Chain of Responsibility pattern example code—Trusty Bank

```
using System;
using System.Collections.Generic;

class ChainPatternExample {

        // Chain of Responsibility Pattern Example        Judith Bishop  Sept 2007
        // Sets up the Handlers as level-based structure
        // Makes use of a user-defined exception if the end of the chain is reached

    class Handler {
      Levels level;
      int id;
      public Handler (int id, Levels level) {
        this.id = id;
        this.level = level;
      }
```

```
    public string HandleRequest(int data) {
      if (data < structure[level].Limit) {
        return "Request for " +data+" handled by "+level+ " "+id;
      }
      else if (level > First) {
        Levels nextLevel = --level;
        int which = choice.Next(structure[nextLevel].Positions);
        return handlersAtLevel[nextLevel][which].HandleRequest(data);
      }
      else {
        Exception chainException = new ChainException();
        chainException.Data.Add("Limit", data);
        throw chainException;
      }
    }
  }
}

public class ChainException : Exception {
  public ChainException() {}
}

void AdjustChain() {}

enum Levels {Manager, Supervisor, Clerk}
static Random choice = new Random(11);
static Levels First {
  get { return ((Levels[])Enum.GetValues(typeof(Levels)))[0]; }
}

static Dictionary <Levels,Structure> structure =
    new Dictionary <Levels, Structure> {
      {Levels.Manager, new Structure {Limit = 9000, Positions =1}},
      {Levels.Supervisor, new Structure {Limit = 4000, Positions =3}},
      {Levels.Clerk, new Structure {Limit = 1000, Positions =10}}};


static Dictionary <Levels, List<Handler>> handlersAtLevel =
    new Dictionary <Levels, List<Handler>> {
      {Levels.Manager, new List <Handler>()},
      {Levels.Supervisor, new List <Handler>()},
      {Levels.Clerk, new List <Handler>()}};

class Structure {
  public int Limit {get; set;}
  public int Positions {get; set;}
}

void RunTheOrganization () {

  Console.WriteLine("Trusty Bank opens with");
  foreach (Levels level in Enum.GetValues(typeof(Levels))) {
    for (int i=0; i<structure[level].Positions; i++) {
      handlersAtLevel[level].Add(new Handler(i, level));
```

Example 8-2. Chain of Responsibility pattern example code—Trusty Bank (continued)

```
        }
        Console.WriteLine(structure[level].Positions+ " "+ level+
            "(s) who deal up to a limit of " + structure[level].Limit);
    }
    Console.WriteLine( );

    int [] amounts = {50,2000,1500,10000,175,4500,2000};
    foreach (int amount in amounts) {
      try {
        int which = choice.Next(structure[Levels.Clerk].Positions);
        Console.Write("Approached Clerk "+which+". ");
        Console.WriteLine(handlersAtLevel[Levels.Clerk][which].
            HandleRequest(amount));
        AdjustChain( );
      } catch (ChainException e) {
        Console.WriteLine("\nNo facility to handle a request of "+
            e.Data["Limit"]+
            "\nTry breaking it down into smaller requests\n");
      }
    }
  }

  static void Main () {
    new ChainPatternExample( ).RunTheOrganization( );
  }

}
```

In the preceding example, the handlers were all instantiated from the same class. But according to the UML diagram (Figure 8-2), the classes can be different, as long as they conform to an interface with a well-defined Request method. In this case, using delegates to set up the chain of request methods might be a useful technique.

Use

The Chain of Responsibility pattern is used in tools that handle user events. It is often employed in conjunction with events and exceptions.

Use the Chain of Responsibility pattern when...

You have:

- More than one handler for a request
- Reasons why a handler should pass a request on to another one in the chain
- A set of handlers that varies dynamically

You want to:

- Retain flexibility in assigning requests to handlers

Exercises

1. Change the enumerated type in the Trusty Bank example so that each constant has an associated value that refers to its limit. Rework the program accordingly.

2. In the Trusty Bank example, set up a completely different `Handler` class called `HeadOffice`. Extend the system to enable requests to go from the `Manager` to `HeadOffice` for approval.

3. Exception handlers work in chains and are themselves an example of the Chain of Responsibility pattern. As an exercise, implement the notion of an exception-handling mechanism without using C#'s built-in exception-handling mechanism.

Command Pattern

Role

The Command pattern creates distance between the client that requests an operation and the object that can perform it. This pattern is particularly versatile. It can support:

- Sending requests to different receivers
- Queuing, logging, and rejecting requests
- Composing higher-level transactions from primitive operations
- Redo and Undo functionality

Illustration

The Command pattern is used in the menu systems of many well-known applications. An example of such an interface is shown in Figure 8-5 (which happens to be the program editor I usually use). Note that there are different insert and copy operations.

The figure shows two ways in which commands can be activated: select them from a drop-down textual menu, or click on the icons that represent each of the operations. In the top menu, there could be a receiver that handles word processing cut-and-paste-type operations, and another for brace matching and changing case. For most of these commands, Undo and Redo functions will also be appropriate; however, some operations are indicated in gray, which means they cannot be undone or repeated. Furthermore, in systems such as this one, there is usually a way of stringing together some commands so that they can be executed in a batch later. These so-called *macro* commands are common in graphics and photo-editing programs.

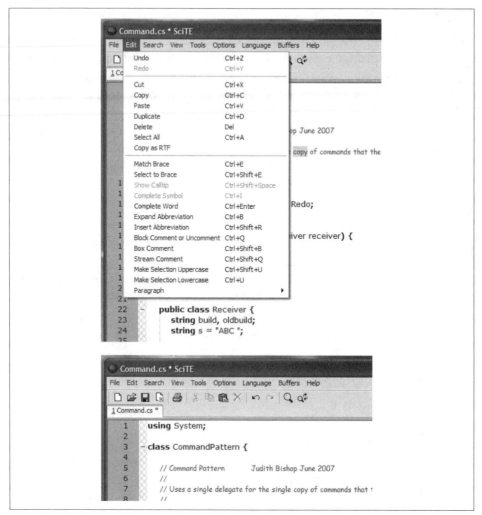

Figure 8-5. Command pattern illustration—menus

Design

The design of the Command pattern is shown in Figure 8-6. The Client has a certain way of saying what is required, usually in high-level and domain-specific terms. It thinks in terms of commands such as Cut, Redo, Open, and so on. The Receivers—and there may be several—know how to carry out these requests. Referring to the menu example, a Cut command for text would go to one part of a system and a Cut command for an image would be handled elsewhere.

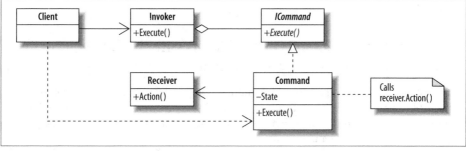

Figure 8-6. Command pattern UML diagram

The Command class forms the interface between the Client and the Receivers. In a Command object, the Client's requests are declared and associated with viable corresponding operations in a Receiver. There might also be a state that the Client wants to pass on to the Receiver, and this must be allowed for. The Invoker is there to distance the Client from the Receiver.

Put simply, the Client issues a call to Execute in the Invoker, and the request goes to the Command and then to Action in the Receiver. In a program, there could be many requests of different types being routed to different Receivers. The ICommand interface ensures that they all conform to a standard form.

The players in this pattern are:

Client
    Creates and executes Commands

ICommand
    An interface that specifies the Execute operation

Invoker
    Asks the Command to carry out the Action

Command
    A class that implements the Execute operation by invoking operations on the Receiver

Receiver
    Any class that can perform the required Action

Action
    The operation that needs to be performed

The Command pattern does seem to have many players, but some of them fall away when delegates are used, as shown in the next section. Other aspects of the design are:

- Commands can be assembled into composite commands in the Command class.
- New commands can be added without disturbing existing ones.

Match the Command Pattern Players with the Cut Request Illustration

To test whether you understand the Command pattern, cover the lefthand column of the table below and see if you can identify its players among the items from the illustrative example (Figure 8-5), as shown in the righthand column. Then check your answers against the lefthand column.

Client	User of the editor, who selects a Cut command on a menu
ICommand	Menu
Command	Holder of a Cut request
Receiver	An object that can perform a Cut
Invoker	Process the selection of a Cut option
Action	Cut

Implementation

The theory code for implementing a simple version of the Command pattern is shown in Example 8-3.

Example 8-3. Command pattern theory code

```
1     using System;
2
3     class CommandPattern {
4
5         // Command Pattern                    Judith Bishop  June 2007
6         // Uses a single delegate for the single type of commands that
7         // the client invokes
8
9         delegate void Invoker ();
10        static Invoker Execute, Undo, Redo;
11
12        class Command {
13          public Command(Receiver receiver) {
14            Execute = receiver.Action;
15            Redo = receiver.Action;
16            Undo = receiver.Reverse;
17          }
18        }
19
20        public class Receiver {
21          string build, oldbuild;
22          string s = "some string ";
23
```

Example 8-3. Command pattern theory code (continued)

```
24            public void Action( ) {
25                oldbuild = build;
26                build +=s;
27                Console.WriteLine("Receiver is adding "+build);
28            }
29
30          public void Reverse( ) {
31              build = oldbuild;
32              Console.WriteLine("Receiver is reverting to "+build);
33          }
34        }
35
36    static void Main( ) {
37        new Command (new Receiver( ));
38        Execute( );
39        Redo( );
40        Undo( );
41        Execute( );
42      }
43    }
44    /* Output
45    Receiver is adding some string
46    Receiver is adding some string some string
47    Receiver is reverting to some string
48    Receiver is adding some string some string
49    */
```

The Invoker and ICommand interface are implemented together as a delegate type (line 9) with its instantiated delegate objects (line 10). The names of the delegate objects (the Invokers) are based on what the client wants; their names are Execute, Redo, and Undo (line 10). The Command associates the delegate command objects with the two methods inside the Receiver, Action, and Reverse (lines 14–16). Execute and Redo both go to Action, and Undo goes to Reverse. The Receiver keeps track of the state and is responsible for output. This arrangement is unlike previous patterns, where the receivers returned values from their fields for the client to display or not. To adopt the same mechanism, we would make the delegate type return a string, as in:

```
delegate string CommandStr ( );
```

This implementation is vastly shorter than many of the standard ones because it uses a delegate type (line 9) and instantiates it for three delegate objects in one line (line 10). The object-based solution would have three separate single-method classes for the three invokers.

 The actual Undo/Redo implementations depend on actual operations to be undone or redone. In the Command pattern, Undo and Redo serve only as abstract placeholders.

Multireceiver commands

What would happen if we had more than one delegate type in the same program, and also more than one receiver? First of all, the names of the delegate types (Invokers) would be different. The Command objects can configure the matches between the delegate objects and different Receiver methods as required.

In the following program, there are two Command classes and two Receivers. Because both Commands use the same delegate objects (Invokers), the Client executes commands first in one Receiver and then in the other; however, that might be an unnecessary constraint. To overcome it, we can either introduce more delegate objects or group them inside the Commands, as shown in the next example.

The multireceiver version of the Command pattern in Example 8-4 illustrates in addition how to handle commands that cannot be associated with anything meaningful in a given Receiver, as shown for the second Command (lines 25–32). Undo is not allowed for this Execute command, so we assign an anonymous delegate to the delegate object that writes out an error message (line 30). Note that the writing is not done when the association is made, but only when (and if) the Client calls Undo.

Example 8-4. Command pattern theory code—multireceiver version

```
1    using System;
2
3    class CommandPattern {
4
5        // Command Pattern - Multireceiver Version      Judith Bishop  June 2007
6        // Has two different delegates for two types of commands
7        // The second receiver uses both of them
8
9        delegate void Invoker ();
10       delegate void InvokerSet (string s);
11
12       static Invoker Execute, Redo, Undo;
13       static InvokerSet Set;
14
15       class Command {
16         public Command(Receiver receiver) {
17           Set = delegate {Console.WriteLine("Not implemented - default of XXX used");
18             receiver.S = "XXX";};
19           Execute= receiver.Action;
20           Redo = receiver.Action;
21           Undo = receiver.Reverse;
22         }
23       }
24
25       class Command2 {
26         public Command2(Receiver2 receiver) {
27           Set = receiver.SetData;
28           Execute= receiver.DoIt;
29           Redo = receiver.DoIt;
30           Undo = delegate {Console.WriteLine("Not Implemented");};
```

```
31            }
32        }
33
34        public class Receiver {
35          string build, oldbuild;
36          string s = "some string ";
37          public string S {
38            get {return s;}
39            set {s = value;}
40          }
41
42        public void Action() {
43          oldbuild = build;
44          build +=s;
45          Console.WriteLine("Receiver is adding "+build);
46        }
47
48        public void Reverse() {
49          build = oldbuild;
50          Console.WriteLine("Receiver is reverting to "+build);
51        }
52      }
53
54        public class Receiver2 {
55          string build, oldbuild;
56          string s;
57
58          public void SetData(string s) {
59            this.s = s;
60          }
61
62          public void DoIt() {
63            oldbuild = build;
64            build +=s;
65            Console.WriteLine("Receiver is building "+build);
66          }
67        }
68
69        class Client {
70          public void ClientMain() {
71
72            new Command (new Receiver());
73            Execute();
74            Redo();
75            Undo();
76            Set("III");
77            Execute();
78
79            Console.WriteLine();
80            new Command2 (new Receiver2());
81            Set("houses ");
82            Execute();
```

Example 8-4. Command pattern theory code—multireceiver version (continued)

```
83              Set("castles ");
84              Undo( );
85              Execute( );
86              Redo( );
87          }
88        }
89
90      static void Main( ) {
91          new Client( ).ClientMain( );
92        }
93      }
94  /* Output
95  Receiver is adding some string
96  Receiver is adding some string some string
97  Receiver is reverting to some string
98  Not implemented - default of XXX used
99  Receiver is adding some string XXX
100
101 Receiver is building houses
102 Not Implemented
103 Receiver is building houses castles
104 Receiver is building houses castles castles
105 */
```

Example: Menu Handler

Consider a very small part of a menu, with just Paste and Print commands. Assume there is a public clipboard, where the client can place strings. The pasting and printing is done by a receiver, which maintains the current copy of the document. On top of that, there are Undo and Redo commands that might or might not be appropriate (for example, undoing a Print operation does not make sense).

There is only one invoker type, but the Paste and Print command classes will implement the Execute, Undo, and Redo invoker objects differently. Therefore, we place them in an abstract class that the commands can inherit. This ensures uniformity for the commands; it is also used in logging, which we will discuss momentarily.

In this example, the commands each have their own delegate objects, so one of them looks like this:

```
class Paste {
  public Invoker Execute, Redo, Undo;
  public Paste(Document document) {
    Execute = document.Paste;
    Redo = document.Paste;
    Undo = document.Restore;
  }
}
```

When the Client calls the commands, the object name is required, as in:

```
Paste paste = new Paste(document);
Print print = new Print(document);

clipboard = "Hello, everyone";
paste.Execute( );
print.Execute( );
paste.Undo( );
```

The rest of the program—including the Receiver that handles the Document—mirrors the simple Command pattern example.

Because command objects are separate from Clients and Receivers, they can undertake system functions such as *logging*. A simple logging operation is to count how many times commands are called—a function of the Invoker type. To implement the logging, we define an extension method on the Invoker delegate type to provide:

- A Log method that increments a count
- A Count method that returns the current count value

This InvokerExtensions class is shown at the start of the program in Example 8-5.

 Recall that extension methods:
- Must be static
- Must be in static classes at the outer level
- Can only have static fields
- Can be applied to delegates

Details are in Chapter 2.

At the end of the program, we can call the Count method to print out the number of calls, as in:

```
Console.WriteLine("Logged "+paste.Execute.Count( )+" commands");
```

Because the count field is static, the count applies to all invoker calls (thus the reference to the instance paste). Execute is a way of getting at this total count. Any invoker instance would return the same value (7). More sophisticated logging methods are explored in the upcoming "Exercises" section. The full menu handler program is shown in Example 8-5.

Example 8-5. Command pattern example code—menu handler

```
using System;
using System.Collections.Generic;

// Command Pattern           Judith Bishop  Jan, July 2007
// Example: simple Paste and Print system
// with Undo and logging

delegate void Invoker ( ) ;
```

Example 8-5. Command pattern example code—menu handler (continued)

```
static class InvokerExtensions {
  static int count;
  public static int Count (this Invoker invoker) {
    return count;
  }
  public static void Log (this Invoker invoker) {
    count++;
  }
}

class CommandMenu {
  abstract class ICommand {
    public Invoker Execute, Redo, Undo;
  }

  // Command 1
  class Paste : ICommand {
    public Paste(Document document) {
      Execute = delegate {Execute.Log(); document.Paste();};
      Redo = delegate {Redo.Log(); document.Paste();};
      Undo = delegate {Undo.Log(); document.Restore();};
    }
  }

  // Command 2 - without an Undo method
  class Print : ICommand {
    public Print(Document document) {
      Execute = delegate {Redo.Log(); document.Print();};
      Redo = delegate {Redo.Log(); document.Print();};
      Undo = delegate{ Redo.Log(); Console.WriteLine("Cannot undo a Print ");};
    }
  }

  // Common state
  static string clipboard;

  // Receiver
  class Document {
    string name;
    string oldpage, page;

    public Document (string name) {
      this.name = name;
    }

    public void Paste() {
      oldpage = page;
      page += clipboard+"\n";
    }

    public void Restore() {
      page = oldpage;
    }
```

Example 8-5. Command pattern example code—menu handler (continued)

```
      public void Print( ) {
        Console.WriteLine(
          "File "+name+" at "+DateTime.Now+"\n"+page);
      }
    }

  static void Main( ) {
    Document document = new Document("Greetings");
    Paste paste = new Paste(document);
    Print print = new Print(document);

    clipboard = "Hello, everyone";
    paste.Execute( );
    print.Execute( );
    paste.Undo( );

    clipboard = "Bonjour, mes amis";
    paste.Execute( );
    clipboard = "Guten morgen, meine Freunde";
    paste.Redo( );
    print.Execute( );
    print.Undo( );

    Console.WriteLine("Logged "+paste.Execute.Count( )+" commands");
  }
}


/* Output
File Greetings at 2007/09/21 01:40:52 AM
Hello, everyone

File Greetings at 2007/09/21 01:40:52 AM
Bonjour, mes amis
Guten morgen, meine Freunde

Cannot undo a Print
Logged 7 commands
*/
```

Use

The Command pattern can be applied wherever domain-specific commands are required and the tool has system-specific operations. Once the separation has been made between the two, extra functionality can be added at the command level.

You have:

- Commands that different receivers can handle in different ways
- A high-level set of commands that are implemented by primitive operations

You want to:

- Specify, queue, and execute commands at different times
- Support an Undo function for commands
- Support auditing and logging of all changes via commands

Exercises

1. In the simple theory code in Example 8-3, introduce a second delegate type for an Invoker that handles commands with a string parameter. Integrate this into the Command class and observe what other changes are required to make the program run using suitable test calls from Main.

2. In Example 8-4, all of the void Invoker objects are set up by one Command object and go to one Receiver, while all of the string Invoker objects are set up by a second Command object and go to a different Receiver. Investigate how to get a mix of Invoker objects to be handled by each Command object and to go to different Receivers. Report on any limitations you encounter.

3. The Photo Library example for the Composite pattern in Chapter 3, as extended with the Prototype pattern in Chapter 5 for the Photo Archive application, has a fairly complex set of commands. Consider an auxiliary program called UpLoad that just takes a set of photos out of a file and creates it as a set in the library. Implement this as a command that calls other commands. Also include an Undo function, and add a logging function that will report on how many photos were uploaded.

Pattern Comparison

A similarity between the Chain of Responsibility and the Command patterns is that they decouple senders and receivers, thus improving the layering and reusability of a system. The Chain of Responsibility pattern supports decoupling by passing a request between potential receivers, whereas the Command pattern supports using a command object to encapsulate a request. The implementation issues are described in Table 8-1.

Table 8-1. Comparison of the Chain of Responsibility and Command patterns

	Chain of Responsibility	Command
Client creates	Handler objects	Command objects
Different kinds of	Handler classes at different levels	Command classes and Receiver classes
Client can work with	Multiple handlers	Different receivers
Client calls	Handler objects	Receiver objects
Work is done in	HandleRequest, in a handler	Action, in a receiver
Decisions based on	Limits in handlers	Routing in commands
Deals with unimplementable requests	Yes	Yes

CHAPTER 9

Behavioral Patterns: Iterator, Mediator, and Observer

The three behavioral patterns we will study in this chapter support communication between objects while letting them keep their independence and, in some cases, their anonymity. The Iterator pattern is a fundamental pattern that has wide application in many situations and is substantially supported by C# 3.0's LINQ or Linq (Language INtegrated Query) extensions. The Mediator and Observer patterns mirror the mailbox and publish/subscribe methodologies that are well-known in distributed systems.

Iterator Pattern

Role

The Iterator pattern provides a way of accessing elements of a collection sequentially, without knowing how the collection is structured. As an extension, the pattern allows for filtering elements in a variety of ways as they are generated.

Illustration

Consider a typical file directory such as that shown in Figure 9-1. Common directory operations include searching for files with particular names or extensions, or files created before or after certain dates. When searching for a file, the directory structure is unimportant and should be abstracted away. For directories of reasonable size, another useful operation is to list their contents in a hierarchy, as shown in Figure 9-2. The loop that displays a directory in a neat format can once again be independent of which item is supplied next. As long as enough is known about each item's position in the hierarchy and its attributes (such as size), a loop should be able to print each line.

A more interesting iterative operation than a simple print would be to calculate the sizes of directories as the sum of the sizes of all their enclosed files and subdirectories. Once again, we can imagine that the loop will be supplied with file or directory sizes

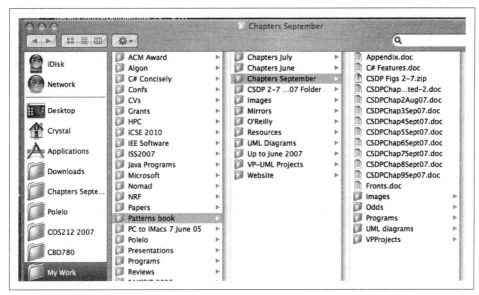

Figure 9-1. Iterator pattern illustration (a)—files and directories

▼ 📁 Patterns book	--
▶ 📁 Chapters July	--
▶ 📁 Chapters June	--
▼ 📁 Chapters September	--
📄 Appendix.doc	68 KB
📄 CSDP Figs 2-7.zip	1.8 MB
📄 CSDPChap2Aug07.doc	788 KB
📄 CSDPChap3Sep07.doc	848 KB
📄 CSDPChap4Sept07.doc	484 KB
📄 CSDPChap5Sept07.doc	440 KB
📄 CSDPChap6Sept07.doc	208 KB
📄 CSDPChap7Sept07.doc	272 KB
📄 CSDPChap8Sept07.doc	536 KB
📄 CSDPChap9Sep07.doc	36 KB
📄 Fronts.doc	44 KB
▶ 📁 Images	--
▶ 📁 Odds	--
▶ 📁 Programs	--
▶ 📁 UML diagrams	--
▶ 📁 VPProjects	--

Figure 9-2. Iterator pattern illustration (b)—hierarchical directories

one at a time and will be told when one directory ends and a new one begins (recursively).

As this illustration shows, there can be many reasons for iterating through a structure. The way in which we iterate might change as well. For example, to do the file size calculation, we need to scan all the inner files and then return to the enclosing directory. For printing, we can print each item in turn as it comes.* However, both operations are independent of how the directories themselves are stored in memory. Now, let's consider the background and design of iterators and match this illustration to the pattern itself.

Design

The concept of iterators and enumerators (also called generators) has been around for a long time. *Enumerators* are responsible for producing the next element in a sequence defined by certain criteria. Such a sequence is said to be *enumerable*. Examples might be the next prime number or the next product order sorted by date. The *iterator* is the means by which we cycle through this sequence of elements from beginning to end.

Over the past five years, developments in language and compiler technology have wrought a revolution in loop programming. Iteration over any collection of any data type is now linked to a more compact, yet versatile, type-specific enumerator. The inspiration for this new way of thinking comes from the database world (SQL) as well as the functional world (Haskell and Mondrian). Consider the following C# 3.0 statements:

```
var selection = from f in mydir
  where f.Date.Year >= 2007
  orderby f.Name
  select f;

foreach (var f in selection) {
  Console.Write(f + "  ");
```

The first statement asks for a selection of files from a collection called `mydir`, with the conditions that they must be dated 2007 or later and that the selection, when made, must be ordered by filename. Note that the statement will work no matter what the type of the collection holding `mydir` is; it could be an array, a linked list, a binary tree, or even a database. This statement works together with an enumerator that:

- Follows the structure of the data type in a prescribed order
- Applies the conditions and ordering as specified
- Operates in a lazy fashion, generating values only when they are needed by an iterator

When the foreach iterator is applied to a collection resulting from an enumerator (in this case, the variable called `selection`), the values are fetched and can be used in the body of the loop.

---

* These operations are known as "tree traversals" in data structures and algorithms terminology. The file size calculation would use a postorder traversal and the printing calculation would use a preorder traversal.

Thus, if a display of the *mydir* directory gives:

```
Full directory
[COS110, 1999]  [COS212, 2007]  [COS341, 2005]  [COS333, 2006]  [CBD780, 2007]
[VRS780, 2006]  [SPE781, 2007]
```

the result of the preceding statements will be:

```
Files from 2007 in alpha order
[CBD780, 2007]   [COS212, 2007]   [SPE781, 2007]
```

Iterators need data to iterate over. Most of the time the data exists, either in memory, on disk, or somewhere on the Internet. However, sometimes an iterator will work with an enumerator that actually generates values (for example, random numbers). An example of the latter case is given in one of the programs we'll look at later.

The Iterator pattern is the one that has received the most assistance from language design in recent years. For this reason, the UML diagram in Figure 9-3 shows the statements that are involved, on an equal footing with the classes. In C# 3.0, the names of the interface (IEnumerable) and its one enumerator method (GetEnumerator) are fixed. GetEnumerator is automatically invoked from the foreach statement. Other enumerator methods can also be implemented and called from the Client. These are indicated by OtherOps in the diagram.

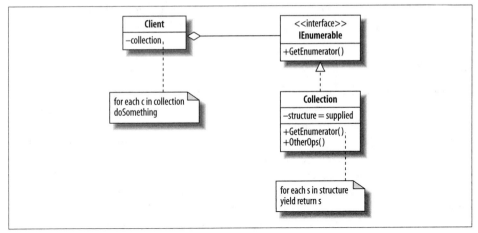

Figure 9-3. Iterator pattern UML diagram

The players in the pattern are:

Client
    Keeps a Collection object and uses a foreach statement to iterate over it

IEnumerable
    A defined interface in C# for the operation GetEnumerator

Collection
    A data type containing or having the ability to generate a collection of values

GetEnumerator

A method that supplies the values in sequence

OtherOps

Other methods that supply Collection values in different sequences with different filters and transformations

---

QUIZ

Match the Iterator Pattern Players with the Directory Illustration

To test whether you understand the Iterator pattern, cover the lefthand column of the table below and see if you can identify its players among the items from the illustrative examples (Figures 9-1 and 9-2), as shown in the righthand column. Then check your answers against the lefthand column.

Client	The user who is iterating over file directories
Collection	A structure of directories and files
GetEnumerator	Returns a single file or directory item
OtherOps	Returns a single file or directory item according to other criteria (such as date>=2007)

Implementation

Iterators range from the very basic to the very powerful. Consider the theory example in Example 9-1, which writes out the contents of an array. Here, the players in the pattern are clearly identifiable. The Client is the Main method (lines 20–27). It aggregates a collection object (line 22) and iterates over it using a normal foreach loop (line 24). The foreach defers to the GetEnumerator method in the Collection class (lines 13–17). Its foreach loop on line 15 seemingly duplicates line 24, but its body uses a new statement, the yield return. The effect of the yield return is to return a value only each time the object returned by the GetEnumerator is called by the Client's foreach. GetEnumerator's foreach remembers where it was after the last yield return and gives the next value.

Example 9-1. Iterator pattern theory code

```
1    using System;
2    using System.Collections;
3
4       class IteratorPattern {
5
6          // Simplest Iterator              Judith Bishop  Sept 2007
7
8          class MonthCollection : IEnumerable {
```

Example 9-1. Iterator pattern theory code (continued)

```
9
10          string [] months = {"January", "February", "March", "April", "May", "June",
11              "July", "August", "September", "October", "November", "December"};
12
13          public IEnumerator GetEnumerator () {
14            // Generates values from the collection
15            foreach( string element in months )
16                yield return element;
17          }
18      }
19
20      static void Main( ) {
21
22          MonthCollection collection = new MonthCollection( );
23          // Consumes values generated from collection's GetEnumerator method
24          foreach (string n in collection)
25              Console.Write(n+"    ");
26          Console.WriteLine("\n");
27      }
28   }
29 /* Output
30 January    February    March    April    May    June    July    August    September
31 October    November    December
32 */
```

The astute reader will wonder why, on line 24, we did not just loop through months. The reason is that months is declared not in the Client, but in its own collection class. Even without the benefits gained from separating iteration and enumeration, it would be bad style for the Client to access months directly

The enumerator does not have exclusive access to the collection. Therefore, enumerating through a collection is not intrinsically a thread-safe procedure. Even when a collection is synchronized, other threads can still modify the collection, which causes the enumerator to throw an exception. To guarantee thread safety during enumeration, you can either lock the collection during the entire enumeration or catch the exceptions resulting from changes made by other threads.

Enumerators can also provide filters, transformations, and projections on the data that can be linked back to the iterators that use them. The enumerators provide methods that do the work, and the iterators can either call the methods directly or use the special LINQ query expression syntax.

Now, let's look at another simple program, shown in Example 9-2, that uses the full power of LINQ. Here, the collection is in the same class as the iterators for simplicity's sake; however, it could easily be placed in a Collection class. The first query is on lines 21–23. It sets up a rule to select from the daysInMonth structure all elements that have names with more than five characters. The next query (lines 25–28) works on the result of the first; it looks for all months that have 31 days, and then orders the results alphabetically. Neither of these statements actually executes until the foreach iterator on line 30 begins. It starts asking for values in the selection collection, and these are supplied by going through the two query expressions. The result is shown in the output.

C# Features—IEnumerable and IEnumerator

IEnumerable is an interface that has one method, GetEnumerator. Classes that implement IEnumerable supply a GetEnumerator method that successively returns a value from a collection using yield return. Each time GetEnumerator is invoked, control picks up after the yield return statement.

All collections in the .NET library implement IEnumerable (i.e., they each provide a conforming GetEnumerator method). That is why they can be used in the foreach statement directly. When yield return appears in a foreach loop, it is making use of the underlying GetEnumerator for the collection it is iterating over, as in:

```
public IEnumerator GetEnumerator () {
  foreach ( string element in months )
    yield  return element;
}
```

In this case, the enumerator for an array (used by months) is invoked.

yield return can appear several times in succession. For example, these statements:

```
public IEnumerator GetEnumerator () {
  yield return 1;
  yield return 3;
  yield return 5;
  yield return 7;
  yield return 11;
}
```

will return the numbers in the sequence given.

yield return keeps the enumerator going for the next iteration. However, a yield break statement has the effect of terminating the loop that called the enumerator.

IEnumerator is a lower-level interface that specifies the Current property and the Rest and MoveNext methods. It is possible to implement this method and thereby satisfy the requirements of the IEnumerable interface.

IEnumerable and IEnumerator exist in generic and nongeneric forms.

cf. C# 3.0 Language Specification Version 3.0, September 2007, Section 8.8.4

C# Feature—Query Expressions

Query expressions provide a language-integrated syntax for queries that is similar to relational and hierarchical query languages such as SQL and XQuery.

A query expression begins with a from clause and ends with either a select or a group clause. In between, these clauses can appear:

- A from clause, which is a generator that introduces one or more iteration variables ranging over a sequence or a *join* of multiple sequences
- A let clause, which computes a value and introduces an identifier representing that value
- A where clause, which is a filter that excludes items from the result
- An orderby clause, which specifies an ordering for the result
- An into clause, which can be used to "splice" queries by treating the result of one query as a generator in a subsequent query

These query expressions are translated into invocations of methods named Where, Select, SelectMany, Join, GroupJoin, OrderBy, OrderByDescending, ThenBy, ThenByDescending, GroupBy, and Cast that are expected to have particular signatures and result types. These methods can be instance methods of the object being queried or extension methods that are external to the object. They implement the actual execution of the query.

For the standard collections, there are default methods present.

cf. C# 3.0 Language Specification Version 3.0, September 2007, Section 7.15

Example 9-2. Iterator pattern LINQ code

```
1     using System;
2     using System.Collections.Generic;
3     using System.Linq;
4
5       class IteratorPattern {
6
7         // Iterator Pattern         Judith Bishop  Sept 2007
8         // Uses LINQ
9
10        static void Main( ) {
11
12        Dictionary <string, int> daysInMonths =
13            new Dictionary <string, int> {
14            {"January", 31},   {"February", 28},
15            {"March", 31},     {"April", 30},
16            {"May", 31},       {"June", 30},
17            {"July", 31},      {"August", 31},
18            {"September", 30}, {"October", 31},
19            {"November", 30},  {"December", 31}};
20
```

Example 9-2. Iterator pattern LINQ code (continued)

```
21          var selection = from n in daysInMonths
22              where n.Key.Length > 5
23              select n;
24
25          selection = from n in selection
26              where n.Value == 31
27              orderby n.Key
28              select n;
29
30          foreach (var n in selection)
31              Console.Write(n+"   ");
32          Console.WriteLine("\n");
33
34      }
35
36
37  /* Output
38  [August, 31]    [December, 31]    [January, 31]    [October, 31]
39  */
```

Example: Family Tree

Suppose we have a family tree, such as that in Figure 9-4. The goal of the example is to traverse the tree and select people with various criteria for printing.

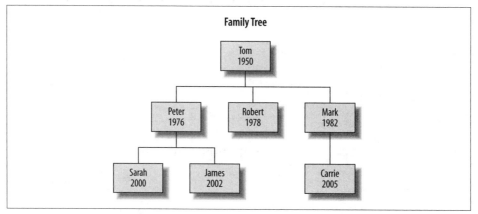

Figure 9-4. Iterator pattern example—a family tree

Because the number of links from one person to the next is unpredictable, family trees are usually represented as binary trees, with the left link to the firstborn and the next link to the right to the next sibling. Given this scheme, an initialization of the tree in Figure 9-4 would be:

```
var family = new Tree <Person> ( new Node <Person>
    (new Person ("Tom", 1950),
     new Node <Person> (new Person ("Peter", 1976),
```

```
      new Node <Person>
        (new Person ("Sarah", 2000), null,
      new Node <Person>
        (new Person ("James", 2002), null,
      null) // no more siblings James
    ),
    new Node <Person>
      (new Person ("Robert", 1978), null,
    new Node <Person>
      (new Person ("Mark", 1982),
      new Node <Person>
          (new Person ("Carrie", 2005), null, null),
      null) // no more siblings Mark
    )),
      null) // no siblings Tom
  );
```

There is no predefined way to handle a tree with nodes of the following kind:

```
class Node <T> {
  public Node () {}
  public Node <T> Left{get; set;}
  public Node <T> Right {get; set;}
  public T Data {get; set;}

  public Node (T d, Node <T> left, Node <T> right) {
    Data = d;
    Left = left;
    Right = right;
  }
}
```

as used in the initialization. Therefore, we need to define our own class, which serves as the Collection class for the Iterator pattern. We'll make the class generic, and in this example, T will stand for Person, which is defined quite simply as having Name and Birth properties. The Tree class is as follows:

```
// T is the data type. The Node type is built-in.
class Tree <T> {
  Node <T> root;
  public Tree() {}
  public Tree (Node <T> head) {
    root = head;
  }

  public IEnumerable <T> Preorder {
    get {return ScanPreorder (root);}
  }

    // Enumerator with Filter
    public IEnumerable <T> Where (Func <T, bool> filter) {
      foreach (T p in ScanPreorder(root))
        if (filter(p)==true)
        yield return p;
  }
```

```
// Enumerator with T as Person
private IEnumerable <T> ScanPreorder (Node <T> root) {
    yield return root.Data;
    if (root.Left !=null)
        foreach (T p in ScanPreorder (root.Left))
            yield return p;
    if (root.Right !=null)
        foreach (T p in ScanPreorder (root.Right))
            yield return p;
    }
}
```

There are two public enumerators. The first is called Preorder, because it will walk
through the tree from left to right and top to bottom. Preorder itself is a front for a
private version called ScanPreorder. ScanPreorder uses recursion to treat the tree as
follows:

Visit a tree

> Visit the root
>
> Visit the left tree
>
> Visit the right tree

Visiting means yielding a value. For the root, the method yields the data at that node
to the iterator in the Client. For the other two cases, it yields a node to the enumerator itself. In this way, the whole tree is traversed. An iterator in the Client such as
this:

```
foreach (Person p in family.Preorder)
    Console.Write(p+"  ");
    Console.WriteLine("\n");
```

will print the following based on the data presented earlier:

```
[Tom, 1950]  [Peter, 1976]  [Sarah, 2000]  [James, 2002]  [Robert, 1978]
[Mark, 1982]  [Carrie, 2005]
```

The other enumerator is the Where method, which also calls ScanPreorder but then
filters out the required Person objects according to the delegate supplied. The type of
the delegate is Func <T,bool>, meaning it takes a T (in this instance, a Person) as a
parameter on each iteration, and returns a bool value. The corresponding iterator in
the client is:

```
var selection = from p in family
    where p.Birth > 1980
    orderby p.Name
    select p;
```

The delegate's parameter is inferred from the from clause type, and the body of the
delegate is provided by the where clause. In older syntax, without the sorting this
would be:

```
var selection = family.
    Where(p=> p.Birth > 1980);
```

Remember that query expressions are not activated until an iterator uses them.

So, it is only when we get to:

```
foreach (Person p in selection)
    Console.Write(p+"   ");
    Console.WriteLine("\n");
```

that the people in the tree are enumerated and filtered, producing finally:

```
[Carrie, 2005]   [James, 2002]   [Sarah, 2000]
```

The full program for this example is in the Appendix. Further examples of iterators will be given in the programs that follow.

In the past, there were many implementation issues to consider with iterators. They have mostly been covered with C# 3.0's query expressions, a very powerful and user-friendly concept (see the earlier sidebar).

Use

The Iterator pattern defines a fundamental separation between the iteration process and the enumeration process. Even in trivial cases the separation is advantageous, but its benefits are really felt when:

- The structure is complex.
- Different iterations are required over it, potentially at the same time.
- The same structure and iterations can be applied to different data.

It is important to keep clear the distinction (in the C# 3.0 context) between enumerators and iterators:

Enumerators
Provided by all the collections in the library, generic and nongeneric. They are supported by the IEnumerable interface and the yield return and yield break statements.

Iterators
Written by clients and supported by the foreach statement and query expressions.

Loops pervade most code. Specifically, we would look to use an Iterator pattern with an iterator/enumerator mechanism when the conditions in the following table apply.

Use the Iterator pattern when...
You are iterating over a collection and one of these conditions holds:
• There are various ways of traversing it (several enumerators).
• There are different collections for the same kind of traversing.
• Different filters and orderings might apply.

Exercises

1. Consider the file directory illustration. The problem to be solved is almost the same as the family tree problem. Realize the data from Figure 9-2 in the form of the initializer given for the family tree. Then rework the client program to get a printout of various views of the hierarchy. You should be able to use the Node and Tree classes as they are.

2. Create a new enumerator for the file directory that will traverse it in postorder to determine the total size of each directory as a sum of its parts. Add this to the Tree class and test it out.

3. Write a simple program that throws two dice. A die can have values from 1 to 6. Encapsulate this information and the enumerator for generating a value at random in a class called Dice. In the client program, create an iterator that will throw two dice together and display their values.

Mediator Pattern

Role

The Mediator pattern is there to enable objects to communicate without knowing each other's identities. It also encapsulates a protocol that objects can follow.

Illustration

The Mediator pattern is all about communication. There are numerous ways of communicating these days. Communication can be between two individuals, or among members of a group. Often there is *protocol* that is observed between the members of a group. Messages might also be vetted for *content*. All of this points to the need for a mediator.

Consider a mailing list whose members are people interested in *C# 3.0 Design Patterns*. People interested in the topic can join the mailing list by subscribing to it using a special message subject ("Subscribe"). Any messages that come in will go to all of the list's subscribers. Members can remove themselves from the list at any time by sending an "Unsubscribe" message.

Of course, mailing lists are seldom so simple. Members expect that messages they receive will not be spam, will come only from other members, and will be relevant to the topic at hand. To enforce this latter rule, the cs3pd group might decide not to permit any messages that mention Java, for instance. Sending out messages and checking their content is termed "moderating" the list. Some of the moderation functionality can be handled by software, and some of it will be done by a designated person in the group (usually referred to as the *moderator*).

Figure 9-5 shows an example of a moderation panel from a mailing list program. The program has trapped a message as potential spam and is asking for confirmation and further action. One of the allowable actions is to automatically reject any future emails from that address.

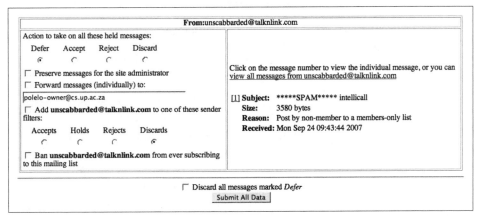

Figure 9-5. Mediator pattern illustration—mailing list moderation

Clearly, the moderation process here is performing part of the role of the Mediator pattern: establishing a communication protocol and content filter. The other part— keeping members unaware of each other—is inherently part of the mailing list concept of mailing to a central address and then broadcasting from there.

Design

Now, let's consider the Mediator pattern at the UML diagram level. As illustrated in Figure 9-6, it consists of only two classes that use messages to communicate:

Colleague
Registers with a Mediator by supplying a Receive method; issues Send requests to other colleagues via the Mediator

Mediator
Broadcasts sent messages to all signed-on Colleagues using the Respond delegate

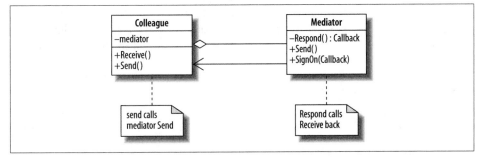

Figure 9-6. Mediator pattern UML diagram

Match the Mediator Pattern Players with the Mailing List Illustration

To test whether you understand the Mediator pattern, cover the lefthand column of the table below and see if you can identify its players and methods among the items from the illustrative example (Figure 9-5), as shown in the righthand column. Then check your answers against the lefthand column.

Colleague	A user subscribed to a mailing list
Mediator	The mailing list moderator
Respond	Calls back the signed-on users
Callback	A means of contacting all users on the list
Send	Mailing a message to the list
Receive	Receiving a message from the list

The Mediator pattern makes provisions for more than one mediator. For example, there may be many different mailing lists created under one mailing system. Each list may have a different moderator, different rules of engagement, and a different list of users, but the structure of the lists is identical. Therefore, creating a new Mediator is merely an instantiation operation and does not require subclassing or an interface.

Implementation

Key points of the Mediator pattern are:

- Each Colleague is passed a Mediator at instantiation and keeps it as a private reference.
- Each Mediator keeps a list of signed-on Colleagues as a private reference.

The callback to the colleagues is a very thin interface—just a method. Therefore, a dictionary list (names with callbacks) of Colleagues in the Mediator would be overkill: we can just use the delegate mechanism to chain the Receive methods. On the other hand, within one mediator system, there could be Colleague types that implement the Receive method differently. This variation is shown in the theory code in Example 9-3.

Example 9-3. Mediator pattern theory code

```
1    using System;
2    using System.Collections.Generic;
3
4      class MediatorPattern {
5
```

Example 9-3. Mediator pattern theory code (continued)

```
 6        // Mediator Pattern                         Judith Bishop  Sept 2007
 7        /* The Mediator maintains a list of colleagues and specifies the
 8          communication methods that it can mediate - in this case, Send.
 9          Receive is implemented at Colleague level and called via a delegate
10          supplied by the colleagues to the mediator on sign-on.
11        */
12
13        class Mediator {
14
15          public delegate void Callback (string message, string from);
16          Callback respond;
17
18          public void SignOn (Callback method) {
19          respond += method;
20          }
21
22         public void Block (Callback method) {
23          respond -=method;
24          }
25         public void Unblock (Callback method) {
26            respond +=method;
27          }
28
29          // Send is implemented as a broadcast
30          public void Send(string message, string from) {
31            respond(message, from);
32            Console.WriteLine();
33          }
34        }
35
36        class Colleague {
37          Mediator mediator;
38          protected string name;
39
40          public Colleague(Mediator mediator,string name) {
41            this.mediator = mediator;
42            mediator.SignOn(Receive);
43            this.name = name;
44          }
45          public virtual void Receive(string message, string from) {
46            Console.WriteLine(name +" received from "+from+": " + message);
47          }
48          public void Send(string message) {
49            Console.WriteLine("Send (From "+name+ "): "+message);
50            mediator.Send(message, name);
51          }
52
53        }
54
55        class ColleagueB : Colleague {
56          public ColleagueB(Mediator mediator,string name)
57              : base (mediator, name) {
```

Example 9-3. Mediator pattern theory code (continued)

```
58                }
59
60                // Does not get copies of own messages
61                public override void Receive(string message, string from) {
62                  if (!String.Equals(from,name))
63                    Console.WriteLine(name +" received from "+from+": " + message);
64                }
65              }
66
67        static void Main () {
68          Mediator m = new Mediator();
69          // Two from head office and one from a branch office
70          Colleague head1 = new Colleague(m,"John");
71          ColleagueB branch1 = new ColleagueB(m,"David");
72          Colleague head2 = new Colleague(m,"Lucy");
73
74          head1.Send("Meeting on Tuesday, please all ack");
75          branch1.Send("Ack"); // by design does not get a copy
76          m.Block(branch1.Receive); // temporarily gets no messages
77          head1.Send("Still awaiting some Acks");
78          head2.Send("Ack");
79          m.Unblock(branch1.Receive); // open again
80          head1.Send("Thanks all");
81        }
82      }
83    /* Output
84    Send (From John): Meeting on Tuesday, please all ack
85    John received from John: Meeting on Tuesday, please all ack
86    David received from John: Meeting on Tuesday, please all ack
87    Lucy received from John: Meeting on Tuesday, please all ack
88
89    Send (From David): Ack
90    John received from David: Ack
91    Lucy received from David: Ack
92
93    Send (From John): Still awaiting some Acks
94    John received from John: Still awaiting some Acks
95    Lucy received from John: Still awaiting some Acks
96
97    Send (From Lucy): Ack
98    John received from Lucy: Ack
99    Lucy received from Lucy: Ack
100
101   Send (From John): Thanks all
102   John received from John: Thanks all
103   Lucy received from John: Thanks all
104   David received from John: Thanks all
105   */
```

This code uses for illustration an example of two people from the head office and one from a branch office communicating about a meeting. The Colleagues are of different types, in that they have different ways of receiving messages: the head office group members always get copies of their own messages (lines 45–46), whereas the branch office members do not (lines 61–63).

The Mediator keeps a private delegate called Respond of a public type called Callback (lines 15–16). The Colleagues use the Callback type to ensure that the Receive methods they register at sign-on are compatible. The Mediator also provides Block and Unblock methods that Colleagues can use to sign themselves in and out of the system. Consider the first three actions on the system:

```
74        head1.Send("Meeting on Tuesday, please all ack");
75        branch1.Send("Ack"); // by design does not get a copy
76        m.Block(branch1.Receive); // temporarily gets no messages
```

and the relevant output:

```
84   Send (From John): Meeting on Tuesday, please all ack
85   John received from John: Meeting on Tuesday, please all ack
86   David received from John: Meeting on Tuesday, please all ack
87   Lucy received from John: Meeting on Tuesday, please all ack
88
89   Send (From David): Ack
90   John received from David: Ack
91   Lucy received from David: Ack
```

At this point, David actively blocks further messages by calling mediator.Block. Later, he calls Unblock to start receiving them again.

Simulating activity by calling methods from the main program presents an unnaturally sequential view of the operation of this pattern. The example we'll look at next shows a more dynamic version.

Although the previous example shows a very simple Mediator, it is possible that mediating between more than two subclasses of colleagues could make the Mediator code quite complex. For example, Mediator might need to be used as a router through which colleague A can address colleague B without contacting colleague C. Nevertheless, the value of the anonymity and the simplicity the colleagues gain is worth the effort.

Example: Chat Room

A chat room is a more dynamic form of a mailing list where the messages are immediately visible to all the members on a window, rather than being sent via email. Consider the sample chat room session in Figure 9-7.

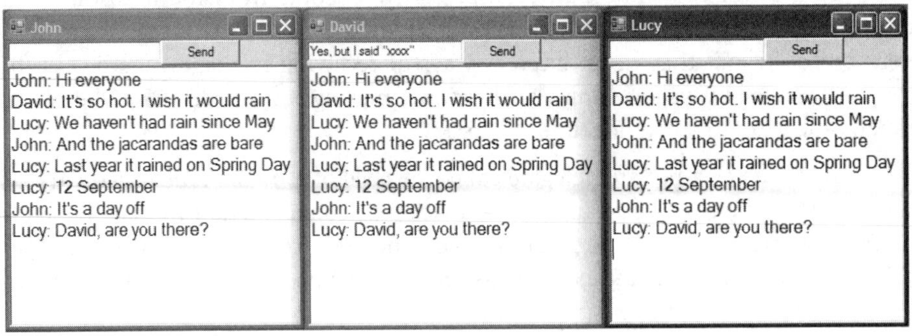

Figure 9-7. Mediator pattern example—chat room

The chat room design closely follows the Mediator theory code, except for two changes:

- The Mediator Send method checks messages before broadcasting them. The rule of this chat room is that no one can mention work, so any message that contains "work" is ignored. In the figure, David sent the message "It's a day off work" and it was not broadcast.

- All the members have the same standing, so there is only one Colleague class.

The full chat room program is shown in Example 9-4. It integrates the Interact class for multithreaded windows, which was first introduced for CoolBook in Chapter 4. The GUI setup of the Interact constructor is not shown in the listing, as it is not too relevant to the pattern.

Example 9-4. Mediator pattern example code—chat room

```
using System;
using System.Collections.Generic;
using System.Windows.Forms;
using System.Drawing;
using System.Threading;

   // Mediator Pattern                          Judith Bishop  Sept 2007
   // This version of the pattern does not need a list of Colleagues in
   // the Mediator. The delegate keeps a record of the methods on its chain.
   // All other information stays in the colleague itself.

namespace MediatorSpace {
   public delegate void Callback(string message, string from);

   // The Mediator is in two parts: Interact handles the GUI;
   // Mediator itself sets up the threads and does the
   // broadcast from the delegate (Send method)
class Mediator {
   Callback Respond;

   public void SignOn (string name, Callback Receive, Interact visuals) {
```

Example 9-4. Mediator pattern example code—chat room (continued)

```
        // Add the Colleague to the delegate chain
        Respond += Receive;
        new Thread((ParameterizedThreadStart) delegate(object o) {
          visuals.InputEvent += Send;
          Application.Run(visuals);
        }).Start(this);

        // Wait to load the GUI
        while (visuals == null || !visuals.IsHandleCreated) {
          Application.DoEvents();
          Thread.Sleep(100);
        }
      }

    // Send implemented as a broadcast
    public void Send(string message, string from) {
      // Message not sent if it contains "work"
      if (message.IndexOf("work")==-1)
        if (Respond != null)
          Respond(message, from);
    }
  }

  class Interact : Form {
    TextBox wall ;
    Button sendButton ;
    TextBox messageBox;
    string name;

    public Interact(string name) {

        // GUI construction not shown but includes
        // sendButton.Click += new EventHandler(Input);
    }

    public event Callback InputEvent;

    public void Input(object source, EventArgs e) {
      if (InputEvent != null)
          InputEvent(messageBox.Text, name);
    }

    public void Output(string message) {
      if (this.InvokeRequired)
          this.Invoke((MethodInvoker)delegate() { Output(message); });
      else {
        wall.AppendText(message + "\r\n");
        messageBox.Clear();
        this.Show();
      }
    }
  }
}
```

Example 9-4. Mediator pattern example code—chat room (continued)

```
class Colleague {
  Interact visuals;
  string name;

  public Colleague(Mediator mediator, string name) {
    this.name = name;
    visuals = new Interact(name);
    mediator.SignOn(name, Receive, visuals);
  }

  public void Receive(string message, string from) {
    visuals.Output(from + ": " + message);
  }
}

class MediatorPattern {
  static void Main () {
    Mediator m = new Mediator();

    Colleague chat1 = new Colleague(m, "John");
    Colleague chat2 = new Colleague(m, "David");
    Colleague chat3 = new Colleague(m, "Lucy");
  }
}
```

The mediator functionality is divided between the Mediator itself, which handles messages as before, and the Interact class, which handles the window I/O. Because the GUI is kept in the Interact class, both the Mediator and Colleague classes closely resemble the theory code for this pattern. The Mediator is set up as a separate thread, as is each of the Colleague's visual objects. The Colleague's Send and Receive methods are altered to work with the window instead of the console.

One major change to the program was required to accommodate the windows. The colleagues each type their messages on their windows and then press the Send button. As shown in the single line from the Interact constructor, a click on Send is directed to an Input event in Interact:

```
sendButton.Click += new EventHandler(Input);
```

Interact then passes this on to InputEvent:

```
public event Callback InputEvent;

public void Input(object source, EventArgs e) {
  if (InputEvent != null)
    InputEvent(messageBox.Text, name);
}
```

In the Mediator constructor, the Mediator's Send method was signed up to InputEvent. So, by this route, a click of the Send button triggers the Send method. The Send method then broadcasts the message as usual.

C# Feature—Events or Delegates?

The construct for providing references to methods is the *delegate*. The keyword event is a modifier that can be used on delegate objects. For almost all purposes, objects designated as delegates and those designated as events are interchangeable. However, events have some added value:[a]

- An event behaves just like a field of a delegate type. The field stores a reference to a delegate that represents the event handlers that have been added to the event.
- An event can be invoked only within the class that declared it; all who can see it can use a delegate.
- Events can be included in interfaces, but delegates cannot.
- Events have Add and Remove accessor methods that can be overridden.

The most significant difference is that one can restrict delegates to be invoked only locally by declaring them as events. In Example 9-4, for instance, both Respond and InputEvent can be events rather than delegates, even though Respond is private and InputEvent is public.

cf. C# 3.0 Language Specification Version 3.0, September 2007, Sections 10.8 and 15

---

[a] Julien Couvier's April 29, 2003 blog entry helped clarify this point (see *http://blog.monstuff.com/archives/000040.html*).

Use

The Mediator pattern is used in many modern systems that reflect a send/receive protocol, such as list servers and chat rooms. But in addition to supporting human interaction, the Mediator pattern has an important role to play as a means of centralizing interconnections between objects. If objects communicate directly with each other, it becomes difficult to move or reuse any one of them. Mediators can be set up to collect and disseminate information about who is connected to whom. For example, within a given application, GUI controls (or widgets) can appear in different forms and locations in different dialog boxes, and they may interact in different ways. For instance, pressing a button in a Continue dialog box may result in very different behavior than pressing the same button in a Print dialog box. This information can be kept in a Mediator for each type of dialog box. The Mediator collects the controls it needs and arranges their interconnections.

The Mediator pattern can have a performance impact on a system. Because all communication must go through the mediator, it can become a bottleneck. Almost everyone has experienced a slowdown in receiving list messages when a system is overloaded. Alternatives to the Mediator are the Observer (which does not check protocols) and the Façade (which is a unidirectional form of providing a convenient interface to complex subsystems).

Use the Mediator pattern when...

- Objects communicate in well-structured but potentially complex ways.
- The objects' identities should be protected even though they communicate.
- Some object behaviors can be grouped and customized.

Exercises

1. Change the chat room example so that individual users can specify which topics they would not like to hear about. This will make the work inside the Mediator's Send method more complex.

2. Investigate the dialog box system mentioned in the "Use" section by designing two such dialog boxes that have a selection of buttons, text boxes, and other controls, and show how Mediators can help to keep their interaction under control.

Observer Pattern

Role

The Observer pattern defines a relationship between objects so that when one changes its state, all the others are notified accordingly. There is usually an identifiable single publisher of new state, and many subscribers who wish to receive it.

Illustration

Once more, we'll look to the world of the Internet for an illustration. The Observer pattern leads us to *blogs*, which are web sites where people write about technical topics, their travels, their lives, and so on. Each blog site is maintained by a single *blogger*. People who come to read about the information put out by a blogger and find it interesting can subscribe to be informed each time a new blog entry is posted. Bloggers don't always post regularly; days or weeks might go by between entries. Therefore, it is more efficient for the blogger to alert interested parties rather than for those parties to constantly poll the blog site.

Figure 9-8 shows a typical blog site. On the right is an "Email alerts" link. In terms of the Observer pattern, those who wish to observe what is going on can click on this link to sign up to be alerted whenever there is a change on the site.

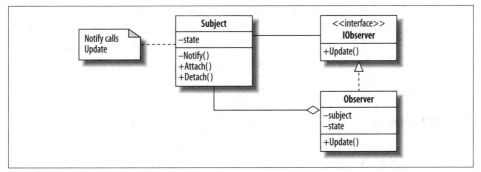

Figure 9-8. Observer pattern illustration—a blog site

Design

The Observer pattern is, like the Mediator pattern, composed of two classes. The Subject is a class whose objects change their state at an independent rate. Observers may indicate that they wish to be informed of these changes, in which case, the Subject will send them notifications. Observers can subscribe to and unsubscribe from such notifications at will. The UML for the Observer pattern is shown in Figure 9-9.

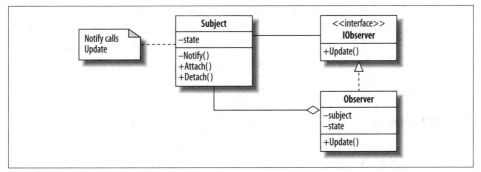

Figure 9-9. Observer pattern UML diagram

The Subject maintains a private event called Notify. Whenever its state changes, it activates the event, sending its state as a parameter to the Update operations inside the Observers. These methods have previously been registered with the Subject via the Attach operation. Each Observer is quite distinct from the Subject and can register an operation of any name to receive the updates, provided it can receive the state.

Here is a summary of the players in the pattern:

Subject
    The class whose instances independently change their state and notify Observers

IObserver
    An interface for Observers specifying how they should be updated

Observer
    A class that provides an Update method to enable its instance's state to stay consistent with the Subject's

Update
    The operation that forms the interface between the Subject and the Observers

Notify
    The event mechanism for calling the Update operation on all Observers

---

QUIZ

Match the Observer Pattern Players with the Blog Illustration

To test whether you understand the Observer pattern, cover the lefthand column of the table below and see if you can identify its players among the items from the illustrative example (Figure 9-8), as shown in the righthand column. Then check your answers against the lefthand column.

Subject	A blogger who writes about C#
IObserver	The "Email alert"
Observer	A programmer interested in C#
Update	Receiving an alert by email
Notify	An email from the blog site to all those signed up
State	A blog

Push and pull models

It should be noted that the state that is sent is not necessarily just text, as in the case of a blog. It could, for example, include values that cause the Observers to react and rearrange their own state accordingly. Sometimes the Subject might want to send a lot of data. In the *push* notification model, the Update interface allows full details related to the change to go through on a Notify (the data is pushed down to the Observers). An alternative mechanism is for the Update interface to merely indicate a change, and for the Observers who are really interested to ask for more information. This is known as the *pull* model. The Observer pattern supports both models.

A particular observer might be interested in only certain aspects of the changing state of a Subject. In this case, the Update interface can be expanded to express such a selection. The Subject will then have several Notify events, and each Observer will be able to choose the ones required. Another option would be to split the work among different Subjects so that Observers can attach to only those that are relevant.

Implementation

The theory code for the Observer pattern is given in Example 9-5. There is one subject that produces numbers. Two observers—center and right—receive and print this information. To simulate the independent nature of the Subject's operation, it is implemented as a thread (line 22), and its data comes from an iterator, the Simulator class (lines 72–80). It will start producing data and sending it out as soon as line 22 is executed. For this reason, we split the instantiation of the Subject from its activation, with the Observers (which need the Subject reference) in between (lines 66–69).

Example 9-5. Observer pattern theory code

```
1     using System;
2     using System.Collections;
3     using System.Threading;
4
5       class ObserverPattern {
6
7         // Observer Pattern                Judith Bishop   Jan 2007
8
9         // The Subject runs in a thread and changes its state
10        // independently. At each change, it notifies its Observers.
11
12        class Subject {
13          public delegate void Callback (string s);
14
15          public event Callback Notify;
16
17          Simulator simulator = new Simulator();
18          const int speed = 200;
19          public string SubjectState {get; set;}
20
21          public void Go() {
22            new Thread(new ThreadStart(Run)).Start();
23          }
24
25          void Run () {
26            foreach (string s in simulator) {
```

Example 9-5. Observer pattern theory code (continued)

```
27                 Console.WriteLine("Subject: "+s);
28                 SubjectState = s;
29                 Notify(s);
30                 Thread.Sleep(speed); // milliseconds
31              }
32          }
33
34          interface IObserver {
35            void Update(string state);
36          }
37
38          class Observer : IObserver {
39            string name;
40            Subject subject;
41            string state;
42            string gap;
43
44            public Observer (Subject subject, string name,string gap) {
45              this.subject = subject;
46              this.name = name;
47              this.gap = gap;
48              subject.Notify += Update;
49            }
50            public void Update(string subjectState) {
51              state = subjectState;
52              Console.WriteLine(gap+name+": "+state);
53            }
54          }
55
56          static void Main () {
57            Subject subject = new Subject();
58            Observer Observer = new Observer(subject,"Center","\t\t");
59            Observer observer2 = new Observer(subject,"Right","\t\t\t\t");
60            subject.Go();
61          }
62
63          class Simulator : IEnumerable {
64
65            string [] moves = {"5","3","1","6","7"};
66
67            public IEnumerator GetEnumerator () {
68              foreach( string element in moves )
69                  yield return element;
70            }
71          }
72      }
73      /* Output
74      Subject: 5
75            Center: 5
76                  Right: 5
77      Subject: 3
78            Center: 3
```

Example 9-5. Observer pattern theory code (continued)

```
79                Right: 3
80   Subject: 1
81        Center: 1
82                Right: 1
83   Subject: 6
84        Center: 6
85                Right: 6
86   */
```

Notify is expressed as an event (line 15), as it is only used locally within the Subject. Its delegate type is Callback (line 13), which is accessible publicly and used by the Observers when they attach with an Update method to the subject's Notify event (line 48). The output shows that the Observers get the state. This example does not illustrate detaching; that is shown next.

Example: Blogs

The next example shows how blogs work. In terms of what Observers can achieve, it is not a very complex example, but it is interactive and therefore enables us to see the dynamics of the pattern. Consider Figure 9-10.

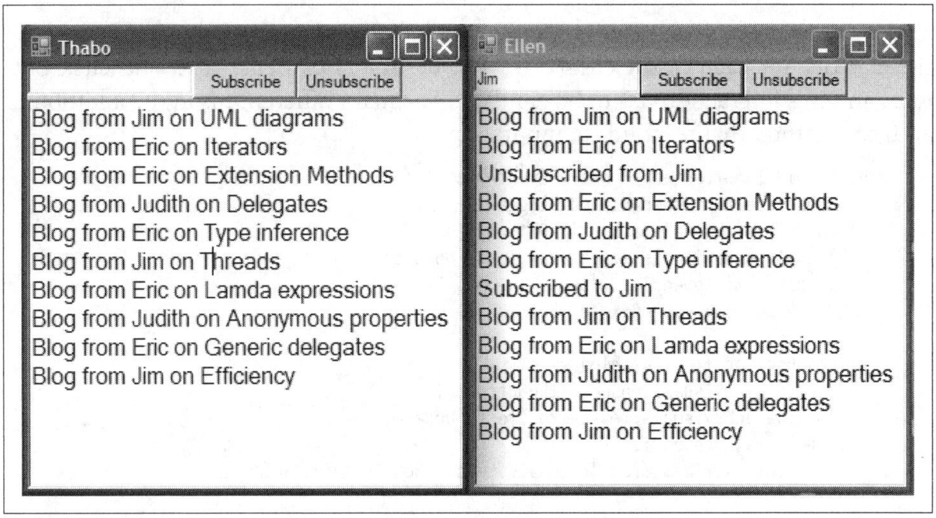

Figure 9-10. Observer pattern example—blogs

There are three bloggers—Eric, Jim, and Judith—who are blogging on programming issues. Thabo and Ellen are initially subscribed to all three blog sites. After Jim's first post, Ellen decides to unsubscribe from his blog. Therefore, Thabo gets Jim's post on Threads, but Ellen does not. A short while later, Ellen resubscribes to Jim's blog and gets his last post on Efficiency.

The full program that implements this system is given in the Appendix. Here, I'll just highlight the points that distinguish it from the theory code.

The first design issue is: are there three Subjects? Because the nature of the state that is being transferred is the same (a blog entry), it is not necessary to have three Subject classes, or even subclasses; instead, we maintain a table of blogger names against their lists of Observers. This is expressed in the Subject as:

```
Dictionary <string,Callback> Notify =
    new Dictionary <string,Callback> ();
```

And the Attach and Detach methods change accordingly:

```
public void Attach(string blogger, Callback Update) {
  Register(blogger);
  Notify[blogger] += Update;
}

public void Detach(string blogger, Callback Update) {
  Notify[blogger] -= Update;
}
```

The Register enables the system to be self-starting. Observers can ask about blogs for someone, even if that person has not yet posted anything. (Try out Peter Subscribe when you run the program.)

The system runs with the Interact class and has four threads: a thread for the blog site and one for each of the Observers. The Observers can enter text and click buttons, and this interaction has to be handled. The main difference is in the addition of an Input method that responds to input:

```
public void Input(object source, EventArgs e) {
  // Subscribe to the specified blogger
  if (source == visuals.subscribeButton) {
    blogs.Attach(visuals.messageBox.Text, Update);
    visuals.wall.AppendText("Subscribed to "+
        visuals.messageBox.Text+"\r\n");
  } else
  // Unsubscribe from the blogger
  if (source == visuals.unsubscribeButton) {
    blogs.Detach(visuals.messageBox.Text, Update);
    visuals.wall.AppendText(
        "Unsubscribed from "+visuals.messageBox.Text+"\r\n");
  }
}
```

Potential extensions to this system are mentioned in the "Exercises" section.

Finally, notice once again that the Iterator pattern has been used to good effect to simulate the irregular appearance of blog entries, thereby supplying data to the Subject. The loop in the Simulator is:

```
public IEnumerator GetEnumerator () {
  foreach( Blogs blog in bloggers )
     yield return blog;
}
```

Use

The Observer pattern is widely used in blog sites and various software systems—
Flickr, cyber-dating web sites, and Microsoft Updates are a few of the places where it
is applied. It also has a formal face as the "publish/subscribe" model and the
"Model-View-Controller" (MVC) architectural pattern.

Use the Observer pattern when...

- There are aspects to an abstraction that can vary independently.
- Changes in one object need to be propagated to a selection of other objects, not all of them.
- The object sending the changes does not need to know about the receivers.

Another good example of the Observer pattern is the way that different graphs
reflecting data in a spreadsheet change when the data changes. The Observers seem
to be working together, although they are independent.

Exercises

1. An important aspect of the Observer pattern is that Observers deal with state differently. Enhance the blog program by creating another Observer that subclasses
   Observer and that reports differently on the blog (i.e., has a different implementation of Update).

2. Repeat exercise 1, this time with a combination of the State pattern and the
   Observer pattern.

3. Change the blog system to implement the pull model. That is, do not send any
   state back with Update, but enable Observers to call back for more information if
   desired.

Pattern Discussion and Comparison

We shall wind up the chapter in two parts. First, we shall consider the Iterator pattern
in more detail, and second, we shall compare the Mediator and Observer patterns.
Although all three patterns support communication between objects, C#'s language
support for the Iterator has projected it into a different category than the other two.
The Observer and Mediator still rely on communication via simple method calling.

Language Support for the Iterator Pattern

Fully 25 years ago, iterators were supported by languages such as Alphard and Clu and could be programmed via functions in Ada.* During the Java and C# 1.0 and 2.0 era, iterators consisted of the methods for the basic elements of a loop: Current, MoveNext, and Reset. If the programmer implemented these methods in a collection, a foreach loop would call them correctly for objects of that collection. C# 3.0's query expressions together with the IEnumerator interface have vastly simplified the handling of loops over arbitrary collections of data. Consider this excerpt from Example 9-2:

```
var selection = from n in daysInMonths
        where n.Key.Length > 5
        select n;
```

In earlier versions of C# iterators, both *lambda expressions* and delegates were used to express queries and interact with enumerator methods. Using lambda expressions, the selection would be expressed like this:

```
var selection = daysInMonths.
    Where(s => s.Key.Length>5);
```

The lambda expression is introduced by the Where keyword and reads like this: "all s such that s.Key.Length>5". Where maps to a method defined for the Dictionary collection. The method returns a value of type "sequence of s", or Dictionary in this case. Expressing this query in an even more primitive form with delegates, we have:

```
foreach (string n in collection.
    Where(delegate(string s) {return s.Length > 5;}))
```

Note the dot after collection on the first line; it indicates that Where is an instance method for collection's type. collection would be instantiated as follows:

```
StringCollection collection = new StringCollection(months);
```

and the class would look like this:

```
public class StringCollection {

  string[] elements;

  public StringCollection(string[] elements) {
    this.elements = elements;
  }

  public IEnumerable<string> Where (Func <string, bool> filter) {
    foreach( string element in elements )
        if( filter(element) == true )
        yield return element;
  }
}
```

---

* J. M. Bishop, "The effect of data abstraction on loop programming techniques," *IEEE Transactions on Software Engineering* 16, no. 4 (1990): 389–402.

The iterator passes a delegate to the enumerator Where. Where applies the delegate, called filter, each time around the loop, yielding only those elements that comply. These more complex forms are necessary for structures and/or criteria not covered by the built-in forms, as shown in the next example.

The advances made in C# 3.0 iterators give the following benefits:

- Hiding the structure of the underlying collection enables it to be changed independently of the program containing the iterator.
- Providing an extensive range of data-filtering mechanisms akin to those available for database queries makes programs short and powerful.
- Generating values in the enumerator only when the iterator needs them is more efficient in terms of space and time.

Mediator and Observer Pattern Comparison

As the examples suggest, Mediator and Observer are very similar patterns. Mailing lists, chat rooms, and blogs all involve communication between individuals who actively sign up to the activity. The difference is that the Mediator *centralizes* the communication between colleagues, whereas the Observer *distributes* control of information by differentiating between subjects (publishers) and observers (subscribers).

The communication in the Mediator pattern is easier to understand. Colleagues send messages to a mediator and the transmission of the information further to whomever is currently in the group is handled there, in one place (consult Example 9-3 again). In the Observer pattern, observers wait to be invoked with (presumably relevant) information from more than one subject. The coupling is closer in the Mediator, as the client or colleagues send messages that will go to other colleagues (though not by name). The example is the chat room. In the Observer, the coupling is one step removed, in that observers do not send any information; they wait to receive it from subjects, who distributed it to all who have subscribed. An example is the blog.

The question of a constraint on communication is answered differently by the two patterns. The Mediator keeps the constraint in the mediator object, deciding how, who, and when should get the next message. In the Observer, there can be a protocol between an observer and subject, but it would be more varied and maintained on both sides. These observations are summarized in Table 9-1.

Table 9-1. Comparison of Mediator and Observer patterns

	Mediator	Observer
Client creates	Colleagues and a mediator	Observers and subjects
Messages initiated by	Client and colleagues	Subject
Messages sent to	Mediator then colleagues	Observers
Constraints	In the mediator	Between the observers and subjects

CHAPTER 10

Behavioral Patterns: Visitor, Interpreter, and Memento

In this chapter, we'll consider the final three core design patterns. The Visitor and Interpreter patterns are well-known in compiler-writing circles. However, they also apply wherever operations are defined on structures according to specific rules, and the operations and structures are defined separately. The Memento pattern rounds out the behavioral group by showing how the state of objects can be saved and restored.

Visitor Pattern

Role

The Visitor pattern defines and performs new operations on all the elements of an existing structure, without altering its classes.

Illustration

This illustration takes us into the realms of student record systems. These days, it's typical for courses to be assessed in several ways, which all add up to a final result. At the start of a course, instructors are required to declare the components that will contribute to the assessment. The students' marks are recorded throughout the semester and then totaled up at the end according to the weights that were specified. For example, consider the extract from a spreadsheet containing the marks for a course on Programming Languages in Figure 10-1. We can deduce that the assessment for the course consisted of:

- Five *laboratories* (or labs) (2 percent each)
- A *midterm* evaluation consisting of a laboratory component (10 percent) and a theory component (15 percent)
- An assignment that is a take-home laboratory (10 percent)
- An *examination* consisting of a laboratory component (15 percent) and a theory component (40 percent)

Programming Languages 2007	Lab 1 Objects	Lab 2 Polymorph	Lab 3 Haskell	Lab 4 Prolog	Lab 5 C# 3.0	Prac Total	Prac Test	Theory test	Assignment	Semester mark	Prac exam	Theory Exam	Final
Weight	2	2	2	2	2	10	10	15	10	45	15	40	100
Maximum	87	95	100	100	85	92	75	99	100	91	75	94	90
Average %	83	75	100	88	67	73	65	75	75	72	68	74	72
Out of	100	100	100	100	100	100	100	100	100	100	100	100	100
Brinch Hansen P	80	0	100	100	85	73	51	52	50	56	57	56	56
Dijkstra E	87	95	100	100	77	92	70	99	100	91	75	94	90
Nygaard K	0	55	100	65	55	55	75	73	74	70	71	72	71

Figure 10-1. Interpreter pattern illustration—a) an XML specification and b) a corresponding GUI

From the columns, we can see that the total of the labs is important, as is the mark obtained from the lab and theory tests done in the middle of the term (the midterm assessment). Other calculations are the averages for the lab work and the theory work, and of course the final result.

Those who have worked with spreadsheets of this complexity will know that the process can be tedious and error-prone. An alternative is to create a program that will process the results in a customized way. To drive such a program, we can define a notation that specifies the weight of each mark and whether it is categorized as Theory or Lab, Midterm, or Exam. The Midterm and Exam can, as shown in the illustration, be further subdivided into Lab and Theory components. Assignments are take-home labs and fall under the Lab category.

An example of specifying the different mark components and their weights based on the sample course would be:

```
COS333 L2 L2 L2 L2 L2 M25 (L40 T60 ) L10 E55 (L28 T73 )
```

where L stands for lab, T for theory, and so on. The only complexity is introduced by the Midterm and the Exam, which have component parts themselves. These are expressed inside parentheses *after* the main component. All weights are given in percentages, with the percentages inside the parentheses indicating the relative weights of the components (i.e., for the Midterm weighing 25%, the split between the lab and theory components is 40:60).

Given this definition of the data, we can set up a data structure in memory that represents a course (Figure 10-2).

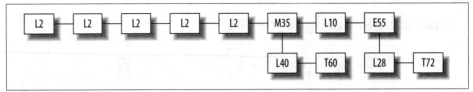

Figure 10-2. Visitor pattern illustration—course structure

Having arrived at this structure, we can now process it in one of two broad ways:

- Categorize and summarize the different types of elements making up the course.
- Apply the structure to the marks recorded for the students to get their results.

Both applications involve the Visitor pattern: we set up the structure and then "visit" it to perform the operations. We'll focus on the first task here and consider the second in the discussion of the Interpreter pattern.

Design

The Visitor pattern has two distinct parts: there are the classes that make up an object structure, and then there are the methods that will be applied to the object structure. These are the *visitors*. The UML for the pattern is given in Figure 10-3.

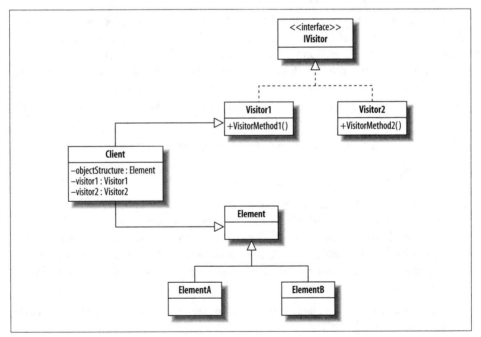

Figure 10-3. Visitor pattern UML diagram

The Client defines and creates an object structure and populates it with data. This process is not part of the pattern, however. The object structure is specified by a hierarchy of Element classes, three of which are shown here: Element, ElementA, and ElementB. The Visitor methods, VisitorMethod1 and VisitorMethod2, are defined in separate classes. Objects of these classes conform to an IVisitor interface. Although the object structure and Visitors are separate, some implementations of the Visitor pattern might require a small change to the objects to make them visitor-ready.

The players in the Visitor pattern are:

Client
: A class that creates and maintains the object structure; instantiates and calls the Visitors

ObjectStructure
: A composite structure of several related element types

Element
: The root element type for the object structure

ElementA *and* ElementB
: Subclasses of Element

IVisitor
: An interface for all the Visitor classes

Visitor1 *and* Visitor2
: Classes that contain methods that iterate through the object structure and apply operations to its elements

Note that the object structure is not necessarily a class hierarchy. In general, one node in the object structure can refer to another object of any type whatsoever, and the visitor can traverse to that other object. The interesting issue with subclass relationships among the object structure nodes is whether the visitor actions can easily be inherited.

The Visitor pattern is intended for object structures, so it is often used in conjunction with the Composite pattern. The Composite pattern is responsible for setting up the multilevel structure on which the Visitor pattern then operates.

Implementation

Because the Visitor pattern is one of those with a distinction between the data and some additional and extraneous behavior, we shall develop it in three parts:

- The object structure
- The visitor(s)
- The client

Match the Visitor Pattern Players with the Course Illustration

To test whether you understand the Visitor pattern, cover the lefthand column of the table below and see if you can identify its players among the items from the illustrative example (Figure 10-1), as shown in the righthand column. Then check your answers against the lefthand column.

Client	The instructor
ObjectStructure	The rules of the course (taken from the notation)
Element	Course
ElementA, ElementB	Lab, Theory, Midterm, Exam
VisitorA	Print the course rules
VisitorB	Summarize the Lab and Theory totals

We shall illustrate this development with a small theoretical example and show two ways of implementing visitors, before going on to the larger example. The small example sets up a structure in levels, and then the client asks the visitor to count the number of top-level nodes. One might imagine that it would be easy to add this functionality to the nodes themselves and simply traverse the structure. However, with the Visitor pattern, we can add new behavior after the object structure has effectively been sealed off. On the other side, the object structure might evolve, and we would like the visiting process to be unaffected. Although this small example does not show the power of the Visitor pattern, it does reveal the independence of the different players and how this independence reduces coupling.

The program is shown in Example 10-1. It starts with setting up the object structure, in a namespace called ObjectStructure (lines 7–37). This is all fairly standard. The initializing of the structure is done in client on lines 70–82, and we can see that it has nine ordinary nodes of the type Element and two of the type ElementWithLink, which go down a next level. The only other business in the client is to instantiate the visitor, call it, and report on the number of elements (lines 84–87).

Example 10-1. Visitor pattern theory code

```
1  using System;
2  using ObjectStructure;
3
4  // Visitor Pattern - Example    Judith Bishop October 2007
5  // Sets up an object structure and visits it
6
7  namespace ObjectStructure {
8
9      abstract class IElement {
```

Example 10-1. Visitor pattern theory code (continued)

```
10          // Added to make the elements Visitor-ready
11          public abstract void Accept(IVisitor visitor);
12      }
13
14      class Element : IElement {
15          public Element Next {get; set;}
16          public Element Link {get; set;}
17          public Element () {}
18          public Element (Element next) {
19              Next = next;
20          }
21          // Added to make the elements Visitor-ready
22          public override void Accept(IVisitor visitor) {
23              visitor.Visit(this);
24          }
25      }
26
27      class ElementWithLink : Element {
28          public ElementWithLink (Element link, Element next) {
29              Next = next;
30              Link = link;
31          }
32          // Added to make the elements Visitor-ready
33          public override void Accept(IVisitor visitor) {
34              visitor.Visit(this);
35          }
36      }
37  }
38
39      // Visitor interface
40      interface IVisitor {
41          void Visit (Element element);
42          void Visit (ElementWithLink element);
43      }
44
45      // Visitor
46      class CountVisitor : IVisitor {
47        public int Count {get; set;}
48        public void CountElements(Element element) {
49              element.Accept(this);
50              if (element.Link!=null) CountElements(element.Link);
51              if (element.Next!=null) CountElements(element.Next);
52        }
53
54        //Elements with links are not counted
55        public void Visit(ElementWithLink element) {
56            Console.WriteLine("Not counting");
57        }
58
59        // Only Elements are counted
60        public void Visit(Element element) {
61              Count++;
```

Example 10-1. Visitor pattern theory code (continued)

```
62         }
63      }
64
65    // Client
66    class Client {
67
68      static void Main( ) {
69         // Set up the object structure
70         Element objectStructure =
71            new Element(
72              new Element(
73              new ElementWithLink(
74                 new Element(
75                   new Element(
76                    new ElementWithLink(
77                    new Element(null),
78                    new Element(
79                    null)))),
80            new Element(
81              new Element(
82              new Element(null))))));
83
84         Console.WriteLine ("Count the Elements");
85         CountVisitor visitor = new CountVisitor( );
86         visitor.CountElements(objectStructure);
87         Console.WriteLine("Number of Elements is: "+visitor.Count);
88      }
89    }
90    /*
91    Count the Elements
92    Found Element
93    Found Element
94    Number of Elements is: 9
95    */
```

Now, we can set up Visitor's communication with the object structure as follows:

1. Add an IVisitor interface listing Visit methods for each type in the structure and make the Visitor implement it:

```
// Visitor interface
interface IVisitor {
   void Visit (Element element);
   void Visit (ElementWithLink element);
}
```

2. In the Visitor class, add implementations for each of these methods, for example:

```
// Only Elements are counted
public void Visit(Element element) {
   Count++;
}
```

3. In the `ObjectStructure`'s namespace, add an interface with one method called `Accept`, and make the top level type implement it:

```
abstract class IElement {
    // Added to make the elements Visitor-ready
    public abstract void Accept(IVisitor visitor);
}
```

4. In each type of the structure, add an `Accept` method of the following identical form:

```
// Added to make the elements Visitor-ready
public override void Accept(IVisitor visitor) {
    visitor.Visit(this);
}
```

Once all this is in place, the Visitor pattern's mechanism can get into action. Within the recursive method `CountElements` (line 48–52), an `Accept` method is called on an object of type `Element`.

The `Elements` are unaware of what visitors to expect, but they do have to supply the "hooks" to accept visits.

Because of the object hierarchy, the actual object could also be `ElementWithLink`. At runtime, the appropriate `Accept` statement in the corresponding class will be called. These small methods simply bounce the call back to the correct `Visit` method in the `CountVisitor` (line 23 goes to line 55 and line 34 goes to line 60). In this way, the Visitor pattern uses a well-known method called *double-dispatch*.

Now, consider how to extend the example. We can add another `Visitor` with its own `Visit` methods and use the same `Accept` methods already build into the structure. That is good news. But what is not such good news, is that we had to add the `Accept` methods in the first place. It is possible that we might not have been able to do so (because the code was not accessible). For this reason, we are going to consider an alternative way of finding the right `Visit` method, without going into the structure to add the `Accept` methods: *reflection*.

Put together, the reflective methods and types outlined in the sidebar form a `ReflectiveVisit` method in the `CountVisitor`:

```
public void ReflectiveVisit(Element element) {
// Use reflection to find and invoke the correct Visit method
    Type[] types = new Type[] {element.GetType()};
    MethodInfo methodInfo = this.GetType().GetMethod("Visit", types);
    if (methodInfo != null)
        methodInfo.Invoke(this, new object[] {element});
    else Console.WriteLine("Unexpected Visit");
}
```

C# Feature—Reflection

Reflection is a feature of the .NET Framework libraries that is available to C# and other .NET languages. Using classes and methods in the `System.Reflection` API, we can discover information about a class or object that we can then use in further executing the program. Typically, reflection can be used in these four circumstances:

- Viewing metadata
- Performing type discovery
- Late binding to methods and properties
- Creating types at runtime with `Reflection.Emit`

The first two relate to the Interpreter pattern (discussed next). Useful classes are:

`Type[]`
> Will hold a list of type names

`GetType()`
> Will return a class name

`MethodInfo`
> Can return all parameters and the return type of a method

`Invoke`
> Will call the method described in a variable of type `MethodInfo`

cf. *http://msdn2.microsoft.com/en-us/library/system.reflection.aspx*

The counting method now calls this method instead of the Accept method in the structures. This sequence of instructions causes the correct `Visit` method inside `CountVisitor` to be called. The method can be put in a class and used by all other Visitors, so it has to be written only once. The full program is given in the Appendix.

The reflective approach has one disadvantage: it is considerably slower (40 to 100 times) than double-dispatch. For small structures, it is adequate, but for large structures with many types, it would be a disaster. However, the dynamic discovery of types can be sped up by adding an optimization that stores the discovered type. This will scale better over hundreds of objects.

Apart from being slow, reflection can be error-prone if the types and their methods don't actually exist. You can test this by commenting out one of the `Visit` methods in `CountVisitor`. The program still compiles, but it will fail at runtime. The Visitor pattern is associated with compile-time checking, however, as supplied by double-dispatch. There are other options for implementing the Visitor pattern, which I will address in the last section of this chapter.

Example: Course Statistics

Now, let's apply the Visitor pattern to our earlier course example. The program code follows the theory code of Example 10-1 quite closely. It starts off with two Visitors: one will print element structures, and one will summarize the values in the individual objects. In this case, we are interested in the total weight for lab components versus theory components. Because we have different visitors and because efficiency is not an issue, we use the reflection solution.

The object structure is built up from five classes—Element plus four others that inherit from it. The Print visitor handles all Elements the same, so it has only one Visit method. The Summarize method in the second visitor has three Visit methods and checks the type in the last one to decide how to handle the weights.

 These Visitors are defined subsequently, independently of the Element classes.

The complete code is shown in Example 10-2.

Example 10-2. Visitor pattern example code—course marks

```
using System;
using System.Reflection;

  // Visitor Pattern - Example    Judith Bishop October 2007
  // Sets up course rules and visits in two ways

class Program {

    abstract class IVisitor {
      public void ReflectiveVisit(Element element) {
        Type[] types = new Type[] {element.GetType()};
        MethodInfo methodInfo = this.GetType().GetMethod("Visit", types);

        if (methodInfo != null) {
            methodInfo.Invoke(this, new object[] {element});
        }
      }
    }

    class PrintVisitor : IVisitor {
        public void Print(Element element) {
            ReflectiveVisit(element);
            if (element.Part!=null) {
                Console.Write(" [");
                Print(element.Part);
            }
```

Example 10-2. Visitor pattern example code—course marks (continued)

```
            if (element.Next!=null) Print (element.Next);
            Console.Write("] ");
        }
    public void Visit(Element element) {
        Console.Write(" "+element.Weight);
    }
}

class StructureVisitor : IVisitor {
    public int Lab {get; set;}
    public int Test {get; set;}

  public void Summarize(Element element) {
        ReflectiveVisit(element);
        if (element.Part!=null) VisitAllLabTest(element.Part.Next);
        if (element.Next!=null) VisitAllLabTest(element.Next);
    }
    public void Visit(Lab element) {
        Lab += element.Weight;
    }
    public void Visit(Test element) {
        Test += element.Weight;
    }
    public void Visit (Element element) {
        if ((element is Midterm || element is Exam)
            && element.Part==null) Test += element.Weight;
    }
}

class Element {
    public int Weight {get; set;}
    public Element Next {get; set;}
    public Element Part {get; set;}

    public void Parse (Context context) {
        string starters = "LTME";
        if (context.Input.Length>0 && starters.IndexOf(context.Input[0])>=0) {
            switch(context.Input[0]) {
              case 'L':
                  Next=new Lab();
                   break;
              case 'T':
                  Next=new Test();
                   break;
              case 'M':
                  Next=new Midterm();
                   break;
              case 'E':
                  Next = new Exam();
                  break;
            }
            Next.Weight = GetNumber(context);
            if (context.Input.Length>0 && context.Input[0]=='(') {
```

Example 10-2. Visitor pattern example code—course marks (continued)

```
                   context.Input = context.Input.Substring(1);
                   Next.Part = new Element( );
                   Next.Part.Parse(context);
                   Element e = Next.Part;
                   while (e!=null) {
                      e.Weight = e.Weight * Next.Weight / 100;
                      e = e.Next;
                   }
                   context.Input = context.Input.Substring(2);
               }
             Next.Parse(context);
         }
      }
   }

   class Course : Element {
      public string Name {get; set;}
      public Course (Context context) {
         Name = context.Input.Substring(0,6);
         context.Input = context.Input.Substring(7);
      }
   }

   class Lab : Element {
   }

   class Test : Element {
   }

   class Midterm : Element {
   }

   class Exam : Element {
   }

class Context {
      public string Input {get; set;}
      public double Output {get; set;}

      public Context(string c) {
          Input = c;
        Output = 0;
        }
   }

   static int GetNumber (Context context) {
        int atSpace = context.Input.IndexOf(' ');
      int number = Int32.Parse(context.Input.Substring(1,atSpace));
       context.Input = context.Input.Substring(atSpace+1);
        return number;
   }

   static void Main( ) {
```

Example 10-2. Visitor pattern example code—course marks (continued)

```
    string rules = "COS333 L2 L2 L2 L2 L2 M25 (L40 T60 ) L10 E55 (L28 T73 ) ";

    Context context;
    Console.WriteLine (rules+"\n");
    context = new Context (rules);
    Element course = new Course(context);
    course.Parse(context);

    PrintVisitor visitor = new PrintVisitor( );
    Console.WriteLine("Visitor 1 - Course structure");
    visitor.Print(course);

    StructureVisitor visitor2 = new StructureVisitor( );
    visitor2.Summarize(course);
    Console.WriteLine ("\n\nVisitor 2 - Summing the weights\nLabs "
                        +visitor2.Lab + "% and Tests "
                        +visitor2.Test + "%");
  }
}
/*Output
COS333 L2 L2 L2 L2 L2 M25 (L40 T60 ) L10 E55 (L28 T73 )

Visitor 1 - Course structure
 0 2 2 2 2 2 25 [ 0 10 15] ] ]  10 55 [ 0 15 40] ] ] ] ] ] ] ] ] ] ]

Visitor 2 - Summing the weights
Labs 45% and Tests 55%
*/
```

Using the same rule as illustrated in Figure 10-2:

```
    COS333 L2 L2 L2 L2 L2 M25 (L40 T60 ) L10 E55 (L28 T73 )
```

we can create an object structure via a Parse method acting on a stream of data.

Use

Clearly, the Visitor pattern is very handy when the behavior of a class hierarchy needs to be extended. As it is specifically intended for hierarchies, it can be found in compilers and other large system software packages that are built with frontends and backends. The class hierarchy is defined so that the frontend can create and populate a parse tree. The backend of the compiler then takes over and adds its own processing of the parse tree with its own methods. These methods should not be muddled up with the frontend's classes, as they are needed at quite different times. The Visitor pattern is ideal for achieving this separation.

A word of caution, however, on the approach taken for implementing the Visitor pattern. To put the performance implications into perspective, some tests were run multiple times on a simple program like the one used here, but with a very large tree.* The reflection approach was between 100 and 200 times slower than the dynamic dispatch implementation. This is a considerable difference, and it's significant enough to make reflection viable only when programs are performing a lot of work in the Visit methods, or they are I/O-bound. In these cases, the effect of the overhead would be diminished.

For applications such as a compiler, dynamic dispatch is the approach of choice; the verboseness of the code is offset by the fact that many compiler generators will emit the methods involved in the Visitor pattern for the parse tree associated with the input grammar.

Use the Visitor pattern when...

• You have a class hierarchy that is effectively sealed.
• There are many distinct operations to perform on it.
• The operations are orthogonal to the core purpose of the types in the hierarchy.
• You need the flexibility to define new operations over time.

Exercises

1. After the course in Example 10-2 has been set up, changes can still be made to the structure during the first two weeks. Suppose that the lab component of the final exam is to be canceled and the weight distributed proportionately among the other components. Thus, the first lab will get 2/15 extra weight. Write a Visitor to perform this operation and alter the weights. Then, call the Print and Summarize visitors again to show the new situation.

2. Take the dynamic dispatch program in Example 10-3 and embellish it with print statements that show the steps taken through the program as a Visitor is activated.

3. In Example 10-1, add some data fields to the structure and invent some visitor behavior that can alter their values.

4. Redo Example 10-2 using double-dispatch.

Interpreter Pattern

The Interpreter pattern supports the interpretation of instructions written in a language or notation defined for a specific purpose. The notation is precise and can be defined in terms of a grammar.

---

* Thanks to Nigel Horspool for suggesting and executing these tests.

Illustration

XML (eXtended Markup Language) is a very popular way of expressing the format of data. XML consists of tags that introduce attributes and associated values in a simple nested and sequential notation. Consider the example in Figure 10-4—(a) shows an XML description of a GUI depicted in (b). The XML corresponds to the controls and parameters of a Windows form. Thus, the following:

```
<TextBox Top="10" Left="100" Name="eurobox" />
```

specifies a TextBox control followed by pixel values for its top-left corner and the name by which it will be known in the program ("eurobox"). The corresponding label at top=10 pixels has the text "Paid on hols" so that will be opposite the eurobox control when it is laid out on the form.

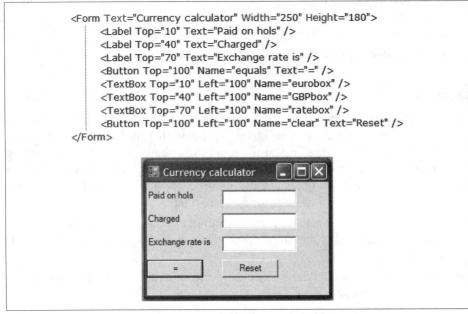

Figure 10-4. Interpreter pattern illustration—XML description of a GUI

The XML specification is read into a program, checked, and interpreted into GUI objects to be displayed on the screen. Thus, this example illustrates the essence of the Interpreter pattern.

Grammars

Languages can be expressed in other notations as well. A familiar form is a grammar of terms. Terms written in sequence must follow each other; alternatives are indicated with a | and repetition by recursive definitions. Given this scheme, we could specify a grammar for the course rules laid out earlier in Example 10-2 as:

```
 1   course          = name restcourse
 2   restcourse      = terminalpart | nonterminalpart | restcourse | empty
 3   nonterminalpart = group ( terminalpart restterminalpart )
 4   terminalpart    = lab | test | group
 5   restterminalpart = terminalpart restterminalpart | empty
 6   group           = midterm | exam
 7   lab             = L weight
 8   text            = T weight
 9   midterm         = M weight
10   exam            = E weight
11   weight          = integer
```

empty is a special term that matches nothing and returns the interpreter to the previous term. L, T, M, E, and integer have their literal meanings.

This grammar is workable for interpreting course rules, although it has one deficiency: both terminalpart and nonterminalpart can start with a group (midterm or exam), and therefore the grammar is ambiguous in the first term as the input is being processed. However, the ambiguity can be resolved by looking ahead to the next few terms. Ambiguous grammars can also be transformed into unambiguous grammars by introducing more terms.

Design

As seen in both the course rules (grammar) and the XML for the GUI (Figure 10-4), there is a distinction between *terminals* and *nonterminals* in the input to the interpreter. In the grammar, terminals are final terms, whereas nonterminals comprise other terms. The Interpreter is an operation defined at all levels to process input as required. The operations are done in the context of some input and output.

The UML diagram for this pattern is given in Figure 10-5.

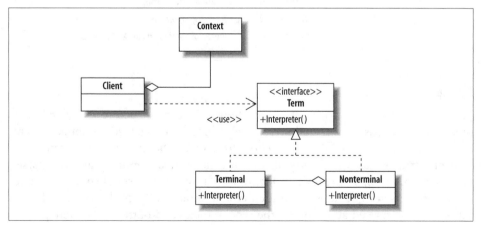

Figure 10-5. Interpreter pattern UML diagram

The players in the pattern are:

Client
> A class that builds an object structure that represents a set of instructions in the given grammar

Context
> A class that contains information for use by the Interpreter (usually its input and output)

Term
> An abstract class that provides an interface for all the classes in the structure and a default for the Interpreter operation

Nonterminal
> A class that implements the Interpreter and also can contain other Term instances

Terminal
> A class that implements the Interpreter

QUIZ

Match the Interpreter Pattern Players with the XML Illustration

To test whether you understand the Interpreter pattern, cover the lefthand column of the table below and see if you can identify its players among the items from the illustrative example (Figure 10-4), as shown in the righthand column. Then check your answers against the lefthand column.

Context	Rule specification and the GUI output
Terminal	An attribute (e.g., Top)
Nontermial	A tag (e.g., TextBox)
Interpreter	Process of transforming the XML to the GUI

Parsing

The Interpreter pattern does not specify how the object structure is created. This process is known as *parsing* and involves matching input against a grammar to create a structure, often known as a *parse tree*. Once the structure is created, the Interpreter starts its work and will match a new set of input against the parsed grammar. For example, the XML in Figure 10-4(a) results in a set of controls that are drawn on the screen. The user can then type in input and press buttons, and these actions are interpreted according to the type of boxes and buttons that were parsed. The process is shown in Figure 10-6.

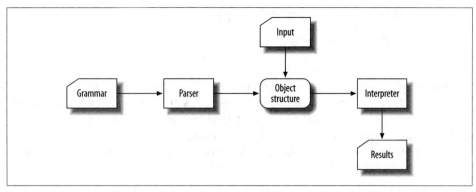

Figure 10-6. Parser and Interpreter diagram

Implementation

Although the UML diagram shows the Interpreter methods as integral to the Term hierarchy classes, it turns out that implementing them as extension methods is a very convenient solution. We'll return to the course example to explore the implementation.

To make our program conform to the ideals of the Interpreter pattern, we replace the object initializer in the Main method with a Parse method inside Element:

```csharp
public void Parse (Context context) {
  string starters = "LTME";
  if (context.Input.Length>0 && starters.IndexOf(context.Input[0])>=0) {
    switch(context.Input[0]) {
      case 'L':
        Next=new Lab( );
        break;
      case 'T':
        Next=new Test( );
        break;
      case 'M':
        Next=new Midterm( );
        break;
      case 'E':
        Next = new Exam( );
        break;
    }
  Next.Weight = GetNumber(context);
  if (context.Input.Length>0 && context.Input[0]=='(') {
    context.Input = context.Input.Substring(1);
    Next.Part = new Element( );
    Next.Part.Parse(context);
    Element e = Next.Part;
    while (e!=null) {
      e.Weight = e.Weight * Next.Weight / 100;
      e = e.Next;
    }
```

```
        context.Input = context.Input.Substring(2);
    }
    Next.Parse(context);
  }
}
```

The Parser's task is to determine whether an element is terminal or nonterminal and, more precisely, what class should be instantiated for the values. It works as an end-recursion method, calling itself on the Next field of each object after it has been created. The switch statement takes care of the terminals (based on the initial character of each), and the if statement after that handles the case when there is a bracketed part, as in M25 (L30 T70).

Finally, we add the interpreter as a visitor. The function of the interpreter is to successively match up against the parsed course rules a sequence of marks such as would be found in this array of three students:

```
int [][] values = new [] {
    new [] {80,0,100,100,85,51,52,50,57,56},
    new [] {87,95,100,100,77,70,99,100,75,94},
    new [] {0,55,100,65,55,75,73,74,71,72}};
```

The Main method calls the Interpreter thusly:

```
Console.WriteLine("\n\nVisitor 3 (Interpreter) ");
foreach (int [] student in values) {
  Console.Write(student.Display());
  course.SetUp(context, student);
  course.Interpreter();
  Console.WriteLine(" = "+context.Output/100);
}
```

resulting in the following output:

```
Visitor 3 (Interpreter)
[80, 0, 100, 100, 85, 51, 52, 50, 57, 56] = 56.15
[87, 95, 100, 100, 77, 70, 99, 100, 75, 94] = 89.88
[0, 55, 100, 65, 55, 75, 73, 74, 71, 72] = 70.8
```

which conforms to the original spreadsheet shown in Figure 10-1. The Interpreter method is:

```
public static int [] values;
public static int n;
public static Context context;

public static void SetUp (this Element element, Context c, int[] v) {
  context = c;
  context.Output=0;
  values = v;
  n = 0;
}

public static void Interpreter(this Element element) {
```

```
// Terminals
if (element is Lab || element is Test) {
  context.Output += values[n]*element.Weight;
  n++;
}
else
  // Potential non-terminals
  if ((element is Midterm || element is Exam)
      && element.Part==null) {
    context.Output += values[n]*element.Weight;
    n++;
  }

  if (element.Part!=null) Interpreter(element.Part.Next);
  if (element.Next!=null) Interpreter(element.Next);
}
}
```

It operates in the same way as previous Visitors, by examining the type of a class and then acting accordingly. The SetUp method is called first to get the marks into a convenient array and clear the context's output. Then, the interpreter works as an end-recursive method, following the Part and Next links as required. The full extended program is shown in the Appendix.

This discussion addressed the implementation issues via a fairly simple example. We'll now consider another, larger example related to the original illustration for the pattern.

Example: Mirrors

In this section, we'll turn our attention to an industrial-strength example of considerable power called *Mirrors*. The Mirrors system is a program that will interpret XML for any .NET API and then call the methods mentioned therein. Figure 10-1(b) was in fact produced from Mirrors using Figure 10-1(a) as the input. In terms of Figure 10-6, Mirrors acts as a combined Parser and Interpreter. It activates XML parsing mechanisms that are built into .NET, and then uses reflection to invoke the methods thus described. As such, Mirrors can be described as a generic reflective Interpreter. It does not mention any API by name and can work with any of them.

The Mirrors system was written by Hans Lombard and was based on an interpreter called Views, which Nigel Horspool, D-J Miller, and I developed before Windows Forms was available with .NET on Linux and Mac OS X. The Views notation was a stylized XML, and the interpreter included a parser and an engine. (See references in the Bibliography at the end of the book.)

Mirrors is particularly useful for creating GUIs. The version included here will access the Windows Forms API and show a GUI, but to conserve space, it does not include the engine to make the resulting GUI operate; this is a small add-on of the size of the Interact class used previously. The events would be specified in the XML and the corresponding methods implemented in extension methods to the Mirrors system.

The main operational part of the Mirrors system is its constructor:

```
1   public Mirror(string spec) {
2     objectStack = new Stack();
3     objectStack.Push(null);
4
5     // Register the commands
6     commands = new List<Command>();
7     commands.Add(new ElementCommand());
8     commands.Add(new EndElementCommand());
9     commands.Add(new AttributeCommand());
10
11    Reader = new XmlTextReader(spec);
12    while (Reader.Read()) {
13      InterpretCommands();
14
15      bool b = Reader.IsEmptyElement;
16      if (Reader.HasAttributes) {
17        for (int i = 0; i < Reader.AttributeCount; i++) {
18          Reader.MoveToAttribute(i);
19          InterpretCommands();
20        }
21      }
22      if (b) Pop();
23    }
24  }
```

XMLTextReader (line 11) accepts the entire XML specification and emits elements one at a time. On line 13, we move to the command interpreter, which operates exactly according to the pattern in Figure 10-5. There are three classes in the hierarchy: ElementCommand, EndCommand, and AttributeCommand.

Each has its own Interpret method. The first one is:

```
public class ElementCommand : Command {
  public override void Interpret (Mirror context) {
    if (context.Reader.NodeType != XmlNodeType.Element) return;
    Type type = GetTypeOf(context.Reader.Name);
    if (type == null) return;
    object o = Activator.CreateInstance(type);

    if (context.Peek() != null)
        ((Control)context.Peek()).Controls.Add((Control)o);
    context.Push(o);
  }

  // Omit GetType method here
}
```

The Interpret method checks that the XML node type from the reader is correct. It then gets the actual type of the node (for example, TextBox), creates an instance of that type, adds the control to the stack, and pushes it down. Correspondingly, an EndCommand (which the Interpreter encounters when it hits a /> symbol in XML) pops the stack. The AttributeCommand class is the only other class:

```
public class AttributeCommand : Command {
  public override void Interpret (Mirror context) {
    if (context.Reader.NodeType != XmlNodeType.Attribute) return;
    SetProperty(context.Peek( ), context.Reader.Name, context.Reader.Value);
  }

  public void SetProperty(object o, string name, string val) {
    Type type = o.GetType( );
    PropertyInfo property = type.GetProperty(name);

    // Find an appropriate property to match the attribute name
    if (property.PropertyType.IsAssignableFrom(typeof(string))) {
      property.SetValue(o, val, null);
    } else if (property.PropertyType.IsSubclassOf(typeof(Enum))) {
      object ev = Enum.Parse(property.PropertyType, val, true);
      property.SetValue(o, ev, null);
    } else {
      MethodInfo m = property.PropertyType.GetMethod
          ("Parse", new Type[] { typeof(string) });
      object newval = m.Invoke(null /*static */, new object[] { val });
      property.SetValue(o, newval, null);
    }
  }
}
```

It too checks the node type, then goes through each of the attributes (e.g., Top or Left) to find their types, and sets the values that follow accordingly (on the last line). This Interpret method makes heavy use of reflection to find out the types of the object attributes.

Assuming the XML specification is in a file called *calc_winforms.xml*, the whole interpreter will be activated by one line:

```
Mirror m = new Mirror("calc_winforms.xml");
```

The full program is shown in the Appendix.

Efficiency

No discussion involving reflection would be complete without mention of efficiency. Any program that relies on reflection has efficiency overheads because for every operation it first has to determine the type of the objects on which it's working. Quantifying these costs for small programs is difficult; however, the overhead is analogous to that incurred in the implementation of the Visitor pattern presented earlier:

- Examining the type of the object using the is operator
- Moving through the classes using dynamic dispatch

Both of these defer object binding to runtime in order to increase flexibility.

Use

The Interpreter pattern is coded up from scratch wherever there is a simple grammar to parse and interpret. For more complex grammars, such as those that describe programming languages or .NET APIs, parsing tools can be employed to set up the object structure. The corresponding `Interpret` methods can still be successfully written from scratch. In the Mirrors example, the `System.Xml` API from .NET provides the parser. In compilers, there are special parser generator tools that construct a parse tree from a grammar.

Many domain-specific languages define their rules in terms of XML and rely on interpreters to activate them. For example, the Windows Vista operating system, in conjunction with Visual Studio, interprets XML for GUIs.

Use the Interpreter pattern when…
You have a grammar to be interpreted and:
• The grammar is not too large.
• Efficiency is not critical.
• Parsing tools are available.
• XML is an option for the specification.

Exercises

1. Program a simple calculator using the Interpreter pattern. To accommodate precedence between addition/subtraction and multiplication/division operations, set the objects involved in the latter operations lower in the object hierarchy.

2. Create the XML for a calculator GUI and run it through Mirrors.

Memento Pattern

Role

This pattern is used to capture an object's internal state and save it externally so that it can be restored later.

Illustration

Many computer games go on for a long time. Having a means to save a game's state so that it can be resumed at a later stage is very handy. It can also be useful to save what are known as "checkpoints" in a game so that it's possible to return to a previous checkpoint after a disastrous move. For example, here is a description of CilkChess, a chess program produced at MIT:

> Cilk jobs may survive machine crashes or network outages despite the fact that Cilk programs have been coded with no special provision for handling machine or network

failures. If a worker crashes, then other workers automatically redo any work that was lost in the crash. In the case of a more catastrophic failure, such as a power outage, a total network failure, or a crash of the file server, then all workers may crash. For this case, Cilk-NOW provides automatic checkpointing, so when service is restored, the Cilk job may be restarted with minimal lost work.

Some of the more humorous aspects of computer chess are summed up in the cartoon in Figure 10-7.[*]

Figure 10-7. Memento pattern illustration—computer chess

Design

As indicated in the preceding quote, the saving of state can be made independent of the object itself, and this is a key point of the Memento pattern. The UML for this pattern is shown in Figure 10-8.

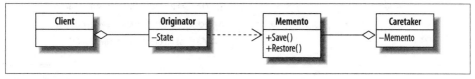

Figure 10-8. Memento pattern UML diagram

The Originator is the class that supports objects with state to be saved; it can decide how much state needs to be saved at any time. The Memento does the saving, and the Caretaker keeps track of the various stored states.

The Memento pattern is interesting because it has two interfaces:

- A wide interface to the Originator that enables it to access everything that needs to be saved or restored
- A narrow interface to the Caretaker that can keep and pass on memento references, but no more

---

[*] From S. Francis, H. Dugmore, and Rico, *www.madamandeve.co.za*, printed with permission.

The Memento class keeps the state of the Originator but does not allow other classes to access that state. It therefore preserves encapsulation boundaries, relieving the Originator of this responsibility.

In sum, the roles in the pattern are:

Originator
> A class that has state to be saved

Memento
> A class for objects representing the Originator's saved state

Caretaker
> A class that is a holder for the mementos

Client
> Keeps a copy of the originator

QUIZ

Match the Memento Pattern Players with the Chess Illustration

To test whether you understand the Memento pattern, cover the lefthand column of the table below and see if you can identify its players among the items from the illustrative example (Figure 10-7), as shown in the righthand column. Then check your answers against the lefthand column.

Originator	The chessboard with pieces on it
Memento	The program that saves the state of the board
Caretaker	A checkpoint of the state of the game
Client	Playing chess on the electronic chessboard

Implementation

The implementation of the Memento pattern relies on the .NET Serialization API, which we saw before when discussing the Prototype pattern. Thus, we'll move straight on to the theory code in Example 10-3. The program shows how strings can be saved out to mementos and then restored if the first character of the line is a *, as in *UNDO (line 131). Thus, mistakes in the data for the Originator can be corrected.

Example 10-3. Memento pattern theory code

```
1     using System;
2     using System.IO;
3     using System.Runtime.Serialization;
4     using System.Runtime.Serialization.Formatters.Binary;
5     using System.Collections.Generic;
```

Example 10-3. Memento pattern theory code (continued)

```
6      using System.Collections;
7
8       // Memento Pattern              Judith Bishop   Sept 2007
9       // Simple illustration with undo
10
11    class MementoPattern {
12
13      // Client
14      static void Main( ) {
15
16      // References to the mementos
17      Caretaker [] c = new Caretaker [10];
18      Originator originator = new Originator( );
19
20      int move = 0;
21      // Iterator for the moves
22      Simulator simulator = new Simulator( );
23
24      foreach (string command in simulator) {
25         // Check for undo
26         if (command[0]=='*' && move > 0)
27             originator.Restore(c[move-1].Memento);
28         else
29             originator.Operation(command);
30         move++;
31         c[move] = new Caretaker( );
32         c[move].Memento = originator.Save( );
33      }
34    }
35
36    // Originator
37    [Serializable( )]
38    class Originator {
39      List <string> state = new List <string> ( );
40
41      public void Operation (string s) {
42        state.Add(s);
43        foreach (string line in state)
44            Console.WriteLine(line);
45        Console.WriteLine("=======================");
46      }
47
48      // The reference to the memento is passed back to the client
49      public Memento SetMemento( ) {
50        Memento memento = new Memento( );
51        return memento.Save(state);
52      }
53
54      public void GetMemento(Memento memento) {
55        state = (List <string>) memento.Restore( );
56      }
57    }
58
```

Example 10-3. Memento pattern theory code (continued)

```
59     [Serializable( )]
60     // Serializes by deep copy to memory and back
61     class Memento {
62       MemoryStream stream = new MemoryStream( );
63       BinaryFormatter formatter = new BinaryFormatter( );
64
65       public Memento Save (object o) {
66          formatter.Serialize(stream, o);
67          return this;
68       }
69
70       public object Restore( ) {
71          stream.Seek(0, SeekOrigin.Begin);
72          object o = formatter.Deserialize(stream);
73          stream.Close( );
74          return o;
75       }
76     }
77
78     class Caretaker {
79       public Memento Memento {get; set;}
80     }
81
82     class Simulator : IEnumerable {
83
84       string [] lines = {
85          "The curfew tolls the knell of parting day",
86          "The lowing herd winds slowly o'er the lea",
87          "Uh hum uh hum",
88          "*UNDO",
89          "The plowman homeward plods his weary way",
90          "And leaves the world to darkness and to me."};
91
92       public IEnumerator GetEnumerator ( ) {
93         foreach( string element in lines )
94             yield return element;
95       }
96     }
97
98   }
99   /* Output
100  The curfew tolls the knell of parting day
101  ========================
102  The curfew tolls the knell of parting day
103  The lowing herd winds slowly o'er the lea
104  ========================
105  The curfew tolls the knell of parting day
106  The lowing herd winds slowly o'er the lea
107  Uh hum uh hum
108  ========================
109  The curfew tolls the knell of parting day
110  The lowing herd winds slowly o'er the lea
111  The plowman homeward plods his weary way
112  ========================
```

Example 10-3. Memento pattern theory code (continued)

```
113    The curfew tolls the knell of parting day
114    The lowing herd winds slowly o'er the lea
115    The plowman homeward plods his weary way
116    And leaves the world to darkness and to me.
117    ========================
118    */
```

The Memento class uses the .NET memory streams and binary formatters to copy data to memory and get it back again. If the data is very large, it could be copied to disk or to the Internet instead.

Example: TicTacToe

Creating an example of chess game or a live Internet computer game would be a bit of a challenge in a book like this, so we'll revert to TicTacToe, which reveals many of the same issues. The game is played on a board between two players. In this example, we'll consider a TicTacToe tutor that pits a human player against the computer. The player learns the better strategies by trial and error and therefore should be able to go back and try different moves if he/she is not winning.

This is an ideal situation for the Memento pattern. The Originator is the board, and its state is saved at every turn. The Caretaker keeps an array of Mementos so that it can roll back more than one turn. See Example 10-4. Its output shows that after a very bad move (line 160), the player rolled back two Mementos and continued with a better strategy.

Example 10-4. Memento pattern example code—TicTacToe

```
1      using System;
2      using System.IO;
3      using System.Runtime.Serialization;
4      using System.Runtime.Serialization.Formatters.Binary;
5      using System.Collections;
6
7        // Memento Pattern              Judith Bishop   Sept 2007
8        // Simulates TicTacToe, where the game can roll back any
9        // specified number of moves. Mementos are kept at each move.
10
11       class MementoPattern {
12
13         // Client
14         static void Main( ) {
15           Console.WriteLine("Let's practice TicTacToe");
16           Console.WriteLine("Commands are:\n1-9 for a position\n"+
17               "U-n where n is the number of moves to undo"+
18               "\nQ to end");
19           Game game = new Game( );
20
21           // References to the mementos
22           Caretaker [] c = new Caretaker [10];
23
```

Example 10-4. Memento pattern example code—TicTacToe (continued)

```
24          game.DisplayBoard( );
25          int move = 1;
26          // Iterator for the moves
27          Simulator simulator = new Simulator( );
28
29          foreach (string command in simulator) {
30            Console.Write("Move "+move+" for "+game.Player+": "+command);
31            if (command[0]=='Q') break;
32
33            // Save at the start of each move
34            c[move] = new Caretaker( );
35            c[move].Memento = game.Save( );
36
37            // Check for undo
38            if (command[0]=='U') {
39              int back = Int32.Parse(command.Substring(2,1));
40              if (move-back >0)
41                game.Restore(c[move-back].Memento);
42              else
43                Console.WriteLine("Too many moves back");
44              move = move - back - 1;
45            }
46            // Otherwise play
47            else
48              game.Play(Int32.Parse(command.Substring(0,1)));
49
50          // Update board and move number
51          game.DisplayBoard( );
52          move++;
53        }
54      Console.WriteLine("Thanks for playing");
55    }
56
57    // Originator
58    [Serializable( )]
59    class Game {
60      // Nine spaces
61      char [] board = {'X','1','2','3','4','5','6','7','8','9'};
62      public char Player {get; set;}
63
64      public Game ( ) {
65        Player = 'X';
66      }
67
68      public void Play (int pos) {
69        board[pos] = Player;
70        if (Player == 'X') Player = 'O'; else Player = 'X';
71        // Preserve player
72        board[0] = Player;
73      }
74
75      // The reference to the memento is passed back to the client
76      public Memento Save( ) {
```

Example 10-4. Memento pattern example code—TicTacToe (continued)

```
77          Memento memento = new Memento( );
78          return memento.Save(board);
79       }
80
81       public void Restore(Memento memento) {
82          board = (char []) memento.Restore( );
83          Player = board[0];
84       }
85
86       public void DisplayBoard( ) {
87          Console.WriteLine( );
88          for (int i = 1; i<=9; i+=3) {
89             Console.WriteLine(board[i]+" | "+board[i+1]+" | "+board[i+2]);
90             if (i<6) Console.WriteLine("---------");
91          }
92       }
93    }
94
95    [Serializable( )]
96    // Serializes by deep copy to memory and back
97    class Memento {
98       MemoryStream stream = new MemoryStream( );
99       BinaryFormatter formatter = new BinaryFormatter( );
100
101      public Memento Save (object o) {
102         formatter.Serialize(stream, o);
103         return this;
104      }
105
106      public object Restore( ) {
107         stream.Seek(0, SeekOrigin.Begin);
108         object o = formatter.Deserialize(stream);
109         stream.Close( );
110         return o;
111      }
112   }
113
114   class Caretaker {
115      public Memento Memento {get; set;}
116   }
117
118   class Simulator : IEnumerable {
119
120      string [] moves = {"5","3","1","6","9","U-2","9","6","4","2","7","8","Q"};
121
122      public IEnumerator GetEnumerator ( ) {
123         foreach( string element in moves )
124             yield return element;
125      }
126   }
127
128   }
```

Example 10-4. Memento pattern example code—TicTacToe (continued)

```
129   /* Output
130   Let's practice TicTacToe
131   Commands are: 1-9 for a position U-n where n is the number of moves to undo Q to end
132
133
134   1 | 2 | 3
135   ---------
136   4 | 5 | 6
137   ---------
138   7 | 8 | 9
139   Move 1 for X: 5
140   1 | 2 | 3
141   ---------
142   4 | X | 6
143   ---------
144 7 | 8 | 9
145   Move 2 for O: 3
146   1 | 2 | 0
147   ---------
148   4 | X | 6
149   ---------
150   7 | 8 | 9
151   Move 3 for X: 1
152   X | 2 | 0
153   ---------
154   4 | X | 6
155   ---------
156   7 | 8 | 9
157   Move 4 for O: 6
158   X | 2 | 0
159   ---------
160   4 | X | 0
161   ---------
162   7 | 8 | 9
163   Move 5 for X: 9
164   X | 2 | 0
165   ---------
166   4 | X | 0
167   ---------
168   7 | 8 | X
169   Move 6 for O: U-2
170   X | 2 | 0
171   ---------
172   4 | X | 6
173   ---------
174   7 | 8 | 9
175   Move 4 for O: 9
176   X | 2 | 0
177   ---------
178   4 | X | 6
179   ---------
180   7 | 8 | 0
```

Example 10-4. Memento pattern example code—TicTacToe (continued)

```
181    Move 5 for X: 6
182    X | 2 | 0
183    ---------
184    4 | X | X
185    ---------
186    7 | 8 | 0
187    Move 6 for 0: 4
188    X | 2 | 0
189    ---------
190    0 | X | X
191    ---------
192    7 | 8 | 0
193    Move 7 for X: 2
194    X | X | 0
195    ---------
196    0 | X | X
197    ---------
198    7 | 8 | 0
199    Move 8 for 0: 7
200    X | X | 0
201    ---------
202    0 | X | X
203    ---------
204    0 | 8 | 0
205    Move 9 for X: 8
206    X | X | 0
207    ---------
208    0 | X | X
209    ---------
210    0 | X | 0
211    Move 10 for 0: Q
212    Thanks for playing
213    */
```

Use

The Memento pattern is used extensively in scientific computing to save the state of long-running computations; in computer games to save the state of play over a matter of hours or days; and in graphics toolkits to preserve the state of a display while objects are being moved around.

Use the Memento pattern when...

- An object's state must be saved to be restored later, *and*
- It is undesirable to expose the state directly.

Exercise

1. Consider how the Memento pattern can be integrated into the Iterator pattern to preserve the state of an iteration and restore it at any time.

Pattern Comparison

Though seemingly dissimilar, there are several ways in which we can compare these three patterns.

Reusability

All three patterns aim to relieve the developer of repeatedly implementing common code. Once Visitors have been set up, they can be used with many different kinds of object structures without change. The success rate for reusability will depend on how much of the actual state the Visitor needs to be aware of. In our examples, the Visitors were dependent only on the type of the elements, and not on their contents, so a high degree of visitor reusability was obtained between the theory example and the course example. The Interpreter pattern was specifically designed to make inputting structures data driven, by means of a Parse method. In the Memento pattern, the Caretaker and Memento classes are data-independent, and only the Originator needs to change for different circumstances.

Working with structures

All the patterns are intended to work with structures. The Memento moves the structure around as a whole, relying on serialization to do the traversing, whereas Visitor and Interpreter require the developer to write the traversing code. These patterns complement each other in that the traversing code is part of the Visitor pattern, whereas getting the data into an object structure in the first place is part of the Interpreter pattern.

Objects as arguments

The Visitor and Memento pattern pass objects around as part of their infrastructure. In the case of the Visitor, the Element object achieves polymorphism in the double-dispatch implementation. In the Memento pattern, the Memento object defined in the Caretaker is the reference to the state that is being saved or restored. In a smaller way, the Interpreter pattern relies on a Context which keeps the evolving state of the input that is being interpreted to output.

This concludes the discussion of the behavioral patterns as well as the set of classic patterns as a whole. In Chapter 11, I summarize all the patterns and make some concluding remarks.

The Future of Design Patterns

This book has introduced and described design patterns, along with the advanced features of C# 3.0, a modern programming language. In many cases, we have found that the language offers substantial assistance in the implementation of the pattern. In this final chapter, we look back at the patterns and what features they needed, and then look forward to what researchers are grappling with for the next iteration of languages.

Summary of Patterns

It is time to collect together all the patterns along with the language features that were used to implement them in this book. It is worth reiterating that in some cases these implementations differ substantially from the traditional forms found with Java, C++, and older C# versions. Thus, in Table 11-1 interpret the Language features column as meaning "modern, good and desirable" rather than "fixed, standard and only." This table is a useful companion to all the theory code programs, which can be found grouped on my web site for the book (*http://patterns.cs.up.ac.za*). In the second column, the features in italics were used in an alternative implementation or in the example, but not in the primary theory code. Most features are written in the plural, but there may be only one instance of them, depending on the size of the system the pattern is being applied to.

The table is ordered by features used so that you can get a feel for which are the "easy" patterns to implement in terms of language knowledge; however, do not confuse this criterion with the pattern itself being easy. My personal experience is that the Adapter and Visitor patterns—which appear in the top half of the table—were two of the most challenging to implement. The difficulties centered around the interplay of types, as both of these are aimed at decoupling types. In a strictly type checked language, such as C#, considerable care has to be taken to get the parameters and object instances to match up correctly, even without considering generics.

Table 11-1. Summary of patterns and language features

Pattern	Language features	Optional and in the examples
Abstract Factory	interfaces	*generic, generic constraints*
Bridge	interfaces	*extension methods*
Builder	interfaces	*generic, generic constraints*
Decorator	interfaces	
Factory Method	interfaces	
Adapter	interfaces, inheritance,	*delegates, anonymous functions, threads, events*
Proxy	interfaces, private	*collections*
State	interfaces, selection statements	
Strategy	interfaces, selection statements	*generics, nullable types*
Interpreter	recursion, selection statements	
Visitor	interfaces, recursion	*reflection*
Façade	namespaces	
Singleton	private, nested classes, static property	
Template Method	method overriding	
Command	delegates	
Mediator	delegates	*threads*
Observer	interfaces, delegates, events	*threads*
Flyweight	interfaces, structs, collections, indexers	*implicit typing, initializers, anonymous types*
Memento	serialization, collections, indexers	
Prototype	cloning, serialization, collections, indexers	
Chain of Responsibility	generics, exceptions	*enumerated types, initializers*
Composite	interfaces, collections, generics, properties	
Iterator	enumerators, foreach, query expressions (Linq)	*generics, recursion*

Another way of looking at patterns is to examine which other patterns they interact with or support. Although somewhat subjective, Table 11-2 gives some idea of the pattern groupings from this angle.

Table 11-2. Pattern interactions

Pattern	Interacts with or supports
Abstract Factory	Bridge, Factory Method, Prototype, Singleton
Adapter	
Bridge	Abstract Factory
Builder	Composite
Chain of Responsibility	Composite

Table 11-2. Pattern interactions (continued)

Pattern	Interacts with or supports
Command	Memento, Composite
Composite	Builder, Decorator, Flyweight, Interpreter, Visitor, Chain of Responsibility, Command, Iterator
Decorator	Composite, Strategy
Façade	Singleton
Factory Method	Abstract Factory, Template Method
Flyweight	Composite, Interpreter, Strategy, State
Interpreter	Composite, Flyweight, Visitor
Iterator	Visitor, Memento, Composite
Mediator	Observer
Memento	Iterator, Command
Observer	Mediator
Prototype	Abstract Factory
Proxy	
Singleton	Façade, Abstract Factory
State	Flyweight
Strategy	Decorator, Flyweight, Template Method
Template Method	Factory Method, Strategy
Visitor	Iterator, Composite, Interpreter

It is not surprising that the patterns with the most interactions are those that create and manage complex structures: Composite, Flyweight, and Abstract Factory. Many of the other patterns rely on these when they have more than a single type to deal with. Adapter and Proxy are not listed as having any interplays, but recall that they were also two of the patterns that came in multiple designs that were related to each other.

A feature of this book has been the examples that illustrate each and every pattern. In several cases, the examples have been carried over several patterns, illustrating the interplays described above. In this way, I was able to strike a balance between variety and continuity. In many of the exercises, further adaptations of the examples using other patterns are suggested. Specifically, the Singleton pattern has not been used much in the book, and it would be a good one to try out with some of the existing programs. For ease of reference, Table 11-3 lists the examples and the patterns they are used in.

Table 11-3. Examples illustrating patterns

Example	
Blogs	Observer
Chat Room	Mediator

Table 11-3. Examples illustrating patterns (continued)

Example	
Course Rules	Visitor, Interpreter
Family Tree	Iterator
Gucci and Poochy (manufacturing)	Abstract Factory, Builder
Menu system	Command
Mirrors	Interpreter
Photo decorator, Photo Library, Photo Groups, Photo sets	Decorator, Composite, Flyweight, Façade, Prototype, Adapter
RCP Game, Tic-Tac-Toe game	State, Memento
Seabird	Adapter
Sorting animator	Strategy, Template Method
Sourcing avocados	Factory Method
SpaceBook, Openbook, Coolbook	Proxy, Bridge, Adapter
Trusty Bank	Chain of Responsibility

Exercises

Summarizing and tabulating are good ways to come to grips with the pattern list. Here are two more to try:

1. Create a table of patterns with a one sentence description of their roles.
2. Create a table of patterns listing at most four major players (no duplicates and ignoring Client).

A Future for Design Patterns

I'll conclude this book with some observations about design patterns and where they are heading.* As we have seen, a design pattern is a formal mechanism of documenting solutions to reoccurring software design problems. Christopher Alexander first introduced the concept of design patterns in civil architecture in 1977; they were later adapted to software design. The academic and commercial interest in software design patterns has grown dramatically over the last few years, and design patterns have been cataloged by a number of researchers.

Design patterns are mostly seen as solutions to software design issues. They are, of course, not the only solution to software design, and they should not be used to the exclusion of all others. Component-based design, software architecture, aspect-oriented programming, and refactoring also have a place. Viewed against the larger

---

* Thanks to Alastair von Leeuwen for researching this topic.

backdrop of software engineering, design patterns can be seen to present some of their own challenges:

Traceability

> The traceability of a design pattern is hard to maintain when programming languages offer poor support for the underlying patterns. The physical implementation of a design pattern in a programming language can be scattered across a number of classes and thus hard to trace. In this respect, the implementations in this book have made considerable strides by using some of the more compact features of C#, such as delegates and query expressions.

Reusability

> Design patterns are used and reused in the design of a software system, but with little or no language support, developers must implement the patterns again and again in a physical programming language. A design pattern does not give a developer the same benefits that a component does, which can encapsulate behavior and be reused as is.

Writability

> Some design patterns have several methods with trivial behavior. Without good programming tools, it can be tedious to write all this code and maintain it. Once again, more compact and powerful language features can alleviate the programmer's burden.

Maintainability

> Using multiple patterns can lead to a large cluster of mutually dependent classes. Mutually dependent classes can lead to maintainability problems when implemented in a traditional object-oriented programming language.

Current research is investigating how to transform design patterns into reusable artifacts so that developers won't have to implement the same patterns over and over. In 1997, Bertrand Meyer defined reusability as "the ability of software elements to serve for the construction of many different applications." In the context of design patterns, a specific language feature, a language library, or a component could solve the pattern implementation reusability problem. Meyer goes on to state that a design pattern "is *componentizable* if it is possible to produce a reusable component, which provides all the functions of the pattern" and that "[a] successful pattern cannot just be a book description: it must be a software component, or a set of components." This work is ongoing.

We have also seen in the course of this book that languages are continually evolving. The Iterator pattern is now fully supported in C# 3.0, and there are good ideas for a Singleton pattern. Others may follow, and pattern and language integration is a fruitful area for research.

Concluding Remarks

This book has given you a tour through 23 design patterns (some with extra variations), 25 C# features, 20 examples, and 25 theory codes. Now, you are ready to reap the benefits of design patterns in C# 3.0. Design patterns offer a number of benefits as they do the following:

- Promote design reuse
- Form a common vocabulary and improve communication within and across software development teams
- Improve documentation
- Help developers restructure a system, regardless of whether it used them up front
- Explicitly capture knowledge that experienced developers already understand implicitly
- Facilitate training of new developers
- Transcend "programming-language-centric" viewpoints
- Exploit and bring out the best in programming languages

You may not have encountered these design benefits in your career yet, except of course the last one, which is the subject of this book. Now, armed with the knowledge and skills here, you will be able to apply each design pattern in the right place and at the right time, knowing that it will be programmed correctly.

Appendix

Pluggable Adapter Pattern Example Code—CoolBook

See the following code for an example of the Pluggable Adapter Pattern:

```
using System;
using System.Collections.Generic;
using System.Windows.Forms;
using System.Drawing;
using System.Threading;

  // Adapter Pattern Example              Judith Bishop  Aug 2007
  // Sets up a CoolBook
  // This is D-J's as changed for the book
  class AdapterPattern {

  // class SpaceBookSystem {

  public delegate void InputEventHandler(object sender, EventArgs e, string s);

  // Adapter
  public class MyCoolBook : MyOpenBook {
    static SortedList<string, MyCoolBook> community =
        new SortedList<string, MyCoolBook>(100);
    Interact visuals;

    public MyCoolBook(string name) : base(name) {
      // Create interact on the relevant thread, and start it!
      new Thread(delegate( ) {
        visuals = new Interact("CoolBook Beta");
        visuals.InputEvent += new InputEventHandler(OnInput);
        visuals.FormClosed += new FormClosedEventHandler(OnFormClosed);
        Application.Run(visuals);
      }).Start( );
      community[name] = this;
```

```
  while (visuals == null) {
    Application.DoEvents();
    Thread.Sleep(100);
  }

  Add("Welcome to CoolBook " + Name);
}

private void OnFormClosed(object sender, FormClosedEventArgs e) {
  community.Remove(Name);
}

private void OnInput(object sender, EventArgs e, string s) {
  Add("\r\n");
  Add(s, "Poked you");
}

public new void Poke(string who) {
  Add("\r\n");
  if (community.ContainsKey(who))
      community[who].Add(Name, "Poked you");
  else
      Add("Friend " + who + " is not part of the community");
}

public new void Add(string message) {
  visuals.Output(message);
}

public new void Add(string friend, string message) {
  if (community.ContainsKey(friend))
      community[friend].Add(Name + " : " + message);
  else
      Add("Friend " + friend + " is not part of the community");
}
}

// New implementation (Adaptee)
public class Interact : Form {
  public TextBox Wall { get; set; }
  public Button Poke { get; set; }

  public Interact() { }

  public Interact(string title) {
    Control.CheckForIllegalCrossThreadCalls = true;
    Poke = new Button();
    Poke.Text = "Poke";
    this.Controls.Add(Poke);
    Poke.Click += new EventHandler(Input);
    Wall = new TextBox();
    Wall.Multiline = true;
    Wall.Location = new Point(0, 30);
    Wall.Width = 300;
```

```
        Wall.Height = 200;
        Wall.AcceptsReturn = true;
        this.Text = title;
        this.Controls.Add(Wall);
    }

    public event InputEventHandler InputEvent;

    public void Input(object source, EventArgs e) {
        string who = Wall.SelectedText;
        if (InputEvent != null)
            InputEvent(this, EventArgs.Empty, who);
    }

    public void Output(string message) {
        if (this.InvokeRequired)
            this.Invoke((MethodInvoker)delegate() { Output(message); });
        else {
            Wall.AppendText(message + "\r\n");
            this.Show();
        }
    }

    protected override void OnFormClosed(FormClosedEventArgs e) {
        // Remove the interact and CoolBook from the community here!
        base.OnFormClosed(e);
    }
}

// The RealSubject (Proxy pattern)
// CANNOT CHANGE
public class SpaceBook {
    static SortedList<string, SpaceBook> community =
        new SortedList<string, SpaceBook>(100);
    string pages;
    string name;
    string gap = "\n\t\t\t\t";

    static public bool Unique(string name) {
        return community.ContainsKey(name);
    }

    internal SpaceBook(string n) {
        name = n;
        community[n] = this;
    }

    internal string Add(string s) {
        pages += gap + s;
        return gap + "======== " + name + "'s SpaceBook =========\n" +
            pages +
            gap + "\n=================================";
    }
}
```

```
    internal string Add(string friend, string message) {
      return community[friend].Add(message);
    }

    internal void Poke(string who, string friend) {
      community[who].pages += gap + friend + " poked you";
    }
  }

  // Target (Adapter pattern)
  // CANNOT CHANGE
  public class MyOpenBook {

    SpaceBook myOpenBook;
    public string Name { get; set; }
    public static int Users { get; set; }

    public MyOpenBook(string n) {
      Name = n;
      Users++;
      myOpenBook = new SpaceBook(Name + "-" + Users);
    }

    public void Add(string message) {
      Console.WriteLine(myOpenBook.Add(message));
    }

    public void Add(string friend, string message) {
      Console.WriteLine(myOpenBook.Add(friend, Name + " : " + message));
    }

    public void Poke(string who) {
      myOpenBook.Poke(who, Name);
    }

    public void SuperPoke(string who, string what) {
      myOpenBook.Add(who, what + " you");
    }
  }

  // }
  // The Client

  static void Main() {

    MyCoolBook judith = new MyCoolBook("Judith");
    judith.Add("Hello world");

    MyCoolBook tom = new MyCoolBook("Tom");
    tom.Poke("Judith");
    tom.Add("Hey, We are on CoolBook");
    judith.Poke("Tom");
    Console.ReadLine();
  }
}
```

Prototype Pattern Example Code—Photo Archive

See the following code for an example of the Prototype Pattern:

```
Here is an
using System;
using System.Collections.Generic;
using System.IO;
using PrototypePattern;

namespace CompositePattern {

    // The Composite Pattern namespace
    // including the Share operations

  // The Interface
  public interface IComponent <T> {
    void Add(IComponent <T> c);
    IComponent <T> Remove(T s);
    string Display(int depth);
    IComponent <T> Find(T s);
    IComponent <T> Share (T s,IComponent <T> home);
    string Name {get; set;}
  }

    // The Composite
    [Serializable()]
    public class Composite <T> : IPrototype <IComponent <T>>, IComponent  <T> {
      List  <IComponent <T>> list;
      public string Name {get; set;}

      public Composite (string name)  {
        Name = name;
        list = new List <IComponent <T>> ();
      }

      public void Add(IComponent  <T> c) {
        list.Add(c);
      }

      // Finds the item from a particular point in the structure
      // and returns the composite from which it was removed
      // If not found, return the point as given
      public IComponent <T> Remove(T s) {
        holder = this;
        IComponent <T> p = holder.Find(s);
        if (holder!=null) {
          (holder as Composite<T>).list.Remove(p);
          return holder;
        }
        else
          return this;
      }

      IComponent <T> holder=null;
```

```csharp
    // Recursively looks for an item
    // Returns its reference or else null
    public IComponent <T>  Find (T s) {
      holder = this;
      if (Name.Equals(s)) return this;
      IComponent <T> found=null;
      foreach (IComponent <T> c in list)  {
        found = c.Find(s);
        if (found!=null)
          break;
      }
      return found;
    }

    public IComponent <T> Share (T set, IComponent <T> toHere) {
      IPrototype <IComponent <T>> prototype =
          this.Find(set) as IPrototype <IComponent <T>>;
      IComponent <T> copy = prototype.DeepCopy() as IComponent<T>;
      toHere.Add(copy);
      return toHere;
    }

    // Displays items in a format indicating their level in the composite structure
    public string Display(int depth) {
      String s = new String('-', depth) + "Set "+ Name +  " length :" + list.Count +
"\n";
      foreach (IComponent <T> component in list)
        s += component.Display(depth + 2);

    }
  }

  // The Component
  [Serializable( )]
  public class Component <T> : IPrototype <IComponent<T>>, IComponent <T> {
    public string Name {get; set;}
    public Component (string name)  {
      Name = name;
    }

    public void Add(IComponent <T> c) {
      Console.WriteLine("Cannot add to an item");
    }

    public IComponent <T>  Remove(T s) {
      Console.WriteLine("Cannot remove directly");
      return this;
    }

    public string Display(int depth) {
      return new String('-', depth) + Name+"\n";
    }
```

```
    public IComponent <T>  Find (T s) {
      if (s.Equals(Name)) return this;
      else
        return null;
    }

    public IComponent <T> Share (T set, IComponent  <T>toHere) {
      IPrototype <IComponent <T>> prototype =
          this.Find(set) as IPrototype <IComponent <T>>;
      IComponent <T> copy = prototype.Clone( ) as IComponent<T>;
      toHere.Add(copy);
      return toHere;
    }
  }
}


using System;
using System.Collections.Generic;
using System.IO;
using System.Runtime.Serialization;
using System.Runtime.Serialization.Formatters.Binary;
using CompositePattern;
using PrototypePattern;

// Prototype Pattern Pattern    August 2007
// Makes use of the Photo Library examples
// Shares (i.e. deep copies) parts of the hierarchy, then makes changes

  // The Client
  class prototypePatternExample {

    static void Main ( ) {
      IComponent <string> album = new Composite<string> ("Album");
      IComponent <string> point = album;
      IComponent <string> archive = new Composite<string> ("Archive");
      string [] s;
      string command, parameter;
      // Create and manipulate a structure
      StreamReader instream = new StreamReader("prototype.dat");
      do {
        string t= instream.ReadLine( );
        Console.WriteLine("\t\t\t\t"+t);
        s = t.Split( );
        command = s[0];
        if (s.Length>1) parameter = s[1]; else parameter = null;
        switch (command) {
        case "AddSet" :
           IComponent <string> c = new Composite <string> (parameter);
          point.Add(c);
          point = c;
          break;
```

```
             case "AddPhoto" :
                point.Add(new Component <string> (parameter));
              break;
             case "Remove" :
                point = point.Remove(parameter);
              break;
             case "Find" :
                point = album.Find(parameter);
                break;
             case "Display" :
                if (parameter==null)
                 Console.WriteLine(album.Display(0));
                else
                 Console.WriteLine(archive.Display(0));
               break;
             case "Archive" :
                archive = point.Share(parameter,archive); break;
             case "Retrieve" :
                point = archive.Share(parameter,album); break;
             case "Quit" :
                break;
             }
        } while (!command.Equals("Quit"));
      }
    }
 }
/*Output
  AddSet Home
         AddPhoto Dinner.jpg
         AddSet Pets
         AddPhoto Dog.jpg
         AddPhoto Cat.jpg
         Find Album
         AddSet Garden
         AddPhoto Spring.jpg
         AddPhoto Summer.jpg
         AddPhoto Flowers.jpg
         AddPhoto Trees.jpg
         Display
Set Album length :2
--Set Home length :2
----Dinner.jpg
----Set Pets length :2
------Dog.jpg
------Cat.jpg
--Set Garden length :4
----Spring.jpg
----Summer.jpg
----Flowers.jpg
----Trees.jpg

         Find Pets
         Archive Pets
         Display Archive
Set Archive length :1
```

```
--Set Pets length :2
----Dog.jpg
----Cat.jpg

        Find Album
        Remove Home
        Find Album
        Remove Garden
        Display
Set Album length :0

        Retrieve Pets
        Display
Set Album length :1
--Set Pets length :2
----Dog.jpg
----Cat.jpg

        Quit
*/
```

Iterator Pattern Example Code—Family Tree

See the following code for an example of the Iterator Pattern:

```
using System;
using System.Collections;
using System.Collections.Generic;
using System.Linq;

  class Person {
    public Person( ) {}
    public string Name {get; set;}
    public int Birth {get; set;}

    public Person (string name, int birth) {
      Name = name;
      Birth = birth;
    }

    public override string ToString ( ) {
      return ("["+Name+", "+Birth+"]");
    }
  }

  class Node <T> {
    public Node ( ) {}
    public Node <T> Left{get; set;}
    public Node <T> Right {get; set;}
    public T Data {get; set;}
```

```
   public Node (T d, Node <T> left, Node <T> right) {
     Data = d;
     Left = left;
     Right = right;
   }
}

// T is the data type. The Node type is built-in.
class Tree <T> {
  Node <T> root;
  public Tree( ) {}
  public Tree (Node <T> head) {
    root = head;
  }

  public IEnumerable <T> Preorder {
    get {return ScanPreorder (root);}
  }

  // Enumerator with Filter
  public IEnumerable <T> Where (Func <T, bool> filter) {
    foreach (T p in ScanPreorder(root))
        if (filter(p)==true)
            yield return p;
  }

  // Enumerator with T as Person
  private IEnumerable <T> ScanPreorder (Node <T> root) {
    yield return root.Data;
    if (root.Left !=null)
        foreach (T p in ScanPreorder (root.Left))
            yield return p;
    if (root.Right !=null)
        foreach (T p in ScanPreorder (root.Right))
            yield return p;
  }
}

class IteratorPattern {

  // Iterator Pattern for a Tree         Judith Bishop  Sept 2007
  // Shows two enumerators using links and recursion

  static void Main( ) {

    var family = new Tree <Person> (new Node <Person>
        (new Person ("Tom", 1950),
            new Node <Person> (new Person ("Peter", 1976),
                new Node <Person>
                    (new Person ("Sarah", 2000), null,
                new Node <Person>
                    (new Person ("James", 2002), null,
                     null) // no more siblings James
                ),
```

```
            new Node <Person>
                (new Person ("Robert", 1978), null,
            new Node <Person>
                (new Person ("Mark", 1980),
                new Node <Person>
                    (new Person ("Carrie", 2005), null, null),
                    null) // no more siblings Mark
            )),
        null) // no siblings Tom
    );

    Console.WriteLine("Full family");
    foreach (Person p in family.Preorder)
        Console.Write(p+"  ");
    Console.WriteLine("\n");

    // Older syntax
    var selection = family.
        Where(p=> p.Birth > 1980);

    // New syntax
    selection = from p in family
        where p.Birth > 1980
        orderby p.Name
        select p;

    Console.WriteLine("Born after 1980 in alpha order");
    foreach (Person p in selection)
        Console.Write(p+"   ");
    Console.WriteLine("\n");
  }

}
```

Observer Pattern Example Code—Blogs

See the following code for an example of the Observer Pattern:

```
using System;
using System.Collections.Generic;
using System.Collections;
using System.Threading;
using System.Windows.Forms;
using System.Drawing;

  class ObserverPattern {

    // Observer Pattern                    Judith Bishop  Sept 2007
    // Demonstrates blog updates. Observers can subscribe and unsubscribe
    // online through a GUI.
```

```csharp
// State type
public class Blogs {
  public string Name {get; set;}
  public string Topic {get; set;}

  public Blogs (string name, string topic) {
    Name = name;
    Topic = topic;
  }
}

public delegate void Callback (Blogs blog);

// The Subject runs in a thread and changes its state
// independently by calling the Iterator
// At each change, it notifies its Observers
// The Callbacks are in a collection based on blogger name

class Subject {
  Dictionary <string,Callback> Notify = new Dictionary <string,Callback> ();
  Simulator simulator = new Simulator();
  const int speed = 4000;

  public void Go() {
    new Thread(new ThreadStart(Run)).Start();
  }

  void Run () {
    foreach (Blogs blog in simulator) {
      Register(blog.Name); // if necessary
      Notify[blog.Name](blog); // publish changes
      Thread.Sleep(speed); // milliseconds
    }
  }

  // Adds to the blogger list if unknown
  void Register (string blogger) {
    if (!Notify.ContainsKey(blogger)) {
      Notify[blogger] = delegate {};
    }
  }

  public void Attach(string blogger, Callback Update) {
    Register(blogger);
    Notify[blogger] += Update;
  }

  public void Detach(string blogger, Callback Update) {
    // Possible problem here
    Notify[blogger] -= Update;
  }
}

class Interact : Form {
  public TextBox wall ;
```

```csharp
  public Button subscribeButton, unsubscribeButton ;
  public TextBox messageBox;
  string name;

  public Interact(string name, EventHandler Input) {

    Control.CheckForIllegalCrossThreadCalls = true;
    // wall must be first!
    this.name = name;
    wall = new TextBox( );
    wall.Multiline = true;
    wall.Location = new Point(0, 30);
    wall.Width = 300;
    wall.Height = 200;
    wall.AcceptsReturn = true;
    wall.Dock = DockStyle.Fill;
    this.Text = name;
    this.Controls.Add(wall);

    // Panel must be second
    Panel p = new Panel( );
    messageBox = new TextBox( );
    messageBox.Width = 120;
    p.Controls.Add(messageBox);
    subscribeButton = new Button( );
    subscribeButton.Left = messageBox.Width;
    subscribeButton.Text = "Subscribe";
    subscribeButton.Click += new EventHandler(Input);
    p.Controls.Add(subscribeButton);
    unsubscribeButton = new Button( );
    unsubscribeButton.Left = messageBox.Width+subscribeButton.Width;
    unsubscribeButton.Text = "Unsubscribe";
    unsubscribeButton.Click += new EventHandler(Input);
    p.Controls.Add(unsubscribeButton);

    p.Height = subscribeButton.Height;
    p.Height = unsubscribeButton.Height;
    p.Dock = DockStyle.Top;
    this.Controls.Add(p);
  }

  public void Output(string message) {
    if (this.InvokeRequired)
        this.Invoke((MethodInvoker)delegate( ) { Output(message); });
    else {
        wall.AppendText(message + "\r\n");
        this.Show( );
    }
  }
}
}

// Useful if more observer types
interface IObserver {
  void Update(Blogs state);
}
```

```
class Observer : IObserver {
  string name;
  Subject blogs;
  Interact visuals;

  public Observer (Subject subject, string name) {
    this.blogs = subject;
    this.name = name;
    visuals = new Interact(name,Input);
    new Thread((ParameterizedThreadStart) delegate(object o) {
      Application.Run(visuals);
    }).Start(this);

    // Wait to load the GUI
    while (visuals == null || !visuals.IsHandleCreated) {
      Application.DoEvents();
      Thread.Sleep(100);
    }
    blogs.Attach("Jim",Update);
    blogs.Attach("Eric",Update);
    blogs.Attach("Judith",Update);
  }

  public void Input(object source, EventArgs e) {
    // Subscribe to the specified blogger
    if (source == visuals.subscribeButton) {
      blogs.Attach(visuals.messageBox.Text, Update);
      visuals.wall.AppendText("Subscribed to "+visuals.messageBox.Text+"\r\n");
    } else
    // Unsubscribe from the blogger
    if (source == visuals.unsubscribeButton) {
      blogs.Detach(visuals.messageBox.Text, Update);
      visuals.wall.AppendText("Unsubscribed from
          "+visuals.messageBox.Text+"\r\n");
    }
  }

  public void Update(Blogs blog) {
    visuals.Output("Blog from "+blog.Name+" on "+blog.Topic);
  }
}

// Iterator to supply the data
class Simulator : IEnumerable {

  Blogs [] bloggers = {new Blogs ("Jim","UML diagrams"),
      new Blogs("Eric","Iterators"),
      new Blogs("Eric","Extension Methods"),
      new Blogs("Judith","Delegates"),
      new Blogs("Eric","Type inference"),
      new Blogs("Jim","Threads"),
      new Blogs("Eric","Lamda expressions"),
      new Blogs("Judith","Anonymous properties"),
      new Blogs("Eric","Generic delegates"),
      new Blogs("Jim","Efficiency")};
```

```
    public IEnumerator GetEnumerator () {
      foreach( Blogs blog in bloggers )
          yield return blog;
    }
  }

  static void Main () {
    Subject subject = new Subject();
    Observer Observer = new Observer(subject,"Thabo");
    Observer observer2 = new Observer(subject,"Ellen");
    subject.Go();
  }

}
```

Visitor Pattern Theory Code—Reflection

See the following code for an example of the Visitor Pattern:

```
using System;
using System.Reflection;
using ObjectStructure;

  // Visitor Pattern - Example    Judith Bishop October 2007
  // Sets up an object structure and visits it
  // in two ways - for counting using reflection

namespace ObjectStructure {

  class Element {
    public Element Next {get; set;}
    public Element Part {get; set;}
    public Element () {}
    public Element (Element next) {
      Next = next;
    }
  }

  class ElementWithLink : Element {
    public ElementWithLink (Element part, Element next) {
      Next = next;
      Part = part;
    }
  }
}

  abstract class IVisitor {
    public void ReflectiveVisit(Element element) {
      // Use reflection to find and invoke the correct Visit method
      Type[] types = new Type[] {element.GetType()};
      MethodInfo methodInfo = this.GetType().GetMethod("Visit", types);
      if (methodInfo != null)
              methodInfo.Invoke(this, new object[] {element});
```

```
      else Console.WriteLine("Unexpected Visit");
    }
  }

  // Visitor
class CountVisitor : IVisitor {
  public int Count {get; set;}
  public void CountElements(Element element) {
      ReflectiveVisit(element);
      if (element.Part!=null) CountElements(element.Part);
      if (element.Next!=null) CountElements(element.Next);
    }

    public void Visit(ElementWithLink element) {
      Console.WriteLine("Not counting");
    }
    // Only Elements are counted
    public void Visit(Element element) {
        Count++;
    }
  }
 }

  // Client
  class Client {

  static void Main( ) {
    // Set up the object structure
    Element objectStructure =
      new Element(
          new Element(
          new ElementWithLink(
           new Element(
                new Element(
                  new ElementWithLink(
                new Element(null),
                new Element(
                null)))),
        new Element(
            new Element(
            new Element(null))))));

    Console.WriteLine ("Count the elements");
    CountVisitor visitor = new CountVisitor( );
    visitor.CountElements(objectStructure);
    Console.WriteLine("Number of Elements is: "+visitor.Count);
  }
}
/*
Count the elements
Not counting
Not counting
Number of Elements is: 9
*/
```

Interpreter Pattern Example Code—Course Rules

See the following code for an example of the Interpreter Pattern:

```
using System;

// Interpreter Pattern Example          Judith Bishop  Oct 2007
// Sets up an object structure and interprets it with given data

static class ElementExtensions {
  public static string gap;

  public static void Print(this Element element) {
    Console.WriteLine(gap+element + " " + element.Weight);
    if (element.Part!=null) {
      gap+="  ";
      Print(element.Part.Next);
      gap = gap.Substring(2);
    }
    if (element.Next!=null) Print(element.Next);
  }

  public static int Lab {get; set;}
  public static int Test {get; set;}

  public static void Summarize(this Element element) {
    if (element is Lab) Lab += element.Weight;
    else if
        (element is Test) Test += element.Weight;
    else if ((element is Midterm || element is Exam)
        && element.Part==null) Test += element.Weight;
    if (element.Part!=null) Summarize(element.Part.Next);
    if (element.Next!=null) Summarize(element.Next);
  }

  public static int [] values;
  public static int  n;
  public static Context context;

  public static void SetUp (this Element element, Context c, int[] v) {
    context = c;
    context.Output=0;
    values = v;
    n = 0;
  }

  public static void Interpreter(this Element element) {

    if (element is Lab || element is Test) {
      context.Output += values[n]*element.Weight;
      n++;
    }
```

```
    else
    if ((element is Midterm || element is Exam)
        && element.Part==null) {
      context.Output += values[n]*element.Weight;
      n++;
  }

    if (element.Part!=null) Interpreter(element.Part.Next);
    if (element.Next!=null) Interpreter(element.Next);
  }
 }

public class Element {
  public int Weight {get; set;}
  public Element Next {get; set;}
  public Element Part {get; set;}

  public virtual string Display() {
    return Weight+"%";
  }

  int GetNumber (Context context) {
    int atSpace = context.Input.IndexOf(' ');
    int number = Int32.Parse(context.Input.Substring(1,atSpace));
    context.Input = context.Input.Substring(atSpace+1);
    return number;
  }

  public void Parse (Context context) {
    string starters = "LTME";
    if (context.Input.Length>0 && starters.IndexOf(context.Input[0])>=0) {
      switch(context.Input[0]) {
        case 'L':
          Next=new Lab();
          break;
        case 'T':
          Next=new Test();
          break;
        case 'M':
          Next=new Midterm();
          break;
        case 'E':
          Next = new Exam();
          break;
      }
      Next.Weight = GetNumber(context);
      if (context.Input.Length>0 && context.Input[0]=='(') {
        context.Input = context.Input.Substring(1);
        Next.Part = new Element();
        Next.Part.Parse(context);
        Element e = Next.Part;
        while (e!=null) {
```

```
            e.Weight = e.Weight * Next.Weight / 100;
            e = e.Next;
          }
          context.Input = context.Input.Substring(2);
        }
        Next.Parse(context);
      }
    }
  }

class Course : Element {
  public string Name {get; set;}
  public Course (Context context) {
    Name = context.Input.Substring(0,6);
    context.Input = context.Input.Substring(7);
  }
  public override string Display() {
    return Name;
  }
}

class Lab : Element {
}

class Test : Element {
}

class Midterm : Element {
}

class Exam : Element {
}

public class Context {
  public string Input {get; set;}
  public double Output {get; set;}

  public Context(string c) {
    Input = c;
    Output = 0;
  }
}

static class IntArrayExtension {
  public static string Display (this int[] a) {
    string s = "[";
    foreach (int i in a)
        s+=i+", ";
    return s.Substring(0,s.Length-2)+"]";
  }
}

class InterpreterPattern {
```

```
static void Main( ) {
  string rules = "COS333 L2 L2 L2 L2 L2 M25 (L40 T60 ) L10 E55 (L28 T73 ) ";
  int [][] values = new [] {new [] {80,0,100,100,85,51,52,50,57,56},
                            new [] {87,95,100,100,77,70,99,100,75,94},
                            new [] {0,55,100,65,55,75,73,74,71,72}};

  Context context;
  Console.WriteLine (rules+"\n");

  context = new Context (rules);
  Element course = new Course(context);
  course.Parse(context);

  Console.WriteLine("Visitor 1 - Course structure\n");
  course.Print( );

  course.Summarize( );
  Console.WriteLine ("\n\nVisitor 2 - Summing the weights\nLabs "
                    +ElementExtensions.Lab + "% and Tests "
                    +ElementExtensions.Test + "%");

  Console.WriteLine("\n\nVisitor 3 (Interpreter) ");
  foreach (int [] student in values) {
    Console.Write(student.Display( ));
    course.SetUp(context, student);
    course.Interpreter( );
    Console.WriteLine(" = "+context.Output/100);
  }
 }
}
```

```
/* Output
COS333 L2 L2 L2 L2 L2 M25 (L40 T60 ) L10 E55 (L28 T73 )

Visitor 1 - Course structure

Course 0
Lab 2
Lab 2
Lab 2
Lab 2
Lab 2
Midterm 25
  Lab 10
  Test 15
Lab 10
Exam 55
  Lab 15
  Test 40


Visitor 2 - Summing the weights
Labs 45% and Tests 55%
```

```
Visitor 3 (Interpreter)
[80, 0, 100, 100, 85, 51, 52, 50, 57, 56] = 56.15
[87, 95, 100, 100, 77, 70, 99, 100, 75, 94] = 89.88
[0, 55, 100, 65, 55, 75, 73, 74, 71, 72] = 70.8
*/
```

Interpreter Pattern Example Code—Mirrors

See the following code for another example of the Intrepreter Pattern:

```csharp
using System;
using System.Xml;
using System.Reflection;
using System.Collections;
using System.Collections.Generic;
using System.Windows.Forms;

   public class Mirror {

      // Mirrors                        Hans Lombard  June 2006, revised Sept 2007
      // Based on Views and Views-2 by Nigel Horspool, Judith Bishop, and D-J Miller
      // A general-purpose interpreter for any .NET API
      // Reads XML and executes the methods it represents
      // This example assumes the Windows Form API only in the final line
      // where Application.Run is called

      Stack objectStack;
      List<Command> commands;
      public object CurrentObject { get { return objectStack.Peek(); } }
      public XmlTextReader Reader { get; set; }
      public object LastObject { get; set; }

      public Mirror(string spec) {
        objectStack = new Stack();
        objectStack.Push(null);

        // Register the commands
        commands = new List<Command>();
        commands.Add(new ElementCommand());
        commands.Add(new EndElementCommand());
        commands.Add(new AttributeCommand());

        Reader = new XmlTextReader(spec);
        while (Reader.Read()) {
          InterpretCommands();

          bool b = Reader.IsEmptyElement;
          if (Reader.HasAttributes) {
            for (int i = 0; i < Reader.AttributeCount; i++) {
              Reader.MoveToAttribute(i);
              InterpretCommands();
            }
          }
```

```
        if (b) Pop( );
      }
    }

    public void InterpretCommands( ) {

        // Run through the commands and interpret
      foreach (Command c in commands)
          c.Interpret(this);
    }

    public void Push(object o) {
      objectStack.Push(o);
    }

    public void Pop( ) {
      LastObject = objectStack.Pop( );
    }

    public object Peek( ) {
      return objectStack.Peek( );
    }
}

public abstract class Command {
  public abstract void Interpret (Mirror context);
}

// Handles an XML element. Creates a new object that reflects the XML
// element name.
public class ElementCommand : Command {
  public override void Interpret (Mirror context) {
    if (context.Reader.NodeType != XmlNodeType.Element) return;
    Type type = GetTypeOf(context.Reader.Name);
    if (type == null) return;
    object o = Activator.CreateInstance(type);

    if (context.Peek( ) != null)
        ((Control)context.Peek( )).Controls.Add((Control)o);
    context.Push(o);
  }

  public Type GetTypeOf(string s) {
    string ns = "System.Windows.Forms";
    Assembly asm = Assembly.Load("System.Windows.Forms, Version=2.0.0.0,
        Culture=neutral, PublicKeyToken=b77a5c561934e089");
    Type type = asm.GetType(ns + "." + s);
    return type;
  }
}

// Handles an XML end element. Removes the element from the object stack.
public class EndElementCommand : Command {
```

```csharp
    public override void Interpret (Mirror context) {
      if (context.Reader.NodeType != XmlNodeType.EndElement) return;
      context.Pop();
    }
  }

  // Applies attributes to the current object. The attributes reflect to the
  // properties of the object.
  public class AttributeCommand : Command {
    public override void Interpret (Mirror context) {
      if (context.Reader.NodeType != XmlNodeType.Attribute) return;
      SetProperty(context.Peek(), context.Reader.Name, context.Reader.Value);
    }

    public void SetProperty(object o, string name, string val) {
      Type type = o.GetType();
      PropertyInfo property = type.GetProperty(name);

      // Find an appropriate property to match the attribute name
      if (property.PropertyType.IsAssignableFrom(typeof(string))) {
        property.SetValue(o, val, null);
      } else if (property.PropertyType.IsSubclassOf(typeof(Enum))) {
        object ev = Enum.Parse(property.PropertyType, val, true);
        property.SetValue(o, ev, null);
      } else {
        MethodInfo m = property.PropertyType.GetMethod("Parse", new Type[] {
            typeof(string) });
        object newval = m.Invoke(null /*static */, new object[] { val });
        property.SetValue(o, newval, null);
      }
    }
  }
}

public class MainClass {
  public static void Main() {
    Mirror m = new Mirror("calc_winforms.xml");
    Application.Run((Form)m.LastObject);
  }
}

/* Input
  <Form Text="Currency calculator" Width="250" Height="180">
    <Label Top="10" Text="Paid on hols" />
    <TextBox Top="10" Left="100" Name="eurobox" />
    <Label Top="40" Text="Charged" />
    <TextBox Top="40" Left="100" Name="GBPbox" />
    <Label Top="70" Text="Exchange rate is"  />
    <TextBox Top="70" Left="100" Name="ratebox" />
    <Button Top="100" Name="equals" Text "="  />
<Button Top="100" Left="100" Name="clear" Text="Reset" />
  </Form>
*/
```

Bibliography

Agebro, E. and Cornils, A. "How to preserve the benefits of Design Patterns." *Proceedings of OOPLSA* (1998): 134–143.

Alexander, C. et al. *A Pattern Language*, New York: Oxford University Press, 1977.

Alexandrescu, Andrei. *Modern C++ Design: Generic Programming and Design Patterns Applied*. Boston, MA: Addison-Wesley Professional, 2001.

Arnout, Karine. "From Patterns to Components." Ph.D. diss., Swiss Institute of Technology, 2004.

Arnout, Karine and Meyer, Bertrand. "Pattern componentization: the factory example." *Innovations in Systems and Software Technology: A NASA Journal* 2, no. 2 (July 2006): 65–79.

Avgeriou, Paris and Zdun, Uwe. "Architectural patterns revisited—a pattern language." *Proceedings of the 10th European Conference on Pattern Languages of Programs* (EuroPlop 2005): 1–39.

Bishop, Judith, Horspool, Nigel, and Worrall, Basil. "Experience in integrating Java with C# and .NET." *Concurrency and Computation: Practice and Experience* 17 (June 2005): 663–680.

Bishop, Judith. "Multi-platform user interface construction: a challenge for software engineering-in-the-small." *Proceedings of the 28th International Conference on Software Engineering* (2006): 751–760.

Bosch, Jan. "Design Patterns as Language Constructs." *Journal of Object-Oriented Programming* 11, no. 2 (1998): 18–32.

Bosch, Jan. "Design Patterns & Frameworks: On the Issue of Language Support." *Proceedings of the Workshop on Language Support for Design Patterns and Object-Oriented Frameworks (LSDF)*, (ECOOP 1997): 133–136.

Budinski, F., Finnie, M., Yu, P., and Vlissides, J. "Automatic code generation from design patterns." *IBM Systems Journal* 35, no. 2 (1996): 151–171.

Coplien, J. O. and Schmidt, D. C. *Patterns Languages of Program Design*. Boston, MA: Addison-Wesley, 1995.

Chambers, C., Harrison, B., and Vlissides, J. O. "A Debate on Language and Tool Support for Design Patterns." *Proceedings of the 27th ACM SIGPLAN-SIGACT Symposium on Principles of Programming Languages* (2000): 277–289.

Gamma, E., Helm, R., Johnson, R., and Vlissides, J. O. *Design Patterns: Elements of Reusable Object-Oriented Software*. Boston, MA: Addison-Wesley, 1995.

Gil, J. and Lorenz, D. H. "Design Patterns vs. Language Design." *Proceedings of the Workshop on Language Support for Design Patterns and Object-Oriented Frameworks (LSDF)*, (ECOOP 1997): 108–111.

Meyer, Bertrand. *Object-Oriented Software Construction*, Second Edition. Upper Saddle River, NJ: Prentice Hall, 1997.

Meyer, Bertrand and Arnout, Karine. "Componentization: the Visitor example." *Computer* 39, no. 7 (2006): 23–30.

Schmidt, Doug. "Using Design Patterns to Develop Reusable Object-Oriented Communication Software." *Communications of the ACM* 38, no. 10 (1995): 65–74.

Index

We'd like to hear your suggestions for improving our indexes. Send email to *index@oreilly.com*.

About the Author

Judith Bishop is a professor of computer science at the University of Pretoria, South Africa. She specializes in the application of programming languages to distributed systems and web-based technologies. She is internationally known as an advocate of new technology, with books on Java and C# published in six languages. Judith represents South Africa on IFIP TC2 on software and is a chair or a member of numerous international conference committees and editorial boards.

Colophon

The animal on the cover of *C# 3.0 Design Patterns* is a greylag goose (*Anser anser*), probably one of the first domesticated animals. Archaeological evidence suggests that domestic geese lived in ancient Egypt and Rome 3,000 years ago.

Fairly large birds, usually weighing between 5–12 pounds, greylag geese have an average wingspan of 59–66 inches and are generally 29–30 inches in length. Their plumage is grayish-brown, their bellies are white, and their lower breasts are shaded gray. Their bills are large and yellow, and their feet and legs are a pink, flesh-like color. (Younger geese have gray legs and feet that turn pinker as they age.)

They are migratory birds that fly south or west in the winter to escape the harsh weather. During the summer, they live in Scotland, Iceland, Scandinavia, as far east as Russia, Poland, and Germany. In autumn, the geese in Iceland migrate to the British Isles, while the rest of the greylag geese in Europe head to places like the Netherlands, Spain, France, and East Africa.

A social bird, it travels long distances in groups, often in the familiar *v*-shape pattern. Their groups range from small families to flocks with tens of thousands of geese.

The time at which their breeding season begins depends on their geographic location. In Scotland, breeding starts in late April; in Iceland it starts in early May; and in Europe, it starts earlier. During breeding season, greylag geese live in marshes and fens—places with a lot of vegetation. Nests are built in high places to keep their eggs safe from predators.

A mother can lay as many as 12 eggs, but she usually lays between 4 and 6. She incubates the eggs for approximately 26 days. Once hatched, the goslings wait until they are dry to leave the nest. Young birds feed themselves with their parents' supervision. Twenty years is their average life expectancy.

Greylag geese thrive on grasses, roots, rhizomes of marsh plants, and small aquatic animals. They also have a taste for some root crops—turnips, potatoes, and carrots—a real concern for farmers in Europe.

Golden eagles, ravens, and hawks are among their predators in the sky; when on the ground, they have to be vigilant for prowling dogs, foxes, and humans. Humans hunt geese for their flavorful meat and their down, or soft feathers. Down is often used to stuff pillows, blankets, and outdoor clothing.

Caesar, the Roman emperor, declared greylag geese as sacred in 390 B.C., and he made it illegal to kill and consume them. Caesar credited them with saving his empire from attack. He believed that when the Gauls tried to invade, the geeses' loud calls alerted the Romans and saved them from occupation.

The cover image is from *Dover Animals Book*. The cover font is Adobe ITC Garamond. The text font is Linotype Birka; the heading font is Adobe Myriad Condensed; and the code font is LucasFont's TheSans Mono Condensed.

Related Titles from O'Reilly

.NET and C#

ADO.NET Cookbook

ADO.NET 3.5 Cookbook, *2nd Edition*

ASP.NET 2.0 Cookbook, *2nd Edition*

ASP.NET 2.0: A Developer's Notebook

Building an ASP.NET Web 2.0 Portal

C# 3.0 in a Nutshell, *3rd Edition*

C# Cookbook, *2nd Edition*

C# Design Patterns

C# in a Nutshell, *2nd Edition*

C# Language Pocket Reference

Exchange Server 2007 Administration: The Definitive Guide

Head First C#

Learning ASP.NET 2.0 with AJAX

Learning C# 2005, *2nd Edition*

Learning WCF

MCSE Core Elective Exams in a Nutshell

.NET and XML

.NET Gotchas

Programming Atlas

Programming ASP.NET, *3rd Edition*

Programming ASP.NET AJAX

Programming C#, *4th Edition*

Programming MapPoint in .NET

Programming .NET 3.5

Programming .NET Components, *2nd Edition*

Programming .NET Security

Programming .NET Web Services

Programming Visual Basic 2005

Programming WCF Services

Programming WPF, *2nd Edition*

Programming Windows Presentation Foundation

Programming the .NET Compact Framework

Visual Basic 2005: A Developer's Notebook

Visual Basic 2005 Cookbook

Visual Basic 2005 in a Nutshell, *3rd Edition*

Visual Basic 2005 Jumpstart

Visual C# 2005: A Developer's Notebook

Visual Studio Hacks

Windows Developer Power Tools

XAML in a Nutshell

O'REILLY®

Our books are available at most retail and online bookstores.

To order direct: 1-800-998-9938 • *order@oreilly.com* • *www.oreilly.com*

Online editions of most O'Reilly titles are available by subscription at *safari.oreilly.com*

The O'Reilly Advantage

Stay Current and Save Money